TEDDY BEARS, ANNALEE'S & STEIFF ANIMALS

Third Series

by
Margaret Fox Mandel

Drawings by
Margot Mandel

COLLECTOR BOOKS
A Division of Schroeder Publishing Co., Inc.

ACKNOWLEDGMENTS

Acknowledgment is gratefully extended to the following who have graciously shared their toys and photographs. All photographs are by the author unless noted otherwise in parenthesis.

Dave and Ann Abbott; Sherilyn Allmond; Carolyn M. Altfather (herself); Charlotte Anderson (herself); Annalee Mobilitee Dolls, Inc.; Debbi Anton (Jacqui Silla); Dottie Ayers (herself); Barbara Baldwin (herself); Sheree Barnes; Mary Benavente (herself); Phyllis Blaser (Pegg Wurdinger); Jeremy Bleecher and Patricia Gallagher (Patricia Gallagher); Elke Block (Nils Vidstrand); Jean Boyda (Jacqui Silla); Kay Bransky (Art Bransky); Fran Cagner; Susie Carlson (Valerie Vann); Sydney Robinson Charles (Valerie Vann); Linda and Laura Lee Croucher (Bill Croucher); Cynthia's Country Store (Cynthia Brintnall); Gwen Daniel (herself); Michelle Daunton (herself); Tammie Depew (herself); Howard Dreier; John Fazendin (himself); Candice Feldstein (Alex Feldstein); Dot Franklin (herself); Rebecca Vaughn Gardner (Polly Judd); Idele Gilbert (Harry Gilbert); Betsy Gottschalk; Catherine Griffin (Harry Gilbert); Stella M. Griffin (Harry Gilbert); Dickie Harrison (herself); Sue Harshman; Isabel Hasselbach (Jason Shpur); Suzanne Hill; Laurie Hix (Randall Giles); Diane Hoffman; Chris Irons (herself); Joy Kelleher (herself); Linda Kuhn (herself); Jim Lambert (himself); Elaine Lehn (herself); Wanda Loukides (herself); Ellyn McCorkell; Carolyn McMaster (Joan Sage); Chris McWilliams (Gene McWilliams); Debbie Masters; Nan C. Moorehead; Rosemary Moran; Mostly Bears, Denver; Kathy Mullin (Joe Finkleman); Ruth Nett; Pam North (herself); Peddler's Wagon; Betty Peil; Marsha Pfenning; Mac Pohlen (herself); Private Collection (Phillip Johnson); Regina Prugh (herself); Harriet Purtill (Peter Pfeffer); Beverlee Reimers; Vivienne Roche (Valerie Vann); Nancy Roeder; Isabel Romer; Beth Savino (Dick Frantz); Maria Schmidt (herself); Karen Silverstein (Carolyn McMaster and Joan Sage); Jean Ann Smith (herself); Patricia R. Smith; Kirk Stines (himself); Marian Swartz; Evelyn Thomas; Kathy Thomas (herself); Bette Todd (herself); Valerie Vann (herself); Larry and Debbie Varner; Marlene Wendt (herself); Susan Wiley (herself); Ingried Wustner (Helmut Wustner); Dana Zastrow.

Additional copies of this book may be ordered from:

Collector Books
P.O. Box 3009
Paducah, KY 42002-3009

@ $19.95. Add $2.00 for postage and handling.

TABLE OF CONTENTS

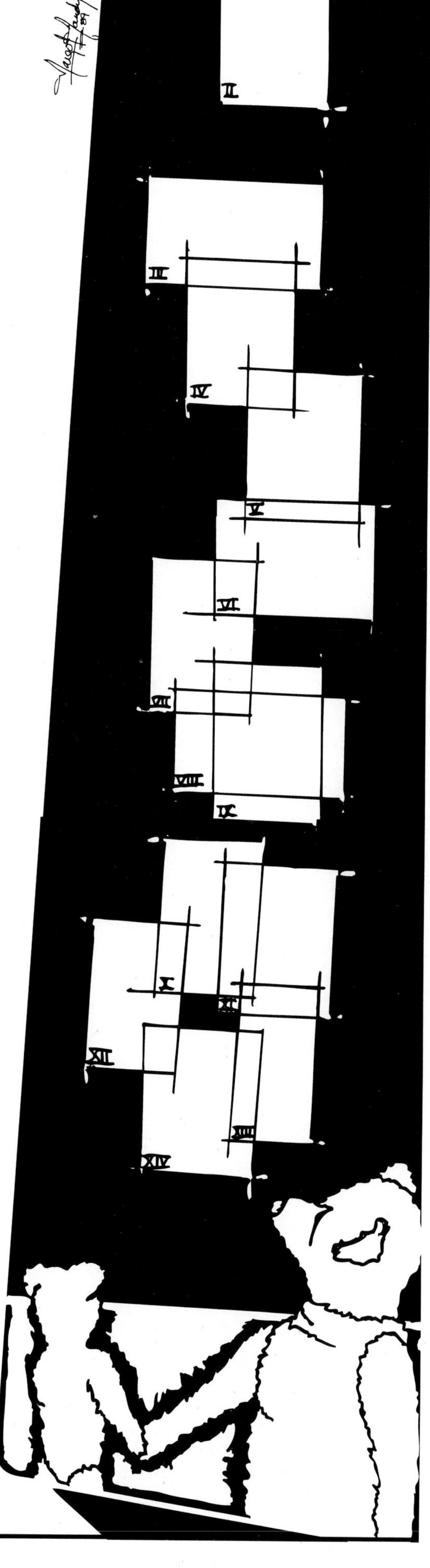

I. INTRODUCTION

Steiff mohair Teddy Bears, (L-R), *Front row*: 13"/33 cm., blond, FF button, ca. 1915; 16"/41 cm. cinnamon, blank button, collar and tie, unusual smiling face, ca. 1905; 18"/46 cm., blond, FF button, collar and tie, ca. 1908. *Middle row*: 30"/76 cm., bright gold, rare size, ca. 1955; 10"/25 cm., honey, soft stuffed excelsior/kapok (early method), ca. 1908; 24"/61 cm., white, 1950s "Original Teddy," RSB; 20"/51 cm., white, 1950s "Original Teddy," RSB 13"/33 cm., champagne, brown nose/mouth, FF button, ca. 1915; 24"/61 cm., champagne, 1950s "Original Teddy," RSB. *Top Row*: 12"/30 cm., honey, blank button, ca. 1905; 13"/33 cm., rare color (cinnamon red), blank button, ca. 1904. All are in *mint condition*.
Courtesy Barbara Baldwin

What is a treasure? The objects in this book are treasures, but not always because of their monetary value. Over 500 soft toys were selected. Some were selected because they are unique or extremely rare; others because they are very old or perhaps were the first of their kind; still others because they are especially fine examples of a type of toy or style of manufacture. All of these toys have stories to tell about the people who produced them and the people who owned them; this is really why we call them treasures.

Collectors should buy with knowledge of the product. Nothing can substitute for study, comparison and the connoisseur's own eye. The market price has dropped for bears in poor condition; it has taken a tremendous leap for pedigreed vintage Teddys in mint to near mint condition, giving them a prominent place in the investment world of collectibles. Rarity and unusual size and/or color are other important variables. Value formulas are complex. The bottom line determination must be made by the collector.

In the Steiff animal line, not all collectors want (or can afford) the super rare. They buy "cute" instead of rare. Toys can be common but popular. There are many kinds of collectors: advanced, beginners, ambitious, those collecting only newer limited editions, those collecting only miniatures, those collecting only

FAO Schwarz exclusives, rabbit and cat lovers and many other types. It is important for collectors to zero in on what interests them the most, define their terms and go after it. It is reported that Steiff made approximately 10,000 different items over the years; it would be impossible for anyone to collect them all. The true collector enjoys the thrill of the chase, trips to shows and auctions, the research, talking with other collectors, and the joy of ownership.

A distinction should be made between **Store New** or **Tissue Mint with all I.D.** (which are the equivalent of the doll collector's **Mint in Box),** and **Mint**, showing no wear or fading of fur and body, and missing no minor parts. Tags may or may not be present in **Mint**. **Near Mint** is applicable to toys which are clean and mechanically sound, have no tears or loss of plush, but have faded airbrushing (aging) and/or missing parts. The substitute of trimmings lowers the value. With the recent price increases one can no longer afford to be casual about such matters. **Very Good:** minimal wear; may be soiled or have a hole but nothing extreme. **Good:** plush may be thin; pads may be worn; might have restoration or loss of parts. **Poor:** dirty; very worn; lost limbs, eyes and/or nose stitching; unrestorable without noticeable additions.

Prices given for Teddys and Steiff dolls are for *that* particular toy, taking into account *condition, rarity, unusual features, special appeal and I.D.* The prices listed in the Steiff animal section are based on Store New condition, button in the ear and paper chest tag, where applicable.

THE CARE OF THE BEAR AND OTHER PLUSH TOYS

Methods of cleaning vary greatly; most give satisfactory results. Some prefer to use foam carpet or upholstery cleaners. The advantage of these is that they don't over-wet the toy. The disadvantage is they tend to leave toys sticky if not thoroughly rinsed. Some use liquid cleaners for fine washables such as Woolite® or special Teddy Bear baths.

First closely examine the toy to be cleaned. Look for rips, split seams, loose eyes, holes, "dry rot" and insect damage. Treat for insects at this time. Generously spray the inside of a clean garbage pail with insecticide to create a vapor. Next completely cover the toy with a pillow case and put it in the tightly covered pail. Leave overnight or longer. Moth balls do not kill most larvae or carpet beetles and therefore are not recommended except as a measure to prevent moths from getting into the material and laying eggs.

Secure loose eyes, limbs and seams. Vacuum carefully. Test for colorfastness of fabric in a hidden place. Start to comb out matted hair by misting animal with cleaning solution in a mist bottle. Gently comb from tips of fur inward to base of fur. Work in small sections at a time. Mist again lightly, being careful to never wet fabric backing. With a clean, white, highly-napped terry towel gently rub the combed out area until it comes clean. Turn towel frequently. Once the area is clean, go on to another area until entire limb or section is clean. If you cannot clean the animal after two attempts -- stop. You will saturate the fabric with water if you continue. Finish cleaning the entire animal and when dry repeat cleaning if necessary. Rinse toy with a clean terry towel tightly wrung from clear water. Gently rub until cleaning solution is removed. Gently recomb damp animal to restore nap. Never comb a dry animal. This pulls out fur and leaves the fur frizzy. Do not blow dry, the heat dries out the mohair and causes excessive shedding. The air makes the animal's fur too "poufy." Let the toy air dry naturally; the fur will lie flat with more shine; if the fur is curly it will dry with more curl.

Some long mohair plush is made of single fibers and some of YARN (spun or plied from 2-3 fibers). The wrong instrument can split the ends and "unspin" the yarn. The comb of choice is a straight steel dog comb, with the spaces between the teeth the same width as the teeth themselves, and with smooth rounded tips on the teeth. Caution is to be exercised at all times, expecially on faces and around tags, embroidered claws, sewn-on ears, and the closing seams, which are often sewn by hand with coarse baseball stitches that the teeth may snag. Wire brushes should not be used on mohair animals. Their use is for "picking seams" and fluffing up monofilament synthetics.

Restoration tips: some patchy fur loss can be repaired by reweaving color-matched mohair from a doll's wig. Do a few strands at a time and clip. Do only for small areas. When the backing is "dry rotted" attach it to another piece of (muslin) cloth; either with tiny stitches in all directions or Stitch Witchery.® As a last resort use iron-on Pellon,® but avoid applying a hot iron to old material if possible.

More words of caution: do not clean "dry rotted" or fragile fabric toys. Do not use fabric softeners or hair cream rinse products on toys. Airbrushed markings, especially those on felt or velveteen, usually fade when cleaned. These fabrics should be cleaned with extreme caution. Do not rub, but blot them. Often cleaning leaves felt and velveteen worse off and water spotted. Sometimes a good going over with an air compressor will forcefully blow dirt from pads, velveteen and felt (including Annalees). Use with caution. Use extreme caution when cleaning excelsior stuffed toys. Do not let the fabric backing become wet. This could result in red stains that are highly acidic and tend to weaken backing fabrics. Do not dry clean or use spot removers or cleaning fluid. Stop combing immediately if the backing fabric starts to rip or disintegrate, if hair combs out in clumps or if excessive shedding occurs. Do not continue to clean these toys.

Work slowly and keep on the lookout for problems. Pre-1930 toys should be cleaned very carefully. If a toy is valuable for any reason leave it to a professional. A clean toy is less attractive to insects and dirt abrasion damage. Keep your toy clean by storing it properly, away from direct light, away from heat sources and in a display case. Place toy on cedar chips or blocks to repel insects and check monthly for insect damage. Vacuum when necessary. When handling, support the toy well; do not lift it by limbs or ears.

Most restoration (past a gentle cleaning) should not be attempted by the inexperienced, for it might cause more harm than good. Before allowing someone else to restore your toys inquire as to their cleaning and repair methods, ask for references or examine before and after repair photos. All repairs should be able to be reversed without damaging the toy and for no reason should glue in any form ever be used on fabric -- never. If you would not approve of a restoration method to restore a fine irreplaceable cashmere coat, do not use that method on your toy

Many old toys are now worth thousand of dollars. Improper repairs and storage can ruin a toy forever. If ever in doubt, it is best to wait until you can consult a professional; better to wait than regret a hasty repair.

You clean your plush toys at your own risk. Neither Collector Books nor the author takes any responsibility for any damage incurred as a result of consulting this guide.

Before **After**

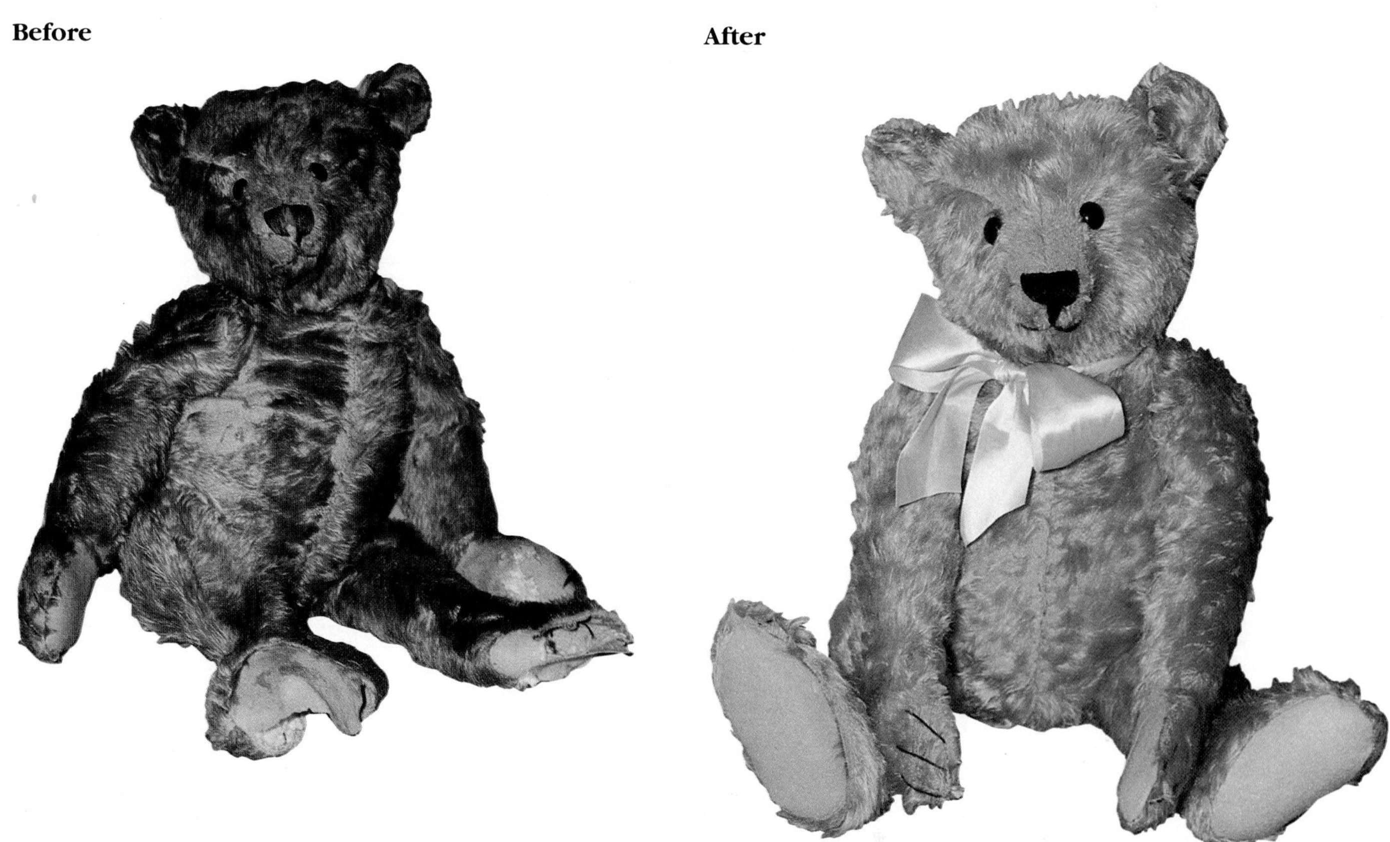

The art of the professional restorer can exceed the art of the original maker as seen in the before and after photos of the 24"/61 cm. Steiff center seam Teddy, ca. 1905. This difficult restoration was achieved by the artist Maria Schmidt.

ANNALEE DAVIS THORNDIKE AND HER COMPANY

The first Annalee Dolls were made in the mid-1930s in Concord, New Hampshire, by Annalee Davis Thorndike. These dolls, made for family and friends, were almost exclusively ski dolls with yarn hair. The superbly talented artist had perfected the art of drawing faces by drawing her own face in the mirror in every possible expression. After WWII, Annalee labored to make dolls at the kitchen table of the family chicken farm. The poultry market had floundered and her husband, Chip Thorndike (a Harvard man), assumed the marketing role. As a result, by the late 1950s Annalee Dolls had been introduced into major department stores in New York. Now the Thorndike sons, Chuck and Town, are committed to the family business. The dream prevails and today the unique dolls and animals hold a high position in the collector field, both here and abroad.

Their collectibility and investment value is ensured. On an average a doll increases ten times in value over its original price. The degree of increase is dependent on *rarity*, *appeal*, and *condition*. In some instances values have increased 3,000%.

Annalee Dolls are entirely an American-made product, employing 350 people at the "Factory in the Woods," Meredith, N.H. Because of the meticulous detail required, 75% of the manufacturing cost is for labor, 25% for materials.

Intermittently, Annalee has designed dolls as a special order for a specific store or event. Over the years animated (motorized) UL – approved figures have been produced as store displays, for which Annalee is also well known.

All Annalee Dolls, be they human or animal, reflect joy, humor and the impishness of childhood; all are handmade from original designs created by Annalee Thorndike; all have painted *felt* faces with sunny expressions that hallmark the dolls as Annalees. Bodies are generally made of felt, although flannel bodies can be found on some dolls, most commonly Santas and rabbits. All Annalee Dolls contain a wire armature that allows imaginative positioning.

Bear with Honey Pot and Bee: **18"/46 cm.; 1986; carries a metal honey pot and wooden spoon. Issued for two years, 1985 and 1986, he is one of 938 produced in 1986; issue price $42.00. The 1985 bear carries a honey pot and spoon dripping with honey. Demand is high for both years. Courtesy Bette Todd.**

ANNALEE GUIDELINES

The evolution of Annalee Dolls:

1936-1950 -- subject was usually ski dolls (limited production).

1950-1954 -- other human figures were added. These had small painted dots for eyes and yarn hair.

1954 -- marked the start of Annalee Mobilitee Dolls, Inc.; the first Santa appeared.

1954-1957 -- skiers, hikers, kids, water skiers and baby angels were among the dolls produced. The eyes on the dolls of this period are almond shaped.

1957-1960 -- the faces changed to a more "character" appearance with impish expressions beginning to emerge. Dolls representing different aspects of life were made: doctors, lawyers, carpenters, bellhops, oil tycoons, bathers, boaters and golfers. These dolls continued to have yarn hair.

1960-1964 -- synthetic plush and chicken feathers as well as yarn were used for hair. Woodsprites, monks, friars and others joined the line.

1975 -- catalogues were first printed.

1964-1982 -- the first facially animated *animals* were introduced by Annalee in **1964-1965**. These included rabbits, mice, ducks and cats. By this time, all the dolls had synthetic plush hair and the whimsical faces similar to those of today. Annalee expanded the subject matter rapidly. Among the great variety of dolls produced since **1964** are Mr. and Mrs. Santas, elves, gnomes, leprechauns, angels, carolers, nuns, drummer boys, skiers, kids, clowns, suns, snowmen, giraffes, frogs, bears, monkeys, dragons, pigs, foxes, reindeer, horses, skunks, scarecrows and turkeys.

1983-1984 marked the beginning of the Folk Hero Series for the 15,000 Annalee Doll Society members. Johnny Appleseed (see Page 9.) and Robin Hood were the first offerings. A new folk hero has joined the others each year. These are the realistically detailed human figures for which Annalee first gained fame. In 1985, Annalee Animals joined the Collectibles for society members -- penguin and chick, unicorn, kangaroo, owl and polar bear. As of June 1989, all new Folk Heroes and Annalee Animals in the Society's exclusive collection will be available for 18 months from the date of issue or until 2,500 are sold, whichever comes first. Since 1985 there is a selection of Artist Proofs sold at the annual Annalee Doll Society auction in June. Approximately one third of the regular line is discontinued each year.

Fabric is one of the most dependable indicators of the year that an Annalee Doll was made. However, in the early years Annalee used whatever scrap of material was available: pieces from her dress or a swatch from her sons' shirts. In 1971 the company purchased fabric by the yard. Since 1974 most of the prints are changed yearly.

Stuffing is another indicator of the date of a figure. Early Annalee Dolls were stuffed with cotton string or cotton batting (the bulge in Santa's tummy was a styrofoam ball). Categories that followed are: cotton string combined with acetate, cotton string with shredded polyurethane, shredded polyurethane alone and shredded polyurethane with polyester fiber. The smaller figures are stuffed entirely with string to enable full contouring of the tiny parts.

The first professional fabric tags -- always red lettering printed on white -- were attached to the dolls in the **1950s**. These carried the company's name and sometimes the date of copyright, *not* the year of manufacture. In the **1960s** tags were made of a white, rayon-type, woven-edged fabric (½"x⅞" after folding) with *embroidered* red lettering; they were sewn in a seam. In the early **1970s** a satin-like ribbon was used. In **1976** the company switched to a ½"x2" (after folding) tag sewn in (any) seam. It is made of a *stiff* material with a *definite* crisscross weave resembling adhesive tape. This tag was printed with the company and copyright information on one side and the figure's contents on the reverse. Finally, **(1980-present)**, a white synthetic non-woven tape (resembling sturdy paper) is folded and stitched into the figure's seam. In **1986** the manufacturing date was added to the label. The green hang tags were used for the first time in **1974**. In **1988** these were changed to navy ink on tan stock paper. For a serious collector wanting a specific or rare piece to round out their collection, the presence of a tag is of little significance. The unique product is self-recognizable, as all art should be.

The values given in the back of this book are derived from the prices realized at annual Annalee Doll Society auctions, sales from the Annalee Antique and Collectible Doll Shoppe (Meredith, N.H.) and documented private sales. In the few cases where there is no record, the value is based on a similar doll.

Johnny Appleseed: 10"/25 cm. was the first in a series of Folk Hero Collector Dolls offered exclusively to members of the Annalee Doll Society. He was made in 1983 in a signed and numbered limited edition of 1,500 which sold out quickly. Originally selling for $80.00, he has commanded as much as $1,500.00 at auction. He was followed by Robin Hood in 1984. Then came Annie Oakley (1985); Mark Twain (1986); Benjamin Franklin (1987); Sherlock Holmes (1988); and Abraham Lincoln in 1989. Courtesy Annalee Mobilitee Dolls, Inc.

KEY

- e.s. indicates "excelsior stuffed" (fine wood shavings).

- f.j. indicates "fully jointed" (swivel head, jointed limbs); disc joints.

- Elephant Button used for a short period (1904-1905).

- Blank Metal Button, two prong attachment (1904-1905).

- <u>FF</u> button indicates pewter color metal ear button; block capitol letters with "FF" underscored; (1905-1950).

- STEIFF button indicates a printed button *without* FF underscored; seen just after WWII (ca. 1950); sometimes in conjunction with US-Zone tag; seldom found.

- RSB indicates "raised script button" (1950-1968).

- IB indicates that the flowing script on the chrome ear button is *incised* (1968-1977).

- S.T. indicates "Stock Tag" attached by ear button showing the exact look of the animal as to posture, covering, height (cm.) and outfit.

- White S.T. used 1908-1926.

- Red S.T. used 1926-1934.

- Yellow S.T. used 1934-1980.

- Cloth S.T. : Yellow or white, used 1980-present. A *white* woven S.T. is used for Limited Editions and Collector Series.

- C.T. indicates paper "Chest Tag."

- Watermelon C.T. indicates the C.T. is a blue bear head with a smiling "watermelon" mouth (1927-1950).

- Red C.T.: For a short time in the early 1950s the animal's name was printed in *red* letters, instead of blue, on the usual (not watermelon) bear's head C.T. with an inverted "V" mouth (1950-1972).

- New C.T. indicates the C.T. is a yellow/red *circle* (1972-Present).

- US-Zone tag indicates "Made in US-Zone Germany"; cloth tag sewn into a seam (1947-1953).

- N.P.A. indicates "No Price Available."

- C.S.P. indicates "Current Sales Price."

- 1 inch equals 2.54 cm.

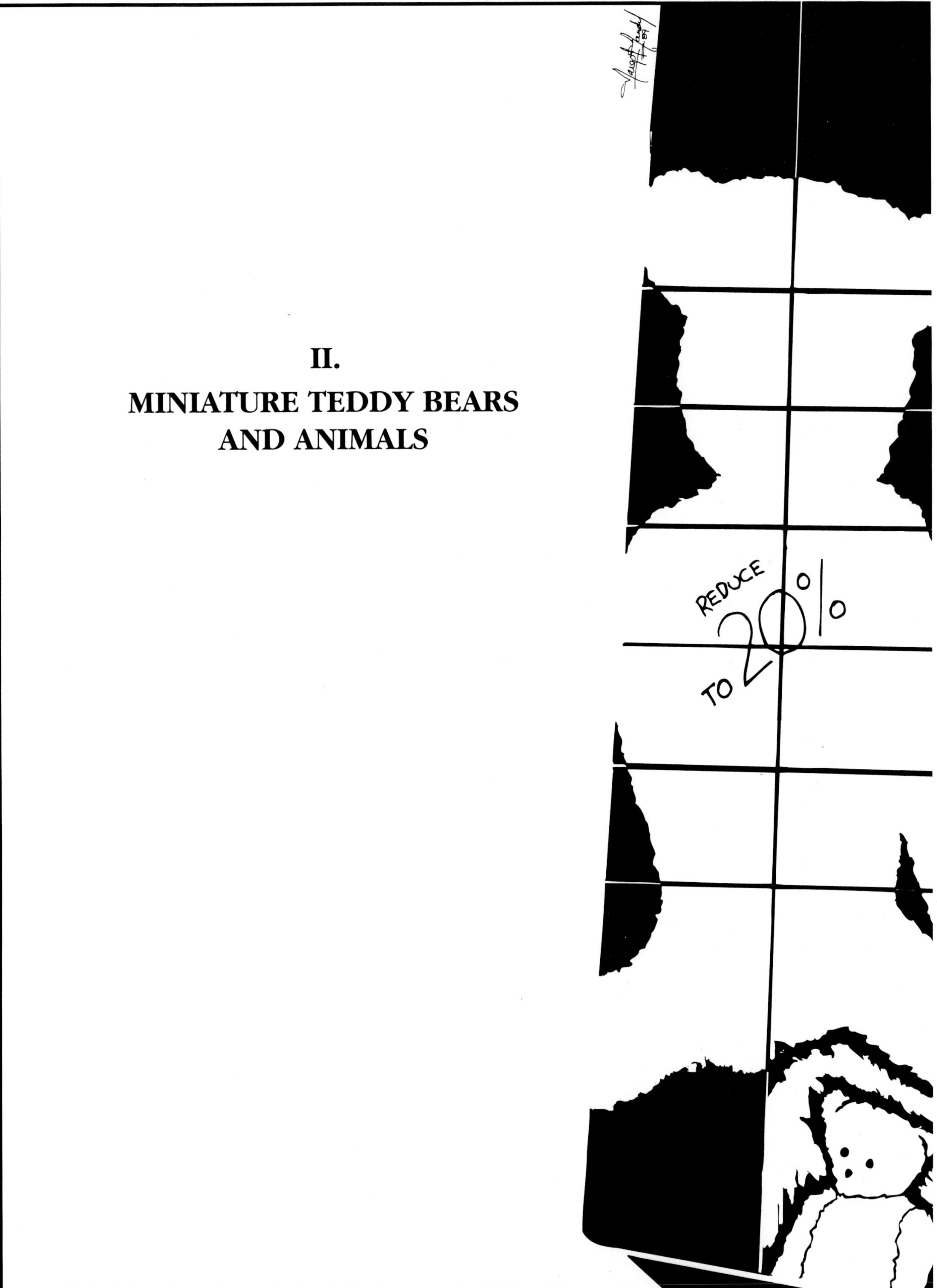

II.
MINIATURE TEDDY BEARS AND ANIMALS

Pincushion manufactured by Steiff with imagination and care. Attached to mushroom (3½"/9 cm.) is a squirrel (2¼/5.7 cm.) and a rabbit (2"/5 cm. not inc. ears); all are velveteen; squirrel's bushy tail is mohair; cotton stuffed; glass eyes; silk thread outlines nose/mouth. Rabbit has original silk ribbon; squirrel holds a nut stem; all are finely detailed. A treasure, ca. early 1900s.
Sitting up nearby is a velveteen rabbit: 5"/12.7 cm. inc. ears; glass bead eyes; pink silk thread nose/mouth; original silk ribbon and brass bell.
Courtesy Jeremy Bleecher and Patricia Gallagher.

Small things possess a tinge of genius. All are velveteen; firmly cotton stuffed; unjointed; have black glass button eyes and share the same construction, ca. 1903.
Tabby cat: 4¼"/10.8 cm.; ELEPHANT BUTTON on *back* of left ear; original ribbon and brass bell; great markings.
Center, Steiff Pug dog: 5¾"/14.6 cm.; special features are *rattle* and original early artificial leather collar.
Right, Steiff dog: 5½"/14 cm.; brown velveteen nose outlined in black floss that extends to mouth; *rattle.* Rare and desirable.
Courtesy Jeremy Bleecher and Patricia Gallagher.

A turquoise kangaroo to refresh the beholder: 6"/15.2 cm. inc. ears; velveteen; e.s.; unjointed; black glass bead eyes; beige floss nose/mouth; Steiff but no I.D., pre-1910. Extremely rare. Courtesy Jeremy Bleecher and Patricia Gallagher.

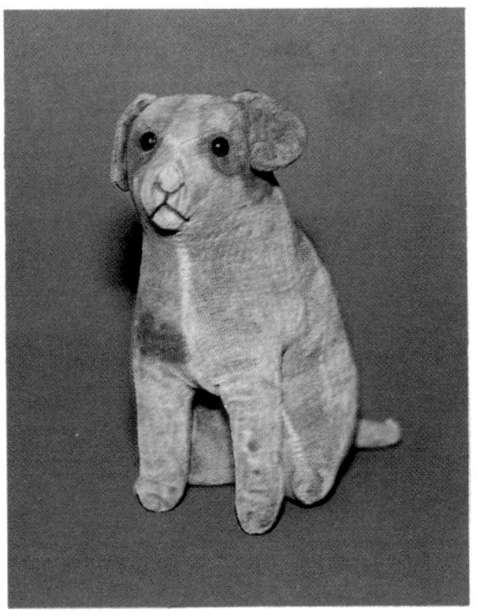

One of the first: 4½/11.5 cm.; *blank button*; e.s.; unjointed; shoe button eyes, ca. 1905. The young and young at heart have always enjoyed the Steiff miniature animals; scarce in excellent condition with I.D. Courtesy Harriet Purtill.

"Hambrick": 5¼"/13.3 cm.; Steiff FF button; white mohair; e.s.; f.j.; black eyes; twisted hard, rust color cotton floss nose/mouth on long pointed snout; no pads. Note, there is a crescent-shaped seam between ears (found on some rod bears). The body is one piece, seamed in front. Good condition, ca. 1908. Miniature Teddys of this vintage are *scarce.* Shown with tin bath, working pump and wooden bucket, ca. 1880.

"Star Gazer": 5½"/14 cm.; pre 1920s Steiff; mohair; glass stickpin eyes. Note the big feet, small hump and wonderful detail on such a *small* Teddy. He looks like a big early bear that shrunk. His head *tilts up*. At night he looks at stars; during the day he looks for rainbows. Rare size for a vintage bear. Courtesy Wanda Loukides.

Steiff Bulldog: 3½"/9 cm. high; FF button; tan velveteen faded from turquoise. This blue shows on inside of ears, bottoms of feet and at neck swivel; tri-color googly glass eyes in white, amber and black; twisted hard, black cotton floss nose; airbrushed mouth and snout; felt tongue; downy-type ruff sewn around neck. Designed as a pincushion and used. There are small dark spots on the head the size of pins. Rare, ca. late 1920s.
Courtesy Kirk Stines.

Snow (Babies) Bears: pink, 2½"/6 cm. high; black, 3½"/9 cm. long; pebbly-textured bisque snow suits and caps; painted features. Stamped "Made in Japan, Pat. 16977." Snow Babies were made both in Germany and Japan and can be of excellent to poor quality from either country. Full of fun and charm, ca. 1930s.
Courtesy Marian Swartz.

The teeny,tiny, highly detailed and expressive all bisque Teddy is ⅞" (2.2 cm.). He is attached by the original green floss leash to the 3"/8 cm. all bisque child, marked "Made in Germany"; a rare jewel from the 1930s.

Carnival-type Panda: 5"/12.5 cm.; painted celluloid head; cotton and rayon body; unjointed; *sawdust stuffed*; original orange silk ribbon, ca. 1930-40.
Right: 2¼"/5.7 cm. high, 2½"/6.5 cm. long; *heavy celluloid* body; hard rubber wheels, ca. 1930s. Rare accents to a Teddy collection.
Courtesy Wanda Loukides.

Three colors and birth dates of miniature Steiff. Left: 6"/15 cm.; beige mohair from 1960s; f.j.; *brown* floss nose/mouth. Note: he has fatter, fuller look than the 1950s bears. Center: 5"/12.5 cm.; pre-1930s; longer white (desirable color) mohair; amber glass eyes; *rust* color floss nose/mouth; small hump, narrow pointy feet and *large ears*; side squeaker. Great demand. Right: 5½"/14 cm. from the late 1940s; gold mohair; excelsior hard stuffed; f.j.; tan glass eyes; *black* floss nose/mouth; large feet turn upward. Note the long snout for this size bear. Courtesy Wanda Loukides.

Steiff 1950s Teddy enjoys looking at his ancestors on the charming postcards published by C.M. Paula Co., Cincinnati, Ohio in 1984. The scoop shovel snout loads him with personality. The mohair bear is 5½"/14 cm. with the typical long turned up toes found on this size and smaller.

Having fun in the children's Christmas tree is the beloved miniature Steiff *Teddy Baby*: 4"/10 cm.; desirable cream color mohair; e.s.; f.j.; glass eyes; twisted hard, brown cotton floss nose and (closed) mouth, ca. 1950s. The clue to this *Teddy Baby* is the velveteen feet. No. I.D. Courtesy Barbara Baldwin.

People collect colors. These 1950s fully jointed 3½"/9 cm. Steiff *Original Teddys* demonstrate the important variables of color, size and condition in determining value. The chocolate brown bears are the most desirable; followed by white, caramel and gold.
Courtesy Barbara Baldwin.

Outfitted in his own trunk: 3¼"/8 cm.; brown mohair; neck is rigid, wire jointed arms and legs move in unison; "stalk" eyes; sliced-in ears faced with felt; long shaved snout; felt overalls and cape.
Maker unknown, ca. 1950.
Courtesy Evelyn Thomas.

Panda: 5½"/14 cm.; mohair; e.s.; f.j.; googly glass eyes; *yarn* nose/mouth, no claws; felt pads; unknown maker, ca. 1950s. The markings on body are not Panda-like. Many collectors prefer Pandas that look like real Pandas, rather than like bears that happen to be black and white.
Courtesy Barbara Baldwin.

Bear family made exclusively for Woodward and Lothrop Dept. Store by Mutzli of Switzerland: 5"/12.5 cm., 6"/15cm. and 4½"/11.5 cm. baby. Though of mohair and high quality workmanship as well as being a special dressed issue, there is little investment potential in *any* unjointed bear. Considered a baby's bear, ca. 1950s. Courtesy Barbara Baldwin.

Limited production, contemporary *Berlin Bear:* 2¾"/11 cm.; mohair over metal body; f.j.; plastic bead eyes and nose; tin crown is embedded in head; removable banner, *"Berlin tut gut"* (Berlin does it right). The Schuco Berlin Bear was originally made in 1962 to celebrate Kennedy's visit to West Berlin. In 1987 Kathy Ann Dolls reissued it in conjunction with the 750th birthday of that city. Other miniature bears of Schuco design with stitched noses are *currently manufactured* in Germany and sold as "old store stock" made by Schuco. The easy way to tell: outside of both the paws and feet there is a staple-like metal protrusion on the reproductions. These should sell for $20.00-30.00. As always, the collector must be armed with knowledge.

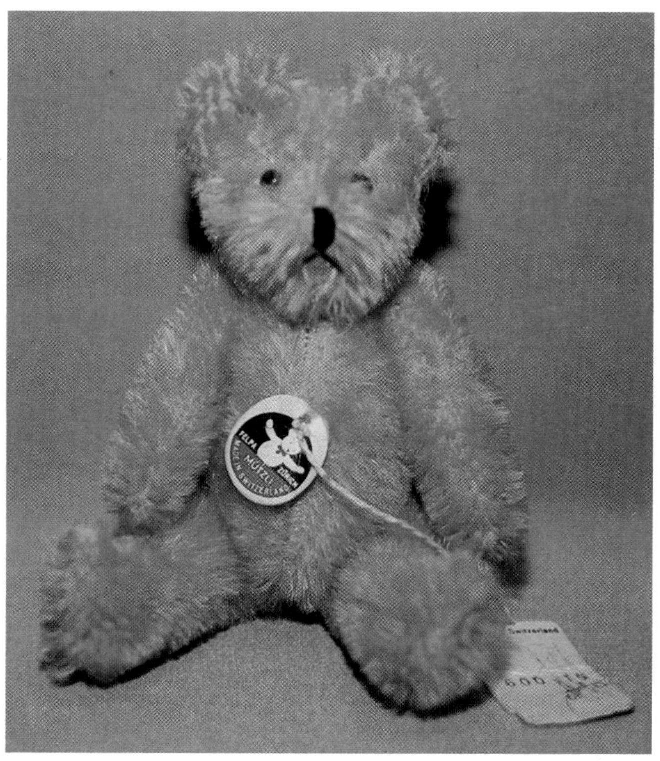

Swiss: 6½"/16 cm.; C.T. "Felpa//Zurich//Mutzli//Made in Switzerland"; mohair; f.j.; black shoe button-type eyes; floss nose/mouth; no claws or pads; original price tag in Swiss currency, ca. 1950-60. Well made. The original tags increase value. *Felpa* means "plush" in Spanish.
Courtesy Wanda Loukides.

III. TEDDY BEARS BEFORE 1940

Teddy Bears: 1903-1912

1912-1920

1920-1930

1930-1940

Teddy Bears 1903-1912

The prized rod bear is an example of something that fits into a collection to be studied and enjoyed. Extremely rare rod bear with *elephant button*, ca. 1903: 20"; mohair; e.s.; hard bodied; metal rods connect the joints; shoe button eyes; floss replaces the sealing wax nose and light brown thread mouth; extra long snout with short, broad forehead; four brown stitched claws; replaced pads. Note: a seam connects the ears. This is found on some elephant button bears and other *early* Steiff Teddys.
Courtesy Karen Silverstein.

The first Ideal Teddy: 18"/45.5 cm.; dense mohair; e.s.; f.j.; besides the triangular face, low set ears and pointy feet, the shoe button eyes give a clue. On an Ideal they are *round* and *shiny* as if lacquered. The nose floss is thicker and the (five) claws are short with the thread often looped slightly onto tip of pad. Price takes a dramatic upturn for the super mint condition and close resemblance to the Smithsonian Bear, ca. 1903. That original Michtom (Ideal) bear is 30" tall. Some collectors prefer an early Ideal to Steiff.
Courtesy Barbara Baldwin.

Birthday gift to a little girl, August 1904: 14½"/37 cm.; mohair; e.s.; f.j.; shoe button eyes; woven nose; cotton floss mouth; three claws; felt pads; no voice box. The triangular-shaped smallish head and oversize ears set low are characteristics attributed to Ideal. More of this "sweet look" bear were made in 1904 because they were more salable than the "hard look" of the bruin-type early Steiff.
Courtesy Jeremy Bleecher and Patricia Gallagher.

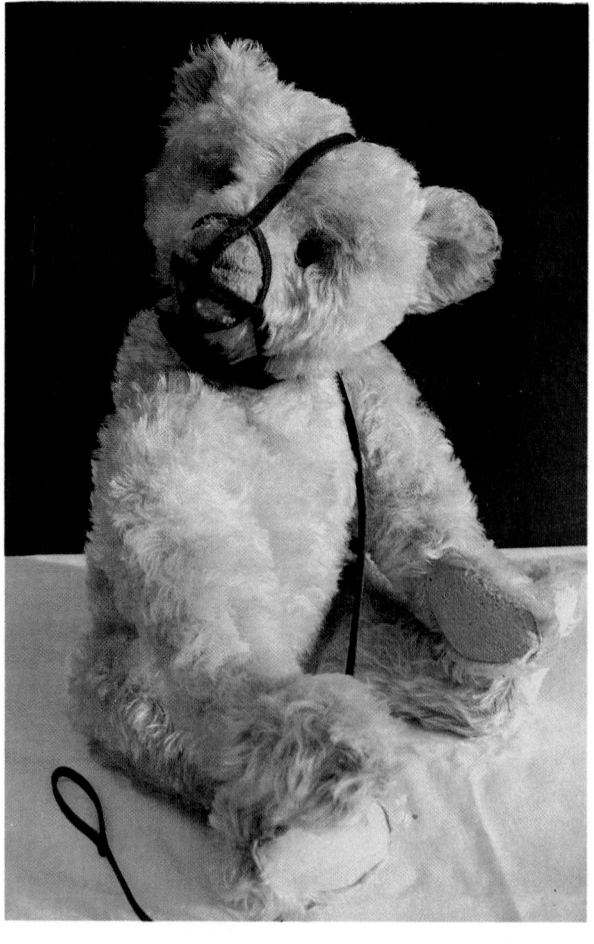

"Attikus,"center seam muzzled bear: 20½"/52 cm.; blank Steiff button (1905-06); long pile silky white dense mohair; stuffed with kapok-excelsior mix (found on earliest bears); f.j.; deep set shoe button eyes; twisted hard, rust color cotton floss nose (reinforced with felt) and mouth; four claws; felt pads reinforced with cardboard and felt; early side squeaker The original leather muzzle is representative of European dancing circus bears and adds value. The rarest as well as most in demand Teddys are: *Dickey*, pre 1912 *Black Bear*, blue eyed *Petsy* and the *Muzzle Bear*; all highly sought after by advanced collectors. This issue is the prototype for Steiff's 1988-89 Muzzle Bear.
Courtesy Ingried Wustner, West Germany.

A collector wants what is rare and wonderful. This can be *color* as in the 20"/51 cm. cinnamon bear with curly mohair, unusual *size* and/or *mint condition*. The white is 10"/25 cm., the honey color is 14"/35.5 cm.; all have blank buttons dating from 1903-04 and are mint. The cinnamon has colored felt under the foot pads and floss nose. On Steiff Teddys felt under the nose can predate colored felt backing of pads. Note the acutely curved paws stressing the ankles. The neck is another stress point because of head weight. Necks and ankles should be examined carefully when purchasing a large expensive bear. Courtesy Diane Hoffman.

The bear who went to Harvard has just won the rugby scrimmage: 16"/40.5 cm,; tiny blank button (tiny buttons are earliest); long dense white mohair; excelsior and kapok stuffed. If the head were opened the kapok would "explode"; deep set shoe button eyes; twisted hard, rust color cotton floss over rust felt nose; floss mouth; *five* claws placed evenly around paw pads (center one is not elongated), four claws on feet. Other early Steiff Teddys have been found with *five* claws, especially on paws. Perhaps one woman in 1904 Germany made all of the five clawed bears. This personable Teddy has the bruin-like "hard look" which is another way to tell an early bear. The Harvard outfit with quilted pants has always been with Teddy and can add $250.00 to value. There is wear to pads and ear. Shown with "Baby Grand" wagon, ca. 1910 and *The Story of the Three Bears* with six richly colored original lithographs by R. Heighway, published by McLoughlin Bros. before 1888. Courtesy Suzanne Hill.

"Smile and say 'honey'" said the photographer to the three 24"/61 cm. center seam Steiff bears, pre 1910: FF button; long pile mohair; e.s.; f.j.; shoe button eyes; nose/mouth on left is *dark brown* twisted hard cotton floss; center and right have black; four claws; felt pads; working tilt-type growlers. Growlers were first used in 1908. The squeeze-type squeaker was introduced in 1912 with the side squeaker being the earliest. Large bears are extremely rare in this beautifully preserved condition. Private Collection.

The aristocrats of Teddybeardom are descendents of the House of Steiff: 28"/71 cm.; FF button; mohair; e.s.; f.j.; shoe button eyes; twisted hard, black cotton floss (vertical) nose/mouth; four claws; felt pads; voice box; rare size; super mint condition, ca. 1905. The pride of ownership of this elegant large Teddy is enhanced by his handsome price appreciation--especially in recent years.
Private Collection.

Outstanding quality and rarity: four Steiff 20"/50.8 cm. Teddys; the first with blank button, the next three are center seam with FF buttons; all have long pile silky golden mohair; e.s.; f.j.; shoe button eyes; twisted hard, cotton floss (vertical) nose/mouth in dark brown, black, black and dark brown; four color matched claws; felt pads and growlers. Pre-1910.
Private Collection.

Only a minority of Teddys and animals are found in mint condition. These command premium prices. Two Teddy treasures: left, 29"/74 cm. and right, 25"/63.5 cm.; Steiff FF buttons; golden mohair; e.s.; f.j.; shoe button eyes; twisted hard, black cotton floss nose/mouth; four claws; felt pads; working voice boxes; extremely desirable sizes, ca. 1906. Steiff STUDIO Dalmation: 15"/38 cm. high, 24"/61 cm. long; RSB; C.T. *Dally*; short mohair spotted black; e.s.; unjointed; glass eyes; twisted hard, cotton floss nose and open felt mouth; three claws; working squeaker, ca. 1950. Rare. Private Collection.

Precious cargo: left, 29"/74 cm.; FF button; extremely rare, long curly cinnamon RED mohair Teddy with the important "cone-shaped" head. His sweet-faced friend is 24"/61 cm. with FF button. The rarest and most desirable sizes of early Steiff are these 24 and 29 inch examples. Demand is less for the 36-40 inch. Both are e.s.; f.j.; have shoe button eyes; twisted hard, black cotton floss nose/mouth; four claws; felt pads and voice boxes; mint, ca. 1905-08. STUDIO *Polar Dog*: 24"/60 cm. high; RSB; S.T. 69a/1360; mohair; e.s.; steel frame; ears fortified with wire so they are always on the alert; swivel head; amber glass bright eyes; pearl cotton nose, open felt mouth; three stitched claws; mohair pads; no voice box; ca. 1950s. Private Collection.

Fine Teddy Bears are moving to the forefront of prestige collecting here and abroad. *Front*: 13"/33 cm.; Steiff blank button; white mohair; mint; appealing sad expression, ca. 1904. *Back*: 24"/61 cm. blank button; center seam; desirable curly cinnamon mohair; e.s.; f.j.; shoe button eyes; faded brown (attractive), twisted hard, cotton floss nose/mouth; four brown claws; felt pads reinforced with red felt, ca. 1904. Steiff bears *over* 20" are in great demand, as is curly mohair. Whether dense or curly depends on mohair maker. The curl comes out of length. If too curly the sculpturesque outline of bear can be lost.
Courtesy Karen Silverstein.

A close conversation between friends who will obviously soon be in each other's arms. Studio portrait taken ca. 1908. The Steiff bear's name was "Teddy" and closely resembles the Richard Steiff bear. Vintage photographs complete the Teddy Bear vision and are a welcome addition to a collection.

"Oskar": 16½"/42 cm.; tiny FF button; silky dense mohair; e.s.; f.j.; deep set shoe button eyes; twisted hard, black cotton floss nose (reinforced with felt); floss mouth; four claws; felt pads on long feet; voice box, ca. 1906. Superb example of the Teddy Bear maker's art in *rare* original condition.
Courtesy Ingried Wustner, West Germany.

Easily loved: 13"/33 cm.; Steiff, no I.D.; mohair at one time; e.s.; f.j.; shoe button eyes; faded black cotton floss nose, missing mouth; pads recovered with coal black fabric; a visual Teddy dressed in her original jumpsuit and attached overskirt with a card suit print (aces, spades, hearts and clubs), ca. 1910.
Courtesy Jeremy Bleecher and Patricia Gallagher.

Teddy Bears come from impressive blood lines, having been named for President Theodore Roosevelt. Each American bear wears a T.R. campaign button. All are mohair, pre-1912; have shoe button eyes and voice boxes. (L-R): 8"/20.5 cm.; e.s.; f.j.; pearl cotton floss nose, no sign of ever having a mouth; three claws; sheared mohair paw pads; rare size. Typical American: 16"/40.6 cm.; excelsior stuffed body, head is *crushed cork*; f.j.; nose is fine black floss in a semi-weaving stitch; five claws; replaced pads. Possible Ideal: 18"/ 45.5 cm.; e.s.; f.j.; cotton floss nose (restored) and mouth; no claws; felt pads; near mint. Note the large fat feet and *slender* ankles that can cause fabric breaks. Pale gold: 12"/30.5 cm.; e.s.; f.j.; restored nose/mouth; three claws on feet, none on paws. Shown with *Teddy Bear's Printing and Drawing Book* by F.I. Wetherbee, New York: The H.B. Claflin Co., 1907.

The finer value points of Teddy: 12"/30.5 cm.; FF button; dense *white* mohair, mint. White bears are desirable and bring higher prices than gold. However, there are a number of white vintage bears in existence. They hold up well because the wool is natural and not dyed by harsh chemicals. Note the perfectly executed nose of twisted hard, rust color cotton floss. Collectors are sensitive about bears' noses; ca. 1907.
Courtesy Barbara Baldwin.

Attributed to Ideal: 12"/30 cm.; long gold mohair; e.s.; f.j.; round and shiny button eyes; thicker twisted floss nose and mouth; five claws; replaced felt pads. Note the triangular (Ideal) shape of head, ca. 1910. The Teddy has "patina." Patina is a surface softening including body shape and facial expression, changes acquired through use and love. It is not grubbiness. Shown with print: 6"/15 cm. x 8"/ 20cm.; signed "St. John"; portrays Roosevelt-type bears going on a picnic, ca. 1915.
Courtesy Marian Swartz.

"Charly Jolly" arrived at his original owner's home Dec. 25, 1908: 11"/28 cm.; light gold mohair; hard stuffed with cotton; f.j.; shoe button eyes; black YARN nose/mouth, no claws; suede *leather* pads; short feet; hump. Note how the snout tilts down to chest. Expressive and high quality bear, but difficult to sell. Unknown maker.
Courtesy Marsha Pfenning.

Special Times. *Left:* 14"/36 cm.; mohair; e.s.; f.j.; shoe button eyes; BROWN FELT NOSE; black floss mouth and four claws; felt pads; mint. Note *long* arms and feet; unknown American maker, ca. 1910. *Right*: 14"/36 cm.; mohair; e.s.; f.j.; shoe button eyes; floss nose/mouth; felt pads. Note five claws, pointy foot pads and triangular-shaped head (characteristic of Ideal).
Courtesy Karen Silverstein.

A comparison of Bruin Manufacturing Co. and Steiff bears. Front, Bruin: 18"/46 cm.; tag sewn to right pad, "B.M.C."; copper tone mohair; e.s.; f.j.; flat shoe button eyes; floss nose/mouth; *six claws*; felt pads. Note the long low-jutting snout on this choice American bear, ca. 1907. Sweater is original to bear; knit from a pattern for Teddy Bears ca. 1908, when Teddy Bear apparel was the rage. Back, Steiff: 20"/51 cm.; FF button, ca. 1908. Teddys enjoy having their own sled on which to ride: 12"/31 cm.; wide, 24"/61 cm. long; bear imprinted on back; no I.D., ca. 1910-20. Courtesy Karen Silverstein.

"Bushy," left: 14"/35.5 cm.; long white mohair; e.s.; f.j.; shoe button eyes; brown pearl cotton nose/mouth; three claws; felt pads; voice will sound by either pressing or tilting. High quality, probably German, ca. 1910. "Bingley," center: 10"/25 cm,; *extra fine* dense old gold mohair; e.s.; f.j.; amber glass eyes; heavily embroidered cotton floss nose/mouth; felt pads; growler. Note the elegantly shaped legs of this Bing Teddy, ca. 1915-20. The snout is very much like a true bear. "Rugby," right: 17"/43 cm.; dense short (1/8") *maroon* mohair (like upholstery fabric); e.s.; f.j.; dark amber glass eyes with an extra high dome; nose and mouth are wool *yarn*; felt pads; no claws; squeaker. Note the unusual color/material often used by manufacturers around WWI. Stands out in a collection. Unknown maker, probably German. Shown with set of three wooden picture puzzles in *Three Bears Puzzle Box*, Milton Bradley, 1907.

Benign and lovable Teddy of fine quality - probably pre-1910 German, but not Steiff. Steiff never mounted the eyes up on the center gusset as in this head construction. Long pile mohair, 13½"/34 cm.; e.s.; f.j.; button eyes; thin ply twisted floss over twill nose; floss mouth and four claws; felt pads on extra long feet. Humpty Dumpty: 13"/33 cm. inc. hat; all felt hard stuffed with cotton; jointed arms and legs; painted features; well defined hands; old repair at wrists and ankles (stress points). At back of sewn on hat tagged, "Humpty Dumpty Doll, Trade Mark Ross and Ross, Oakland, Cal. Pat. May 22, 1917." Unusual.
Courtesy Marian Swartz.

Woolly Teddy: 7"/18 cm.; FF button; mohair; e.s.; f.j.; shoe button eyes; twisted hard, black cotton floss nose and mouth; four claws; no paw pads on bears of this size. Small Steiff bears are in great demand especially with unusual features like the *woolly mohair.* This size is difficult to find from any era prior to 1950. Ca. pre-1920.
Courtesy Barbara Baldwin.

The unmistakable elongated profile of Bing (German) bears. Left, "Peddler," 12"/30.5 cm.; right, "Theodore," 15"/38 cm.; both are mohair; e.s.; f.j.; have *long pointed* snouts, red-amber glass eyes and heavily stitched noses, ca. 1910. "Peddler" is worn but nonetheless shares a place of honor. There is a good chance that many vintage bears casually identified as Steiff may be Bings.
Courtesy Kay Bransky.

Early Americans: left, 13"/33 cm.; off-white medium pile mohair; excelsior stuffed head, soft body/limbs; f.j.; shoe button eyes; black *felt* nose, floss mouth; five claws; replaced pads. Note the cone-shaped head, long neck and wide-set legs; unknown maker, ca. 1912. Good condition. Right: 18"/45.5 cm.; medium pile mohair; e.s.; f.j.; shoe button eyes; black *twill* nose, floss mouth; four claws; replaced pads; working squeaker. Note the small body, large arms and widely set legs; similar to the 1907 "White House" Teddy Bear (Schoonmaker, Ill. 43). Shown with lithographed alphabet blocks, ca. 1900.

Columbia *Laughing Bear*: 18"/46 cm.; *bright gold* mohair (also made in rust color); e.s.; f.j.; glass eyes; floss nose; mouth lined with red paper; painted teeth; two milk glass lower teeth fit into holes above. When tummy is pressed, he emits a deep "bark" and opens his mouth; mouth opens soundlessly when head is turned. This is activated by a spool with string around it in the stomach which winds tighter when tummy is pressed or head is turned, ca. 1907-12. Important bear that commands attention.

Teddy Bears 1912-1920

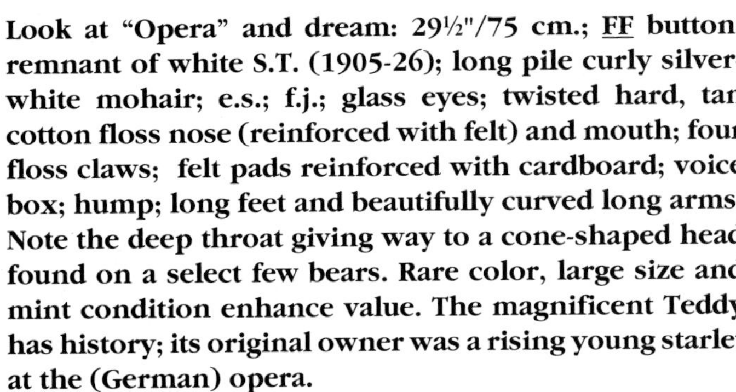

Look at "Opera" and dream: 29½"/75 cm.; FF button; remnant of white S.T. (1905-26); long pile curly silver-white mohair; e.s.; f.j.; glass eyes; twisted hard, tan cotton floss nose (reinforced with felt) and mouth; four floss claws; felt pads reinforced with cardboard; voice box; hump; long feet and beautifully curved long arms. Note the deep throat giving way to a cone-shaped head found on a select few bears. Rare color, large size and mint condition enhance value. The magnificent Teddy has history; its original owner was a rising young starlet at the (German) opera.
Courtesy Ingried Wustner, West Germany.

"Opera" was given to Evamaria Bohn when she was born, Nov. 16, 1915. Since then, he was a member of the family and in on everything. Teddy was at ease among the dolls and other Steiff animals; he went to boarding school and then to the College of Music in Nuremberg; he lived through the air raids of WWII and finally moved to the daughter's family. There too, he again sat among dolls on the couch and dominated. He was a personality -- he saw us and we spoke to him.
(Translated from German.)

Comical Steiff to bring smiles. Right: 12"/30cm.; FF button; e.s.; f.j.; TINY original shoe button eyes set close together (bears in real life have tiny beady eyes); twisted hard, dark brown cotton floss nose (missing mouth); four claws. The stuffing has separated out of the nose tip giving a hooked nose appearance, ca. 1912. Left: white mohair, 11½"/29 cm.; hard stuffed with early cotton enabling the bear to hold form; f.j.; clear glass eyes. The nose/mouth and five claws are rust color thin ply *yarn*; felt pads; low set ears and desirable conformation; unknown maker, ca. 1912.
Courtesy Marian Swartz.

"Mr. Perky": 12"/30cm.; mohair; firmly e.s.; f.j.; shoe button eyes; black twisted floss (vertical) nose with fabric backing; floss mouth and five claws; felt pads/cardboard innersoles; hump; squeaker. He has the proper number of "toes" for a real bear. Most Teddys have fewer. Note his long snout and well proportioned body and limbs. Maker unknown, ca. 1915-20. The hump and excelsior alone do not indicate age. Japan still stuffs with excelsior; many old bears had no hump and new ones do.
Courtesy Pam North.

Exact dating of 1917 from the original owner, rare *large* Steiff Teddy: 30"/76 cm.; light golden aged to light brown long curly mohair; e.s.; f.j.; large shoe button eyes (shoe button eyes were used into early 1920s); twisted hard, black cotton floss nose, missing mouth (easily restored by a skilled artist and not appreciably affecting value); four claws; felt pads; working growler. Note how feet flop outward, a desirable characteristic of early Steiff Teddys. Prong marks are present, button missing. There are dangers in following ONLY Steiff marks. Look at quality first when identifying Steiff. Tricycle is from the early 1900s.
Courtesy Linda Croucher.

The perfectly featured body of the Aetna (American) Teddy Bear: 20"/51 cm.; oval stamp on right foot; golden mohair; e.s.; f.j.; shoe button eyes; heavy floss nose, mouth and five claws. Felt foot pads are reinforced with cardboard which serves as a hard surface for applying the stamp. Rare mark and mint condition, ca. 1915. The name Aetna has instant recall for doll collectors. In 1909 they bought the American Doll and Toy Co. who produced "Can't Break'em Dolls." Aetna then made these composition heads for Horsman.
Courtesy Barbara Baldwin.

American bear: 20"/51 cm.; dense short mohair; e.s.; f.j.; wide set shoe button eyes; large, low-set ears; brown floss nose/mouth; three radiating-type claws; felt pads on acutely curved paws and pointy feet; squeaker, ca. 1915. Sweet-faced bear, desirable because of looks rather than lineage. Courtesy Barbara Baldwin.

"Old Glory," American Clown: 18"/46 cm.; sparse red, white and blue mohair; e.s.; swivel head, wire jointed limbs; glass eyes; black floss nose/mouth; three claws; felt pads; squeaker; original yellow felt collar. The right ear was replaced at factory by an integral stuffed mohair clown hat; ca. WWI era (1917-18).

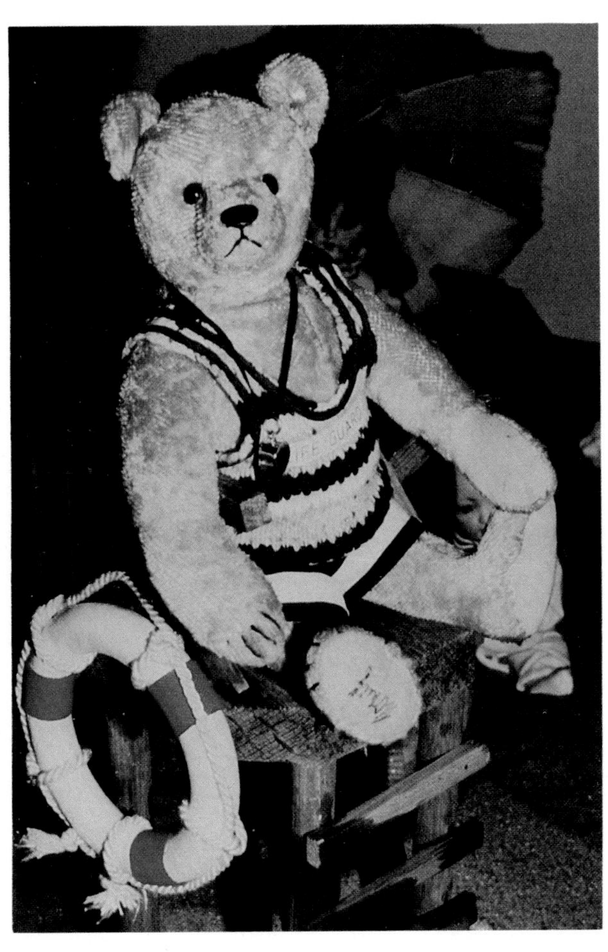

Lifeguard in the spotlight: 11"/28 cm.; FF button; upholstery-type woven fur covering with a silky feel; e.s.; f.j.; shoe button eyes; twisted hard, black cotton floss mouth and nose done in outline style as found on smaller Steiff bears; four floss claws; *muslin pads*; squeaker. The pads help to date him shortly after WWII when only the cheapest materials were available. Other Steiff Teddys from this period are found with *muslin pads*. Many collectors feel that a recent Steiff signature on the pad of a vintage bear does NOT enhance value. Though not the sought after long mohair, this example would be hard to replace. Mint condition from original owner.
Courtesy Debbie Masters.

"Barney," left: 20"/51 cm.; mohair; e.s.; f.j.; sliced-in ears; glass eyes/glass stems; floss nose/mouth; five claws on feet, four on hands; felt pads. He has a shallow (manufactured) hole in center of mouth which probably held a peg for a ring and chain. Unknown maker, ca. 1918. "Reddy Kilowatt": 13½"/34 cm.; mohair; e.s.; jointed arms only; light bulb eyes (switch inside of left ear); black felt nose, missing mouth; felt pads reinforced with cardboard. American electric eye bears did not give satisfaction. The batteries wore out and the glass, bulb small eyes broke easily. Rare today. Unusual small size and red color, ca. 1915-20.

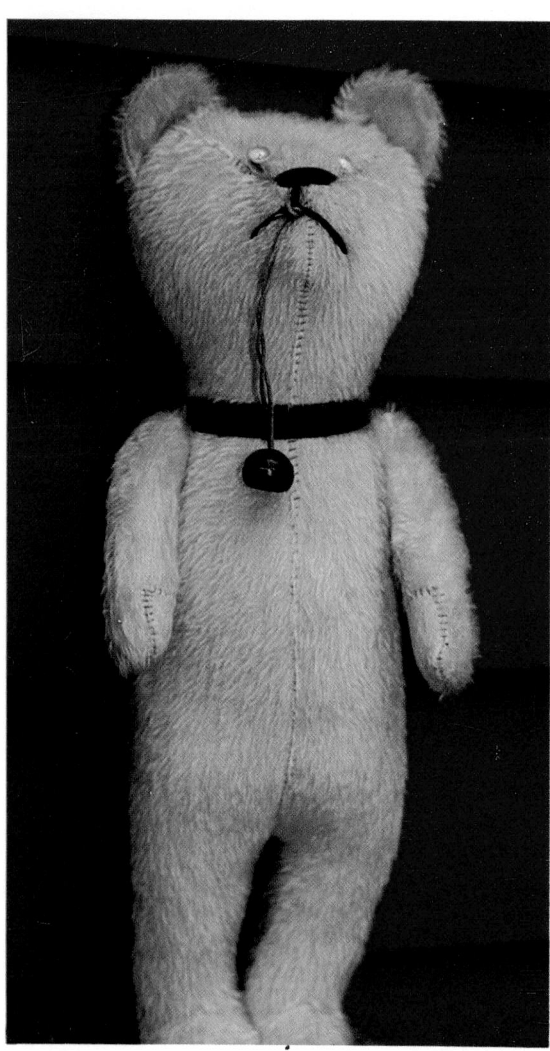

Electric Eye Bear that enjoyed a trial period of twelve years, 1907-1919: 20"/51 cm.; cream mohair (unusual color); *firmly* stuffed with excelsior; jointed head and arms only; bulb eyes; black yarn mouth with *cloth* nose; felt pads. Large dark stitching around paws and body seams indicate an early (pre-1920) American bear. Original collar and cord/knob. Push button in knob to light up eyes; battery pack inside back. Difficult to find in excellent condition. Neat bear!
Courtesy Barbara Baldwin.

Speaker for the group: 14"/35.5 cm.; short pile mohair; e.s.; f.j.; shoe button eyes; floss (pyramid shape) nose/mouth; no claws on long feet; nice hump; unknown American maker, ca. 1918. Sometimes it can be difficult to distinguish a white Teddy from a lighter gold one. The *fabric backing* on white bears is white; the *backing* on light gold is gold.
Courtesy Betty Peil.

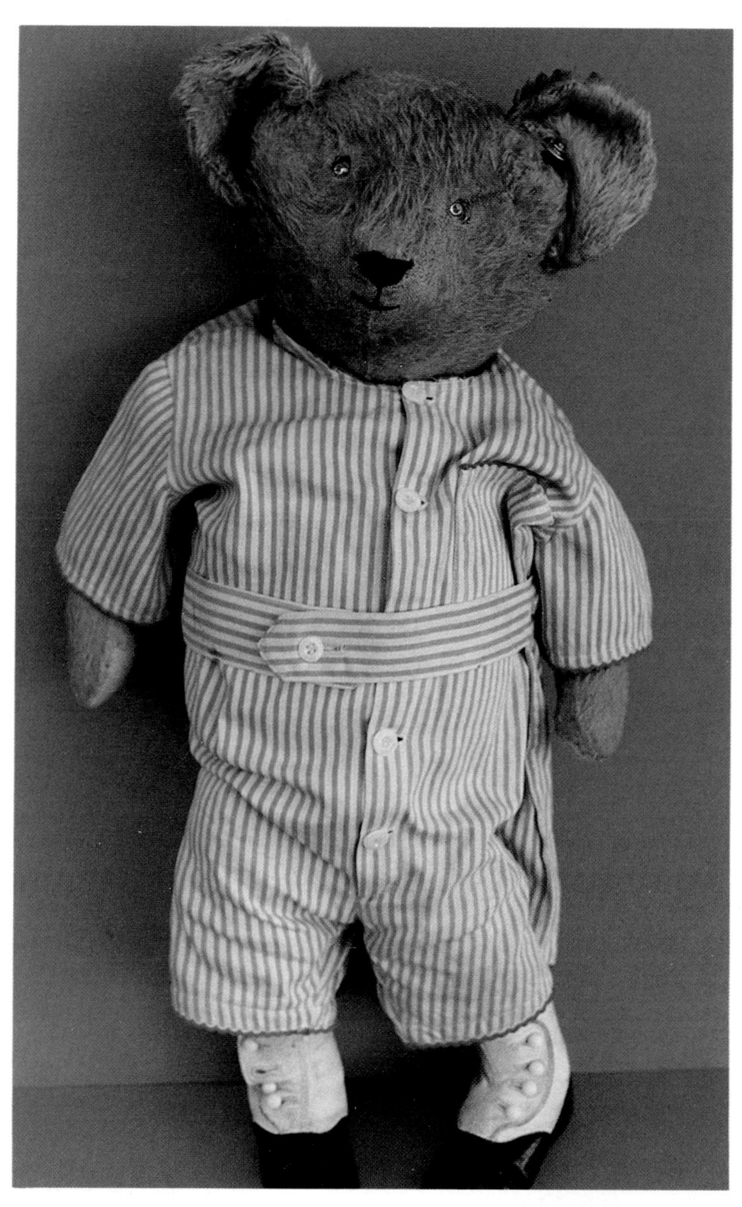

The big stuffed animal sensation of 1914: Electric Eye Bear, 26"/66 cm.; long pile mohair; e.s.; f.j. (among Electric Eye Bears full jointing is rare); flashlight bulb eyes; black embroidery floss nose and tiny mouth; lightweight felt pads; no claws. The battery operated push button switch is in ear. The suit and four button child shoes have always been on bear.
Courtesy Diane Hoffman.

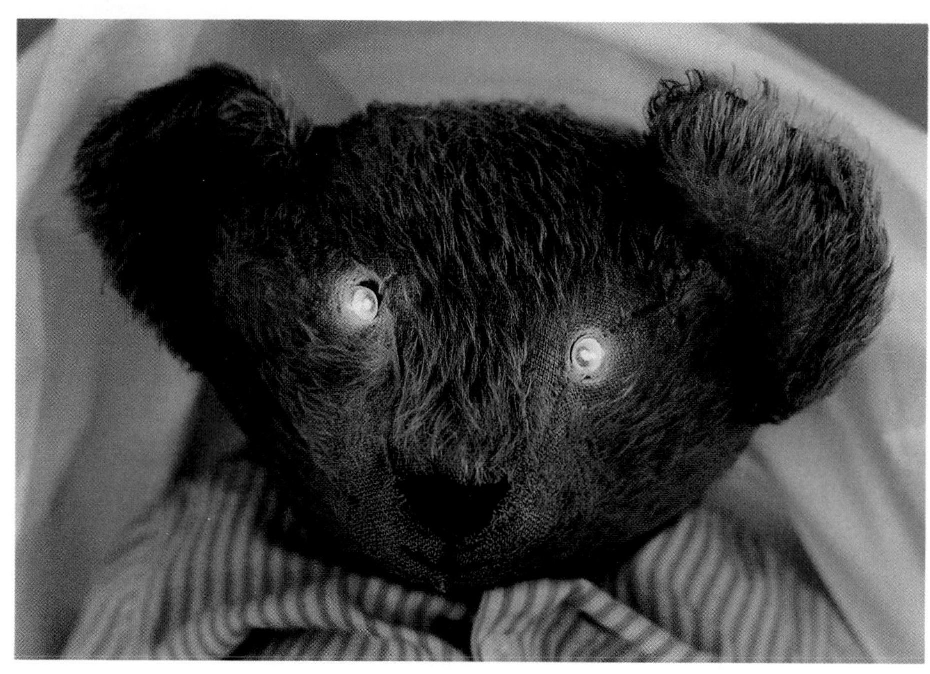

Teddy's oversize ears have cardboard inserts. Mohair: 15"/ 38 cm.; head, hands and feet stuffed with excelsior; kapok stuffed torso, arms and legs; shoe button eyes; coarse floss outlines nose where twill piece once was; floss mouth and three (double strand) claws; thick thighs contour to skinny ankles; unknown maker, ca. 1915. Note close resemblance to "Mighty Bear" (without cardboard inserts).
Courtesy Diane Hoffman.

"Mighty Bear," named after his long time friend "Mighty Mouse": 12"/30.5 cm.; silky dense mohair; excelsior/kapok stuffed; kapok is the mass of silky fibers surrounding the seeds of the silk-cotton tree; f.j.; glass eyes; twill nose, floss mouth; three claws; felt pads; no voice box; unknown maker, ca. 1915-20. He has ears that would fit on a bear twice his size. This gives him an extraordinarily appealing look and is reflected in his price.
Courtesy Fran Cagner.

Teddy Bears 1920-1930

Bing: 18"/46 cm.; copper color mohair; e.s.; f.j.; glass eyes; floss nose/mouth; four claws; felt pads; heavy mechanism in torso (perhaps an inoperative music box); ca. 1920s. Note the mischievous expression; *very long* and pointed shaved snout; straight arms. Excellent patterning dramatized by LONG FINE mohair. Rare German Teddy in mint condition.
Courtesy Karen Silverstein.

Bing Werke (German) Teddy: 24"/61 cm; frosted mohair; e.s.; f.j.; shoe button eyes replace the distinctive Bing dark (red) amber glass eyes/black pupil; *heavily sewn* floss nose on a *very long shaved* snout to give the individual Bing look; attached ears. However, on some earlier Bings the ears are part of the back headpiece; replaced pads; three floss claws. Note the tiptoe foot placement. The growler emits an unusual (weird) sound. Metal red-orange Bing tag attached to outside wrist, ca. 1920. Unique bear.
Courtesy Barbara Baldwin.

Glass eyed Steiff Teddys: the middle one has center seam. These large bears, 25"/63.5 cm. encapsulate the collecting trend at this time. All have FF buttons; shades of golden mohair; e.s.; f.j.; twisted hard, black cotton floss (vertical) nose/mouth; four claws; felt pads; tilt-type growler. Note their super mint condition. The center seam dates from early 1920s; left and right have remnants of *red* S.T. (1926-34). Teddys from this period are extremely hard to find and often missing from Steiff collections. A premium must be paid for the center seam. For any year only every eighth bear made had a center seam due to the process of placing the center of the head gusset on the selvage and piecing together. This was done to save mohair; so the patterning is usually only found on the 16" and larger sizes.
Private Collection.

Beautiful Steiff: 8"/20 cm. high, 10"/25.4 cm. long; RSB; red S.T.; long curly white mohair; appears to be stuffed with paper (crunchy sound); unjointed; glass eyes; twisted hard, light brown floss nose/mouth on the gently upturned snout; 4 claws; *peachy* felt pads (indicate his mintness), ca. 1920s. He is strikingly similar to one of the rarest bears in the world--the wild Kermodei Bear from the Skeena River, around Terrace, British Columbia. In 1928 Dr. Kermode concluded the Kermodei was not an albino, but a true and extremely rare subspecies of the common North American Black Bear. Exciting toy for a collection.
Courtesy Barbara Baldwin.

"Teddy Red Socks": 18"/45.5 cm.; dense mohair; excelsior stuffed head, soft stuffed body and limbs; f.j.; glass eyes; black *yarn* nose and falling down mouth giving a friendly expression; felt pads; three yarn claws. Note how head is in a permanent tilt. A nice bear to have around. Dating from original owner, ca. 1920s; probably American, maker unknown.
Courtesy Linda Croucher.

A skilled artisan made Teddy from a camel hair coat. Left: 16"/40.6 cm.; lumpy excelsior stuffing except for the long snout which is hard stuffed with cotton; f.j.; glass eyes; floss nose/mouth; five claws; beaver felt pads. The arms and legs are muscular from stuffing with excelsior by a non-factory method, ca. 1920.
The early Steiff shaping is due to METHOD of excelsior stuffing as much as the wonderful pattern. They used either a "green excelsior" or wrapped moist excelsior around a stuffing tool. These segments then fit together like a jigsaw puzzle and are found especially on riding toys. The process achieved a HARD SCULPTED LOOK not present here. To date no Bear Artist has mastered the early technique with excelsior. The old excelsior was not dry and brittle to crack and had a red content that caused staining to the backing if the toy was submerged. Right: 14"/35.6 cm. white mohair showing more wear than most collectors will tolerate. Note: low set ears, rust color yarn nose/mouth on long snout; four claws; felt pads on pointy feet; straight arms with small paw pads; hump; unknown maker, ca. 1920.
Courtesy Diane Hoffman.

Coveted 1927-28 Steiff Petsy: 18"/46 cm.; brass color mohair; e.s.; f.j.; deep blue glass eyes; light brown pearl cotton nose/mouth; felt pads; four claws; working squeaker; patchy fur loss. Head pattern is seamed in center front and back, crosswise from ears in back; "V" gusset from center of mouth to neck. The large ears are held erect by inner wire loops. There is no difference in value between the *frosted Petsy* (pg. 46, *TB&SA, Second Series*) and the brass *Petsy*. In the late 1920s Steiff exported far fewer bears than in the early 1900s, thereby guaranteeing the extreme rarity of certain models; price doubles if store new. *Tabby Cat:* 6"/15 cm. long; FF button; *red* glazed S.T. 1314,0; watermelon C.T. "Tabby"; tan mohair with deeper tan airbrushed stripes; unjointed; two tone blue-green glass eyes; floss nose/mouth; squeaker, ca. 1920s. Terrier: 6"/15 cm. long; mohair; e.s.; unjointed; glass eyes; black pearl cotton nose/mouth; unknown maker, ca. 1930s. Shown with natural colored sandstone blocks; set dated 1945 but popular for many decades earlier.

**The Steiff Clown Bear must be considered in the parade of the rare and unusual: 18"/46 cm.; FF button; remnant of *white* S.T. indicating he is one of the earliest of this line; sewn on felt hat stuffed with excelsior; missing ruff. In 1926 the Clown was available in brown-tipped pink or gold mohair with either pink or blue trimmings and in many sizes.
Courtesy Gwen Daniel.**

"Irish," a large friendly bear with blue eyes, became the traveling companion of his new owner between California and Chaumont, France, his future home, in 1930. The bear appears to be the 1928 Steiff Petsy and sold for $25.00 that year.

American Gold: 20"/51 cm.; dense, medium pile mohair; e.s.; f.j.; replaced glass eyes.The iris color differs from the rich amber color of antique glass eyes. Learn to distinguish old from new. Black *yarn* nose/mouth on the upturned snout; football shape torso (unpopular); short arms with slightly curved paws; lightweight felt pads (tend to "ball"); short feet; no claws, ca. 1920.
Courtesy Diane Hoffman.

Platform horse: 24"/61 cm. high, 23"/58 cm. long; upholstery-type grey mohair covering over a wooden frame contoured with excelsior; painted wooden nose and hoofs; glass eyes, leather ears nailed on; steel rod supports horse on wooden platform; red wheels with black rubber tires. Germany, ca. 1920s. American bear: 20"/51 cm.; long mohair; e.s.; f.j.; shoe button eyes; definite snout; thick floss (horizontal) nose; five claws on short feet; no paw claws; felt pads; ca. 1920s.
Courtesy Marian Swartz.

Enjoying a lazy day at the pier is a little American boy: 11"/ 28 cm.; gold cotton plush; e.s.; rigid head, jointed (short) arms and legs; glass eyes; coarse, hemp-type, floss nose/ mouth; no claws on stubby feet, ca. 1920s. For those wishing an affordable old Teddy to bring sunshine.
Courtesy Debbie Masters.

Blue Ribbon Winner: 16"/40 cm.; long blond mohair frosted with brown (blaze on face); e.s.; f.j.; glass eyes with worn painted backing appear clear; black twisted floss nose/mouth; three claws of single strands; felt pads. Key wind music box plays "Blue Danube." In these expensive models the growler was replaced by a fine Swiss music box. Note, the ears are set close together and the eyes set high to give special expression to the desirable Teddy; maker unknown, ca. 1920-30. Steiff sitting rabbit: 5"/12.5 cm. high; RSB; mohair; e.s.; swivel head; red twisted floss nose/mouth.
Courtesy Larry and Debbie Varner.

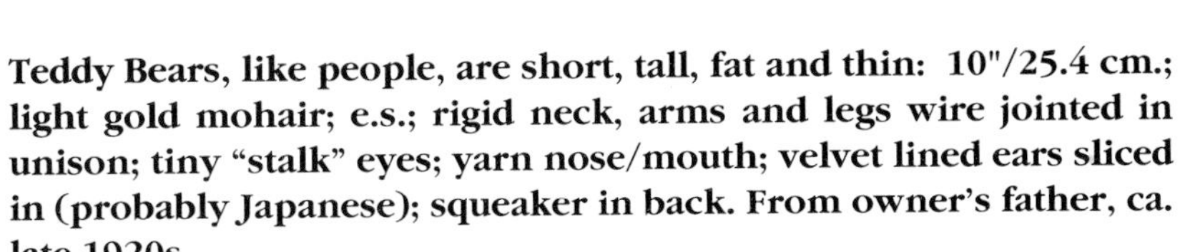

Teddy Bears, like people, are short, tall, fat and thin: 10"/25.4 cm.; light gold mohair; e.s.; rigid neck, arms and legs wire jointed in unison; tiny "stalk" eyes; yarn nose/mouth; velvet lined ears sliced in (probably Japanese); squeaker in back. From owner's father, ca. late 1920s.
Courtesy Dave and Ann Abbott.

Inflatable giant bear with provenance: 36"/91.5 cm.; thick gold mohair; glass eyes; twisted hard, black cotton floss nose/mouth. During 1929 in Vienna, Austria, the original owner was given the inflatable Teddy. Since her family traveled to America regularly this feature was a definite plus. The innertube lasted less than a year and was sent back to the (Steiff) factory for a new one. That too went in less than a year. At this point her mother returned the bear to the factory for stuffing, which was done. Note the slit in the right foot pad where the mouth of the tube could be pulled out. She remembers him being blown up and slowly "coming to life." He is fully jointed – mysteriously, he was even with the innertube. The 1920 Dean's catalogue show they made patent "Blow-Me-Up" toys of plush. Dean's advertised a specially manufactured india rubber bladder which is inflated by blowing through a tube. The inflatable feature was a popular concept in 1920s Europe. No I.D. Attributed to Steiff. When a pattern is enlarged to this extent inexplicably the "look" changes.
Courtesy Charlotte Anderson.

"Miss Mildred": 24"/61 cm.; mohair; e.s.;f.j.; glass eyes; the (vertical) nose/mouth are floss in a distinctive style; squared off (pug) longish snout; cardboard reinforced pads; three claws. A large armful, probably English, ca. 1920-30. Some wear.
Courtesy Linda Croucher.

"James": 12"/30 cm.; aged white woolly plush; f.j.; clear glass eyes; coarse floss nose/mouth. The pads are worn from squeezing and kissing by the child. Affordable bear with personality. Unknown maker, ca. 1920-30.
Courtesy Beverlee Reimers.

Teddy Bears 1930-1940

Petz: 22"/56 cm.; milk glass button in chest, red printing in ornamental cross "Petz"; medium pile (½") mohair; e.s.; f.j.; amber glass eyes; black cotton floss nose/mouth; three long claws; beige felt pads; growler. Features: body of a single piece with seam in back, darts in front to shape; sharp upturn at wrists; foot pads pointed at toes, ca. 1930s. Fine condition. Polar Bear, standing: 5"/12.5 cm. long; "Petz" button and oblong cloth tag in right front leg with woven blue letters: "Original PETZ//US-Zone Germany"; white short (¼") mohair; hard stuffed; swivel head only; amber glass eyes; black cotton floss nose/mouth, no claws or pads, ca. 1950.

Bessie Kate has an affecting presence: 15"/38 cm.; gold rayon/cotton plush; e.s.; f.j.; glass eyes, black string nose and five claws radiating from the center stitch; sliced-in ears indicate Japanese origin; upturned snout in the old style. She wears Patsy-type clothes, ca. 1930s.
Courtesy Evelyn Thomas.
American: 11"/28 cm.; long brown mohair, gold mohair inset snout; excelsior head, cotton stuffed body/limbs; f.j.; glass eyes; heavy floss nose, no claws; velveteen pads; wears bib overalls from a Buddy Lee doll of same 1930-40 era.
Courtesy Sheree Barnes.

"Old Yellow" from early 1930s: 15"/38 cm.; gold mohair; e.s.; f.j.; glass eyes; floss nose/mouth; felt pads, no claws; Note the low set ears and acutely curved paws; unknown maker. Although this Teddy is approaching sixty years of age, demand is limited.

Rare small size of 1930s *Teddy Baby:* 8½"/21 cm.; FF button; C.T.; light tan mohair; e.s.; f.j.; glass eyes; rust color pearl cotton nose; open felt mouth; four claws; voice box; original *spiked* leather collar (distinguishing him as 1930s); brass bell. Uncommon and desirable. Reading to: 5"/12.7 cm. Steiff; FF button; worn but cute, ca. pre 1920. Courtesy Jeremy Bleecher and Patricia Gallagher.

Four Musical Bears. Knickerbocker, Character and other American bears from the mid-1930s have potential as well as real value. Left front, Knickerbocker: 14"/36 cm.; long brown mohair; inset snout; kapok stuffed; f.j.; floss nose/ mouth; felt pads; wind-up music box. Left rear: 14"/36 cm.; white mohair ; same as above except white velveteen pads. Right rear: 15"/38 cm.; tagged "Character"; mohair. Right front: 13"/33 cm.; mohair with short mohair inset snout; velveteen pads; probably Character. Note the difference in head shape between the two Knickerbockers on left and the marked Character bear. These two makers are very much alike; ca. 1930-50. The musical features enhance value. Courtesy Susie Carlson.

Pooh-like look: 25"/64 cm.; e.s.; f.j.; glass eyes. The Steiff button has been added; the golden mohair is *not* Steiff quality; the twisted hard, cotton floss nose/mouth is the same type used by the Steiff Co.; five floss claws. Thought to be English, a possible Farnell, ca. 1930s. Note the center seam in head gusset (not to be confused with a Steiff center seam bear) and the long shaved snout that is not inset. He was purchased in West Germany in 1985 WITH the button. Thus, the proper Steiff button on a Steiff bear is *not adding value as it once did.* N.P.A.

Pals: left, 14"/35.5 cm.; mohair; e.s.; f.j.; amber glass eyes; floss nose/mouth; felt pads; four floss claws; squeaker. Probably American, top of the line, ca. 1920-30. Right, "Tough Eddy": 13½"/34 cm.; mohair; excelsior stuffed head, kapok body; amber glass eyes; floss (vertical) nose/mouth giving a "tough guy" expression; worn rexine pads; squeaker. Note the long torso and short legs; English ca. 1930. Courtesy Isabel Hasselbach.

"Dirty Harry": 23"/58 cm.; mohair; firmly cotton stuffed; f.j.; slight hump; amber glass eyes; black twisted cotton floss (horizontal) nose/mouth; no claws; pads recovered; the original tan twill pads have stitching on the right foot that held a label ½" x 1½". Of special note are the ears: sliced-in at back, sewn on at front. Probably English, unknown maker, ca. 1930.
Courtesy Pam North.

The study of paws is important in identification. Merrythought Teddy with *web embroidered* paw pads: 22"/60 cm.; long curly mohair; e.s.; f.j.; button eyes; faded black floss (vertical) nose & mouth; felt pads; three claws and cardboard innersoles on feet. Tag sewn to chest says, "I Growl," ca. 1930s. Dressed in boy's shirt, ca. 1890. Fine English Bear.
Courtesy Karen Silverstein.

English, maker unknown: 18"/45.5 cm.; fine, dense, silky mohair; excelsior stuffed head; kapok stuffed body/limbs; f.j.; deep amber glass eyes; black pearl cotton nose/mouth; velveteen pads/cardboard innersoles; four claws; squeaker; ca. 1930s. Unfortunately, someone shaved initials on his tummy reducing value. Shown with the Latin translation of *Winnie the Pooh* (translated by Alexander Lenard). New York: Dutton, 1960.

Cutout Bear: 24"/61 cm.; printed by lithography on polished cotton; stuffed with fine wood wool, ca. 1930s. These simple toys, cut and sewn from sheets, are gaining collector popularity along with similar doll series. Many styles are reproduced today. Courtesy Pam North.

An example of large size, rare color and mint condition increasing Teddy's value: 25"/64 cm.; FF button; luxurious dark brown mohair; e.s.; f.j.; glass eyes; twisted hard, black cotton floss nose/mouth; four claws; felt pads; working growler; crossover type of "look" between 1930s-40s. *Hoppel-dackel* (Dachshund *Lumpi*): 8"/20 cm. high, 11"/28 cm. long; RSB; C.T. pet name; S.T. 1328,1; mohair; unjointed; moves realistically with wheels because of flexible tummy; glass eyes; pearl cotton nose, open felt mouth/tongue; four painted claws; Velcro pads attach to metal plates on axles. Sold with or without wheels. Uncommon toy, ca. 1968-69. Private Collection.

Austrian and German: left, 16"/40.5 cm.; bright orange-gold medium pile mohair; e.s.; f.j.; amber glass eyes; black wool *yarn* nose/mouth; three claws; muslin pads; working squeaker. Features: body from one piece of fabric with back seam; sharp upturn to tiny hands; small, pointy foot pads; unknown Austrian maker, ca. 1930s. Right, German 14"/35.5 cm.; silver foil hang tag; obverse, picture of bear, "EM *Das Zeichen fur qualitat"* (the symbol of quality); reverse, picture of doll, *"Original EM Spieltiere u. Puppen"* (play animals and dolls); light tipped dark brown medium pile mohair, tan napped wool snout; e.s.; f.j.; amber glass eyes; cotton floss nose/mouth, no claws; felt pads, ca. 1960s.

"J.B." (for "Jolly Boy"): 25"/64 cm.; curly cotton plush, cotton velour snout and feet; e.s.; f.j.; glass eyes; floss nose; the open red felt mouth is outlined in black; double sewn red felt tongue; felt pads reinforced with cardboard; four floss claws; German maker. The excelsior stuffed ears indicate possible Schuco, ca. 1930-40. Unique and special with an endearing quality, fitting for even an advanced collection. *Peck Peck* bird described in Schuco section.

A Teddy Bear for the historian: 12"/30.5 cm.; cotton plush two-sided; stuffed with grey waste cotton; unjointed; unusual eyes with a tin pupil embedded in orange plastic; heavy twisted floss nose/ mouth, red felt tongues. This ca. 1940s example would be difficult to replace, yet demand is limited unless you happened to own a similar bear as a child.
Courtesy Diane Hoffman.

Sweet expression, left: 17"/43 cm.; *long* silky, curly mohair; e.s.; f.j.; clear glass eyes; floss nose/mouth; short pile mohair pads; three stitched claws; growler. The black "spots" on feet are knots of claw floss, the only careless feature of the well-made Teddy. Unknown maker, ca. 1930s. Right, The Hermann Plush Co. (Hermann-Speilwaren GmbH), not to be confused with Gebr. Hermann KG. See close-up of tag sewn into left shoulder. Frosted mohair: 16½"/42 cm.; short mohair inset snout; e.s.; f.j.; glass eyes; pearl cotton nose/mouth; thin flannel-like pads; growler. Fur and construction are excellent except for poor quality of felt pads (often seen on early bears from *both* Hermanns). Rare tag, ca. 1930s.
Courtesy Valerie Vann.

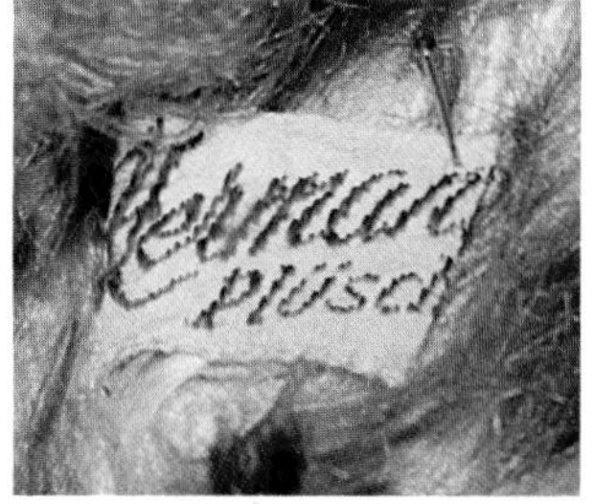

Tag of white matte rayon folded in center; green woven lettering, "Hermann Plusch-Spieltier, Munchen." This soft toy manufacturer is located in Cottendorf near Neustadt, West Germany. Mr. Rolf Hermann, in charge of the Hermann Plush Co., is distantly related to the Gebr. Hermann KG family. They are two different firms.

Mending fences: 17"/43 cm.; fine quality white mohair; cotton stuffed; f.j.; glass eyes; black floss (vertical) nose; small straight mouth with dropped stitch; no claws; felt pads. Note center gusset seam; snout is deeply inset back to eyes. Gold mohair, 17"/43 cm.; old cotton stuffed f.j.; rayon velour lined ears; *black* glass eyes; horizontal stitched nose/mouth, single stitch of red floss at mouth; three floss claws overlap felt pads. Note contoured legs and disproportionately large heads of both bears; unknown maker, ca, 1930s.
Courtesy Nancy Roeder.

Raggedy Ann is a real American folk doll, HIGHLY COLLECTIBLE, and complements a Teddy Bear collection. She was first made commercially in 1918. The merry *Raggedy Andy* appeared in 1920. He is even more collectible than *Raggedy Ann* because not as many were given to past generations. This pair of handmade dolls was lovingly conceived and brilliantly executed by a skilled artist from a (McCall's) pattern. Ann, 30"/76 cm.; Andy, 29"/74 cm.; oil painted features including heart on chest; striped socks are oil painted on the all cotton dolls. The *auburn* yarn hair and the *black outlining* of the noses indicate ca. late 1930s. The made-to-body pointed shoes are silk. Friend: 11"/28 cm.; shaggy mohair; excelsior stuffed head, cotton stuffed body/limbs; f.j.; glass eyes; pearl cotton (horizontal) nose/mouth; no claws; pointy velveteen pads. Probably American, ca. 1930s.

Timeless and well made: 29"/74 cm.; tagged, "Johnny Gruelle's Own Raggedy Ann & Andy, Georgene Novelties, 1947"; large flat shoe button-type eyes; printed heart, "I love you"; the original clothes came in many different prints; large size in good condition. Shown with cinnamon bear: 15"/38 cm.; woolly plush; cotton stuffed head and limbs, excelsior stuffed torso; f.j.; clear glass eyes; snout not inset; floss nose/mouth; three claws on hands, none on feet ; worn mohair pads; squeaker; unknown maker, ca. late 1940s.
Courtesy Isabel Romer and Dana Zastrow.

Pandas were made to be adored. "Ma Jong," left: 17"/43 cm.; light tan and black mohair; cotton stuffed; f.j.; inset black mohair ovals around the humanized glass eyes with red felt below accentuating the contrast of amber iris to black pupil; fuzzy long pile wool snout; *felt* nose, floss mouth; black felt pads; squeaker. Note the long robust torso, short legs and hands turned downward, as in Teddy Baby. Probably English, maker unknown, ca. 1930s. "O'Donnell," 12"/30.5 cm.; square white cloth tag, left foot, inner seam; woven red letters, "Made in//Republic//of Ireland": mohair; soft stuffed; jointed limbs only; black felt squares under amber glass eyes; *oilcloth* nose, floss mouth; taupe color rexine pads pointed at heel.

Panda from 1939: 10½"/26.7 cm.; FF button; off-white mohair. The Panda details were created with black airbrushing rather than inset seaming found in the 1950s models. The fur has aged to a beautiful silvery grey with cream. Any attempt to clean this Panda would be disastrous, as the natural (and attractive) fading of the black airbrushing with time and handling shows that the dyes were not fast. Note his feet are shorter mohair with airbrushed "toes"; pads are greyish coarse weave cotton with cardboard reinforcing the foot pads. *Rare and desirable*. Courtesy Vivienne Roche.

IV.
TEDDY BEARS
1940-Present

Teddy Bears–1940-1960

1960-1990

Artist Bears

Teddy Bears 1940-1960

"Buffy": 18"/45.5 cm.; extremely curly and silky natural "Spanish Lambskin" sewn furrier-style (by machine) with butted seams joined by fine stitches; stuffed with mix of cotton, wool, yarn and thread waste; floppy "hinged" limbs; amber glass eyes; imitation leather seamed and shaped nose; no mouth or pads; *tail*. Note arms are semi-crescent shape. American, ca. 1941. Childhood bear of owner. Right, "Brother's Bear": 9½"/24 cm.; woolly mohair; kapok stuffed; f.j.; glass eyes; wool floss (horizontal) nose/mouth; small embroidered tongue; beige velveteen pads. The hand pads are tear-drop shape, common on American bears. Note the short limbs typical of the shift in American taste to chubby Teddys. Advertised in the 1940 John Plain Catalog as "Honey Bear." Owner's brother's childhood bear.
Courtesy Valerie Vann.

White Steiff bear in the North Woods: 17"/43 cm.; FF button; yellow S.T. 5343,2; US-Zone tag in right arm seam; mohair; e.s.; f.j.; *clear* glass eyes with worn paint backing; twisted hard, *brown* cotton floss nose/mouth; four claws; felt pads; growler. A BROWN (not rust color) nose is found on white bears in the 1930s-40s. Note the *long* curved arms, big feet and hump; all elements of the earlier design. The composite of identifying marks indicate ca. 1947. If the US-Zone tag was removed one would date the bear 1935-40.
Courtesy Marlene Wendt.

Three decades of Steiff: late 1930s; dressed in homemade clothes as old as the bear; ¼" FF button, remnant of yellow S.T. ; some wear. Late 1940s: rich chocolate brown (extremely desirable and scarce color found in this era); ¼" shiny silver button "Steiff" in block capitals (not underlined), US-Zone tag in right upper arm seam. Late 1950s: RSB; larger head; shorter, straighter arms; shorter feet. All are 17"/43 cm. and have growlers.

Cuddlesome: 16"/40.5 cm.; mohair; excelsior stuffed head, kapok stuffed body/limbs; f.j.; amber glass eyes; black twisted floss (vertical) nose/mouth; gold *velveteen* pads with four claws *stitched onto pads* (a Chiltern feature); squeaker. Probably Chiltern (English) *Hugmee* bear from 1947.
Courtesy Isabel Hasselbach.

Bat-eared bear with stubby *tail:* 18"/45.5 cm.; mohair; velveteen snout and pads; stuffing unknown; jointed head only; flat black eyes; black floss (horizontal) nose/mouth, red floss denotes tongue; squeaker, ca. 1940s. Probably Knickerbocker. Right, 14"/35.5 cm.; reddish brown and white cotton plush; f.j.; red felt backs *red* glass eyes/dark pupil; black floss (vertical) nose; white felt snout; peach felt open mouth and red felt tongue; white curly mitten hands with *thumb*, white curly pads reinforced with cardboard; three floss claws; growler, ca. 1940s. Demand is greatest for *fully jointed mohair* Teddys, but these two have their own merits.
Courtesy Isabel Hasselbach.

Teddy, 21"/53.3 cm.; long pile mohair; excelsior stuffed head and arms, soft stuffed body/legs; jointed arms only; ears are set well forward; clear glass eyes; black yarn nose/mouth, no claws. Made-to-body brown velveteen overalls. Probably English, ca. 1940-50. Limited demand for the collector. Madame Alexander's Little Shaver: 10"/25 cm.; cloth; ca. 1940. Elsie Shaver originated the painting of Victorian Children, ca. 1930s.
Courtesy Diane Hoffman.

"Minnie": 9"/23 cm.; short straight white mohair; f.j.; glass eyes; pearl cotton nose/mouth; no claws; felt pads; squeaker. This type of Teddy is often found. Unknown maker, ca. 1940s. Courtesy Beverlee Reimers.

Farnell Toys: left, "Alfie," terrier: 11"/28 cm.; long; tag sewn on stomach, woven blue letters, "FARNELL'S, ALPHA TOYS, MADE IN ENGLAND"; white (1½") long silky mohair; soft stuffed; unjointed; *clear* glass eyes; black floss nose/mouth, red felt tongue; no claws or pads, ca. 1936. Center, "Farni": 19"/48 cm.; "(Greek alpha) FARNELL" label sewn into left body seam. This Rupert-looking bear has dense, glossy white medium pile mohair; soft stuffed; f.j.; amber glass eyes; black cotton floss nose/mouth; no claws; red felt pads; growler, ca. 1960s. Shown with *More Adventures of Rupert.* A Daily Express Publication (London); inscribed with date, 1953; Right "Alpha": 12"/30.5 cm. high; dense, curly white wool plush; hard stuffed; swivel head; orange plastic cat eyes; pink floss nose/mouth; no claws or pads. Special feature: key-wind music box in cat's seat; small lever to stop ("Jingle Bells") music when cat is put down. Key extends through label: woven blue letters, "ALPHA TOY, MADE IN ENGLAND," ca. 1945-50. A choice cat. The J.K. Farnell Co. went out of business in 1968.

Tagged "Anker-Munich, Made in Germany": 12"/30.5 cm. (available in other sizes); brown mohair; lt. tan velveteen snout, mitten hands, feet and ear linings; kapok stuffed; unjointed; wonderful glass eyes in three tones (clear, white and reddish brown) accented by black floss lines; black floss nose and outlined mouth painted red which also trims wrists and feet; squeaker; ca. 1940-50. Smile at the innovative and self recognizable design. Hard to find. Courtesy Isabel Hasselbach.

"Timmie": 13"/33 cm.; cotton plush; waste cotton stuffed; unjointed; yellow plastic heart-shape eyes (probably replaced) give character; black twisted floss nose/mouth; remnants of red felt tongue. Expensive mohair was used only in small pieces for the pads and ear linings; post WWII, 1950. American buddy of Howard Dreier.

Noteworthy *orange* color among the carnival quality Teddy Bears manufactured in West Germany, ca. 1950s. These synthetic plush examples cannot be ignored in the scheme of collecting. They are often found and should be identified. Courtesy Sue Harshman.

Walking Bear: 16"/40.6 cm.; brown tipped rayon plush body, beige flannel snout and inner ears; *papier mache body*; amber glass eyes; black floss nose; pinkish flannel open mouth; felt pads on hands. The foot pads are patterned heavy cotton. When a limb is moved manually, the bear walks, swinging his arms and turning his head. The mechanism is similar to that found on Alexanderkin and Ginny dolls of his era, ca. 1950s. A Teddy for the true collector.

Big Teddy Bears have big appetites! This 28"/71 cm.; Chad Valley prepares himself a snack. Tagged in right side seam, "Hygienic Toys Made in England by the Chad Valley Co., Ltd."; high quality (1") long mohair; excelsior stuffed head; excelsior/kapok mix in torso; kapok stuffed limbs; glass eyes; soft twisted floss widely stitched nose on pleasing snout (not inset); velveteen pads with vestige of foot label. Note: center seam in head gusset is undoubtedly to conserve material on this large size Teddy, ca. 1950s. Chad Valley bought Chiltern in 1967 (Chiltern bears are lower quality than Chad Valley). In 1978 Palitoy bought Chad Valley.
Courtesy Ellyn McCorkell.

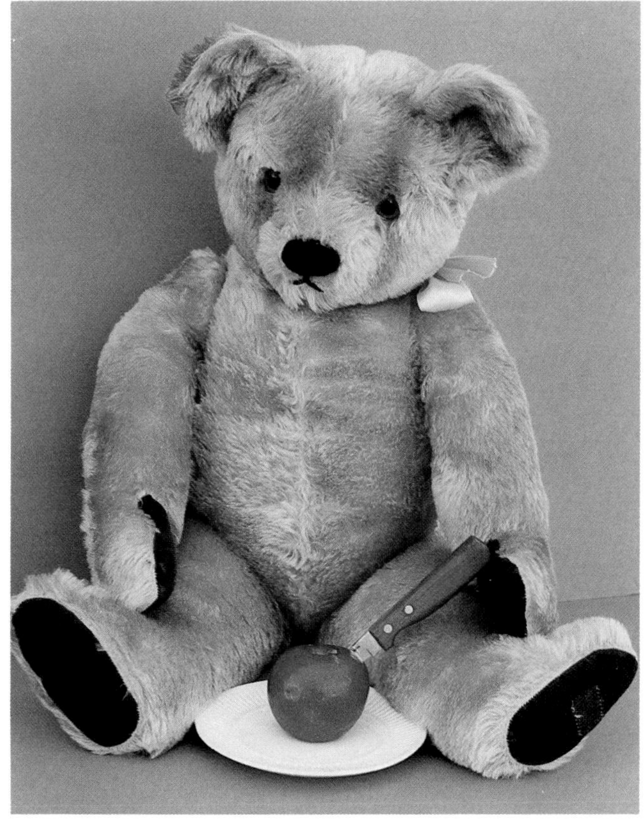

Zottys **with lovely shade variations, even in the standard sandcolored frosted mohair. (L-R) front row: rare and most desirable size, 6½"/16 cm.; standard mohair, unusually long and curly for this size; wonderful face, ca. 1950s. 10"/25 cm.; rare white, ca. 1960s; unusual "redwood" tone commanding a higher price; tan felt circles behind eyes, ca. 1950s; 9"/23 cm.; frosted curly light tan, pale yellow short mohair chest; fine expression, ca. 1950s. Back row: 10"/25.4 cm.; standard; 17"/43 cm.; standard beige with light tips, darker at roots than earlier examples; blue rayon ribbon sewn through the bowknot to back left neck. The desirable chest tag reads, "Zotty (im Steiff Kinderbuch)" -- child's book. In the mid 1960s Steiff released their storybook animals -- *Zotty, Piff* and a giraffe are some -- in conjunction with a child's storybook. The animals and books were sold together; 15"/38 cm.; standard; happy look; well formed mouth; no claws on this size, ca. 1950s. From the 1970s, 8"/20 cm.; curly, dark tan at roots, light frosting; no voice; soft stuffed; ribbon not sewn down; brighter pinky-peach pads; nose probably machine stitched in *fine* twisted floss.**
Courtesy Valerie Vann.

Orsi**: 8½"/22 cm.; RSB; C.T. pet name (very rare to have *Orsi* with his C.T.); caramel colored mohair; e.s.; jointed head and arms only; amber glass eyes; twisted hard, brown cotton floss nose; open felt mouth/ painted tongue; four claws; felt pads; felt bib. The desirable character bear was also made in 15" size. Either size can have a blue or red bib; short production, 1956 only. Since the 1950s, Steiff has named other (completely different and much less collectible) bears *Orsi*. These also have open mouths.**
Courtesy Barbara Baldwin.

Comparative mohair *Zottys*. Left, Hermann: 10½"/27 cm.; lack of contrasting chest plate, *upper* lip outlined in *floss* and square shaped nose with outermost floss stitches extending down past others distinguish Hermann from Steiff. The good quality teardrop shape paw pads turn backward like Steiff, ca. 1960s. Demand for Hermann is SLOWLY rising. Center, Grisly: 9"/23 cm.; metal and foil tag (Grisly shield trademark) sewn to chest; glass eyes not first quality (pupil sizes noticably different); short mohair ear linings, snout and pads. The nose shape and floss outline on upper lip are in the style of Hermann. The disproportionately large head and normal (in-facing) hand pads are characteristic of Grisly, ca. 1950-60. Little demand except to round out a *Zotty* collection. Right, Steiff *Zotty:* 10"/25.4 cm.; standard *Zotty* colors; airbrushed line on lips; the smallest size made with felt circles behind the glass eyes; the largest size with four floss claws and squeaker, ca. 1950s.
Courtesy Valerie Vann.

Cute pug face of the Steiff Zotty: 20"/51 cm.; IB; S.T. 0300/50; long curly mohair; foam rubber stuffed; f.j.; plastic eyes; open felt mouth/painted tongue; felt pads, ca. 1968. Hard to find large size. His friendly growl does not frighten his faithful companion. Terrier: 10½"/27 cm.; woolly mohair, felt facing to underside; e.s.; unjointed; amber glass eyes with worn paint backing; perfectly executed dark brown twisted floss nose in downward points; gently airbrushed pink tongue on the floss mouth; no claws; curled tail. One of the many high quality and lovable Terrier-types from the 1930s-50s. Unknown maker.
Courtesy Ellyn McCorkell.

A totally different bear from Spain. "Pip": 11"/28 cm.; tan synthetic plush over a composition-like body; fully jointed but strung with elastic like a doll. The unusual eyes are pale green glass with an applique of milk glass and black pupil; brown hair eyelashes, red felt mouth and green felt nose; felt pads on feet only; squeaker. The cheeks and inner ears were rouged at the factory. The snout, tail and tummy are a lighter shade of plush. Tagged, "G. Fali's//Osito (baby)//Made in Spain," ca. 1959. Adorable; hard to replace.
Courtesy Pam North.

Bright contrasting colors and chubby shape with short legs typical of American taste in Teddys (post WWII): 10½"/27 cm.; mohair; soft stuffed; f.j.; clear glass eyes; floss nose stitched (vertically) in a square; velveteen inner ears and pads; possibly American or Asian, unknown maker, ca. 1950-60.
Courtesy Valerie Vann.

Friends from the 1950s. Left bear, "Coco": 8½"/22 cm.; fuzzy long pile wool; cotton stuffed; f.j.; glass eyes; floss nose/mouth; squeaker; Knickerbocker cat: 10"/25.4 cm.; mohair; soft stuffed; unjointed; green plastic eyes with green almond-shape felt backing; no pads or tail. Character made a similar cat. Bear, tagged "Character": 13"/33 cm.; white mohair (1½"); kapok stuffed; f.j.; glass eyes; floss nose/mouth; claws airbrushed on tip of felt pads (typical of Character), squeaker. Gold mohair: 13"/33 cm.; at back of head tagged, "Pedigree, Made in Ireland"; shredded foam stuffed; unjointed; plastic eyes; pearl cotton nose/mouth; three double strand claws on hands only (no pads); sheared mohair foot pads. The unique head pattern has inset snout shaped by darts, elongated to join seam at neck. The face and front of the ears are one piece; back of head and ears are treated the same except two pieces with a vertical seam.
Courtesy Susie Carlson.

Teddy Bears 1960-1990

Fine examples made by the Schenker Co. of Austria. They are noted for making animals of real fur. Left, cat: 9"/23 cm. long plus tail; soft, sheared goat fur; f.j.; pale green glass cat eyes; pink cotton floss nose/mouth; nylon whiskers; no claws or pads; rigid tail, ca. 1960s. Teddys, front and back: 4½"/11.5 cm. (seated), 6"/15 cm., 13"/33 cm.; in left ear the large bear has a white satin oblong tag with brown print, "Schenker, Made in Austria." All have white sheepskin covering; hard stuffed (probably wool); f.j.; amber glass eyes; black pearl cotton nose/mouth; *red leather* pads; the smallest have *red leather* inner ears, ca. 1950s. Right, Polar Bear: 6"/15 cm. long; sheepskin; embroidered eyes; long pointed snout.

Grisly Twins: 15"/38 cm.; older metal shield imbedded in chest shows Grisly logo (needle and thread superimposed on a standing bear); gold foil tag; #465/40; pink mohair, cream color mohair inset snouts; excelsior-type stuffing; f.j.; glass eyes, black floss nose/mouth; felt pads, stitched claws; working squeaker, ca. 1960. Increase value for *pink* color. Courtesy Idele Gilbert.

Schwika bears from Austria. Left, 15"/38 cm.; metal button on a loop of red string in left ear, "Pluschtiere (plush animals), Schwika/Graz"; medium pile woolly plush; open felt mouth, lined upper lip; felt tongue; napped grey cotton pads; growler. Note the acutely curved slender wrists and the upturned feet. Center, 11"/28 cm.; button (raised letters) "Schwika"; (1") long mohair. Right, 15"/38 cm.; curly pink (desirable color) rayon plush; fuzzy wool snout; open felt mouth; coarse cotton pads; growler; some wear. The (rare) I.D. adds to value. All are excelsior *hard* stuffed; f.j.; have amber glass eyes and pearl cotton noses, ca. 1950s-1960s.
Center bear courtesy Susie Carlson.

Tag attached to side seam of bear, "Chiltern Hygienic Toys, Made in England": 26"/66 cm.; mohair; excelsior stuffed head, kapok body; unjointed; amber glass eyes; molded plastic nose (a Chiltern feature); snout and decorated pads are shaved mohair, ca. early 1960s. All eyes fall on the huge feet (5" wide, 8½" long).
Courtesy Isabel Hasselbach.

A rare example of the common *Cheeky* bear that came into production in 1957. This *Cheeky* was made in 1962: 11"/28 cm.; honeysuckle nylon plush giving a white woolly appearance; f.j.; glass eyes; velvet snout and open mouth; overstitched brown felt pads; tagged on right foot "Merrythought Ironbridge Shop, Made in England, Reg. & Design," Her original dress has a buckram petticoat. There is a jingle bell in her ear, a sign of the times and of *Cheeky*.
Courtesy Sherilyn Allmond.

Fechter (Austria) Teddys can be confused with the Steiff "Zotty." They are of equal quality and in the same price range. Sizes shown here are 8"/20.3 cm. to 16"/40.6 cm.; tagged, "Fechter Spielwaren" on the right ear. All are quality mohair; excelsior stuffed; fully jointed; have either glass eyes or B&W googly plastic eyes. Their open felt mouths are accented by a black painted line on upper lip. Note the red felt tongue not present on Zotty. Pads are usually of the same mohair as the inset snout, but can be felt or velour; no claws. The 15" bear, 2nd from the left, and the two 16" bears, back, have growlers. Bought as old store stock, these are mint with original ribbons from 1960-70. Learn to recognize the distinctive set of the ears and special facial features. Do not identify by chest plate and backward facing paws alone. At far right stands a humanized cat tagged "Fechter." She is grey mohair; 7"/18 cm.; e.s. f.j.; green enamel-backed glass eyes with round pupil; red pearl cotton nose/mouth; white mohair pads. Her original felt apron has a green center pocket holding a pink checked cotton hankie. The tail is stitched upright to back.

Fechter bears are from a cottage industry begun in Austria after WWII. They are of high quality materials and craftmanship displaying great variety of size and color. The founder, Mrs. Fechter, died in 1973. Her grandson tried to keep the factory going until 1978, at which point it went bankrupt. With few exceptions, the bears have a tan satin label in *right* ear, brown printing, "*Fechter Spielwaren* (toys)"; outline of bear on back. All of the above are mohair except "Snowball" who is white Dralon with a tan mohair inset snout. All are excelsior stuffed; fully jointed (exception small greys who have rigid heads and wire jointed limbs). All have amber glass eyes and noses stitched with pearl cotton. The white and royal blue models have an open felt mouth, black band airbrushed on upper lip and a *red felt tongue*. The pads can be felt, mohair or cotton velour; no claws. The larger bears have growlers. Sizes range from 5¾"/14.6 cm. to 14"/35.6 cm. and date from 1960-78. Of special interest is the blue "Alice": 13½"/34 cm.; oblong tan taffeta label in *left* ear with brown woven, "*Fechter/Rein Mohair* (pure mohair)" reverse is picture of bear woven in brown. A rare color enhances value. At far right sits another Austrian, "Saffie": 11"/28 cm.; square black cloth label in ear with woven white monogram "SAF" in circle shape; grey mohair; dark brown enamel-backed glass eyes; open felt mouth with no airbrushing or tongue; grey *flannel* pads; three stitched claws; growler. Body is formed of a single piece of fabric with seam in back; arms are straight, ca. 1960s.

Unidentified Flying Bear: 24"/61 cm.; tagged "Possum Trot"; brown synthetic plush with made-to-body silver flying suit; polyester stuffed; bendable arms and legs; black plastic eyes; snout and ear linings are beige plush; no nose, mouth or pads; plastic see-through helmet and space pack; a sign of the times, ca. 1977; soon discontinued. Courtesy Marlene Wendt.

***Sebastian* (set No. 1), bespectacled and dignified in his watch plaid vest: 24"/61 cm.; finely carved wooden face and paws of cypress; fully jointed to enhance his unique personality. Designed by artist Robert Raikes for Applause; a signed and numbered Limited Edition from 1985 when retail was $90.00.**

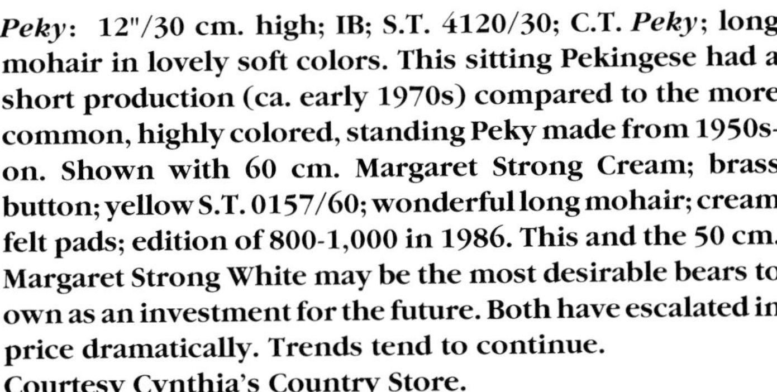

***Peky*: 12"/30 cm. high; IB; S.T. 4120/30; C.T. *Peky*; long mohair in lovely soft colors. This sitting Pekingese had a short production (ca. early 1970s) compared to the more common, highly colored, standing Peky made from 1950s-on. Shown with 60 cm. Margaret Strong Cream; brass button; yellow S.T. 0157/60; wonderful long mohair; cream felt pads; edition of 800-1,000 in 1986. This and the 50 cm. Margaret Strong White may be the most desirable bears to own as an investment for the future. Both have escalated in price dramatically. Trends tend to continue. Courtesy Cynthia's Country Store.**

Molly: 10"/25 cm.; high; RSB; S.T. 3325; C.T. pet name; mohair; swivel head; store new, ca. 1958. Extremely rare and desirable largest size. Margaret Strong White, 50 cm.; white S.T. 0158/50; long mohair and *leather* pads; Ltd. Ed. of 750 worldwide, 1986; no certificate or collector box; excellent bear for enjoyment and investment. *Dally*: 11"/28 cm. high; RSB; S.T. 3328; C.T. *Dally* attached to collar; mohair; swivel head; store new, ca. 1958; rare and desirable largest size. Rabbit from *Alice and her Friends* set: 8"/20 cm.; brass button; white S.T. 0147/20; Ltd. Ed. 2,000, 1986; mohair; original outfit with watch. May also be found undressed or with yellow S.T.; limited and collectible.
Courtesy Cynthia's Country Store.

Manschli or *Buddha Bear*: 7"/19 cm. sitting brass button; S.T. 0310/19; mohair; soft stuffed; unjointed; large plastic eyes; fine floss nose, airbrushed mouth; short mohair pads, no claws; fat belly; stubby tail and devilish expression. Scarce and collectible; made 1983-84 only. Right front, undressed mouse from *Alice* (Gibson doll) *and her friends* set: 5"/13 cm.; brass button; white S.T. 0148,13; Ltd. Ed. 2,000, 1986. Left back, *Teddy Rose*: 16"/41 cm.; brass button; white S.T. 0171,41; Ltd. Ed. 10,000; issued in 1987; boxed with signed and numbered certificate; 1925 replica in unusual rose color mohair with center seam. Very collectible. Right back, *Grey Giengen:* 12½"/32 cm.; first issued in 1985; open stock bear at an affordable price. Outfit design from Cynthia's. Courtesy Cynthia's Country Store.

"Once Upon A Time" by Gae Sharp: 10"/25.4 cm.; high quality plush; bean bag effect from stuffing of clear plastic beads (not recommended for children); jointed arms and legs only; black floss nose/mouth; felt pads on especially long legs. Note the closely set (plastic) eyes and the protruding foreheads. Each is limited to 750-1000. Gae was the first artist to do a floppy bear, ca. late 1980s.
Courtesy Mostly Bears.

Teddy Baby, (11½"/29 cm.) *and Wolf*, 5"/13 cm.; Ltd. Ed. 1,000 to celebrate the 85th anniversary of the firm Paul Wolff OHG *Spielwaren* (toys). Mr. Wolf is a third generation nephew of Margarete Steiff. Since 1903 the store (pictured) has been a sales station for Steiff products. This outstanding set is boxed with attractive sepia tone lithographs of Giengen and the message, "The Wolf protects the bear." Both are made of mohair and have white S.T. 0177/00; the bear's tag is numbered on reverse side to correspond with the certificate in German. Available only in Germany, the demand was greater than the supply; perhaps the nicest Steiff set of the 1980s.

Artist Bears

COVER BEAR: *Kodi's* expression is his fortune. Only with dedicated study of the antique masters can a Bear Artist achieve this perfection. Maria Schmidt's newest and favorite design: 27"/69 cm.; tagged in side seam, "The Charlestowne Bear//Created By//Maria Schmidt"; honey mohair (1"); f.j.; unforgettable expression is due to her *superb* pattern, careful eye placement and clipping of the facial fur. Only a few artists attempt to make this difficult size. A most distinctive large Teddy characteristic of Maria's art and meticulous workmanship.

***Oliver Fox* designed and handmade by artist Maria Schmidt in honor of Margaret Fox Mandel. This perfectly sculpted center seam Teddy is 21"/53 cm.; tagged in right side seam, "The Charlestowne Bear//Created By//Maria Schmidt"; mohair (5/8"); f.j.; has glass eyes and wool felt paws. The classic (early German) conformation shows exceptionally fine construction which is also *consistently* excellent, bear after bear. A top end Artist Bear.**

A hat for fun. The Artist Bears are 3¼"/8 cm. and under. There are over 20 bears attached to hat with safety pins. Visible in the photo are: (L-R), Cindy Martin, white mohair; Cappy Warnick, mohair; Beverly Mark, yellow mohair; Hillary Hulen, rabbit; Kimberly Port, mohair; Dickie Harrison; Cathie Levy, clown; Elke Block, muff; Carol Stewart, gold bear. Courtesy Elke Block.

Separate popular artists working together: Linda Kuhn's 2"/5 cm. "Rock Canyon Bear"; superbly constructed and perfectly styled in the manner of antique bears. The Limited Edition is entirely handsewn with all work done exclusively by the artist from her original copyrighted design. Short plush fur; f.j.; fiberfill stuffed; glass bead eyes; floss nose, mouth and claws. The "Golli and Me" Golliwog was inspired by the original Florence Upton doll that had a leather face. The leather face with a fully formed nose combined with real fur hair is the personal trademark of artist Kathy Thomas. The unique Golli is 5"/13 cm.; handsewn; f.j.; the non-removable ultrasuede clothes are in traditional Golliwog colors. He has glass bead eyes; ultrasuede mouth; quality leather hands and shoes; original copyrighted design in a numbered edition of 125.

Laurie Sasaki is a talented California Bear Artist known for her attention to detail. Her exquisite bears are a sellout at every show she attends. "The Bearrie Patch" Panda: 2¼"/5.7 cm.; synthetic velvet fur. Open mouth Baby Bear (reproduction in miniature of a Teddy Baby type): 3½"/9 cm.; mohair with velveteen snout and feet, airbrushed details; move tail and head says "No-No"; red leather collar with numbered brass tag; Limited Edition of 50. Bellhop Bear, 2¼"/5.7 cm.; synthetic velvet fur head, hands and feet; made-to-body felt costume. Muzzle Bear, 2½"/6.4 cm.; synthetic velvet fur; removable leather muzzle; numbered Limited Edition of 30. Antique style Teddy, 3⅝"/9.1 cm.; hand dyed cinnamon color vintage mohair; all have glass bead eyes and are fully jointed.

Delightful miniatures designed and handmade by prize-winning artist Dickie Harrison: 1"/2.54 cm. bear on goose; kapok stuffed (all others are polyester stuffed); 2"/5 cm. rabbit on goose; 2½"/6.5 cm. Jester Bears and rabbit. This bunny sports a jewel decorated ultrasuede jacket. All are highly detailed, beautifully scaled and skillfully crafted from short pile acrylic fabric; fully jointed and have glass bead eyes. Dickie's motto is, "If it's worth making at all, it's worth trying in miniature."

Kathy Mullin makes carefully crafted bears and has become known for her innovative costuming, especially military and Renaissance. She loves antique laces and trims, making optimum use of these in her award-winning designs. "Mulbearry's" range in size from 6"/15 cm. to 30"/76 cm. and include a full line of rabbits. All Mulbearry's are made of European mohair or acrylic, are firmly stuffed with polyester fiberfill, are fully jointed with glass eyes; and have hard cotton floss handstitched noses and ultrasuede pads. Back: 22" Heinrich von Mulbearon; 30" Abernathy Augustus; 30" Sgt. Major Maxwell Mulbeary. Front: 13" McMurtry; 13" pair Bear Brummels; 22" Bronwyll Merriman.

Cindy Martin's superlative 30"/76 cm.; ***Phantom of the Opera:*** the book placed in left hand serves as a third leg, otherwise his feet would have to be larger and flatter to support the magnificent size. His arms and legs are asymmetrical enabling him to stand with drama--not straight like regular bears. The mask is sculpted to a custom fit over the llama fur head; the "scarring" is leather; wool felt body and suit; cuffs and dickey are antique Arrow shirt; cape is antique material trimmed with old jet beads; hands and feet are of antique opera gloves; fingers are wired to bend. A specialized work of art by a leading Bear Artist. Courtesy Regina Prugh.

Jennifer created by Ann Inman; a Castle Edition for Edinburgh Imports, Inc. She is reading her friends the storybook ***Annie and the Wild Animals*** by Jan Brett. The 24"/61 cm. German mohair bear is mechanical. Her head and arms move while the candle adds light. Shown with assorted Steiff animals from the 1950s and 1960s: (L-R), ***Zooby*** bear; ***Gussy***, deer; fawn; racoon; ***Murmy***; velvet frog; two sitting foxes; skunk; badger; boar; wolf and bird. Courtesy Elke Block.

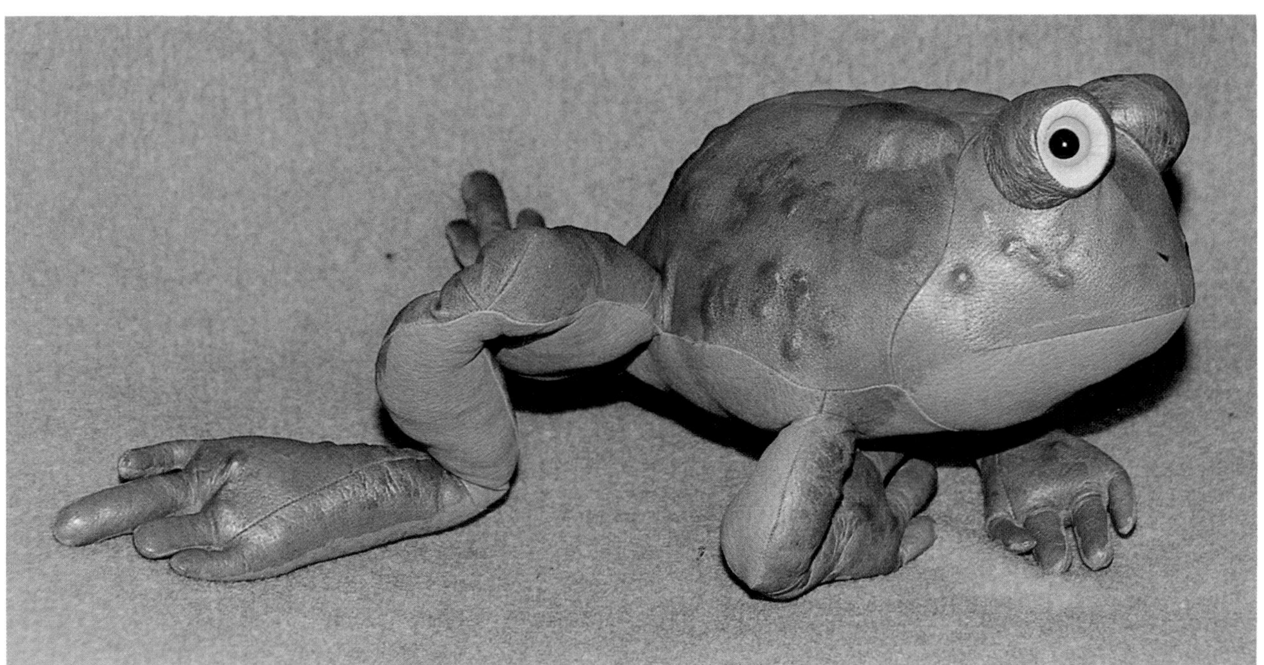

Artist Frog: 11"/28 cm. high, 23"/58.5 cm. long inc. legs; written in dye on belly, "625 Charleen Kinser 1986": cloth and paper tags are in seam of left hind leg; leather body stained and mottled brown; hinged legs; large yellow eyes. Note the hard, realistic "warts." Life-like, poseable, beautifully designed and executed.
Courtesy Valerie Vann.

Tumbler Bears by Joan Woessner: 11"/28 cm.; long pile mohair; stuffed with plastic beads allowing flexibility; f.j.; German glass eyes; brown pearl cotton nose/mouth; touch of mink at the eyelashes; signed card is registered and numbered. Bear Artists continue to change and adapt their creations to meet the demands of an expanding commercial market. Innovation and refinements continue almost always within the context of strong traditional values.
Courtesy Mostly Bears.

Teddy Roosebear: 13"/33 cm.; Ltd. Ed. bear with *two* faces by innovative Bear Artist Pam North. One side of the jointed head features a whimsical bear face, reversing to a likeness of Teddy Roosevelt. Faces and paws are individually hand sculpted of Polyform clay. The body is of dense high quality synthetic plush, fully jointed and firmly stuffed. *Bernie Bruin*, sitting: 4½"/11 cm.; made of durable bisque-like clay with wire jointed limbs. The finely detailed fur is shaded brown. Reminiscent of antique bisque bears.

Contemporary bears by Joyce O' Sullivan: *Joshua*, 17"/43 cm.; yellow long pile mohair; polyester stuffed; f.j.; glass eyes, pearl cotton nose/mouth on shaved snout; no claws; leather pads. He carries his music for when he might sing; #7 of 15. *Chocolate Parfait*, 14"/35.6 cm.; similar construction but felt pads. Original designs handmade with love, care and quality.
Courtesy Mostly Bears.

Wee Wanderer, #42 of a limited edition by Kathy Sandusky, 1988: 12"/30 cm.; German mohair; f.j.; glass eyes; finely clipped snout; pear shape torso; hump; European hiking garb including glued on felt hat and walking stick stitched to his paw. This stick serves as a tripod leg to make him self supporting. The narrow stitched (pearl cotton) mouth contributes to the overall look of a weary forest traveler. Successful design. Courtesy Carolyn Altfather.

Many collect the works of a particular artist such as Janet Reeves. Left: 17"/43 cm.; silky cream imported synthetic plush 1" in length; ultrasuede pads; handloomed scarf with name "Na-Nooq." *Country Blue Bear*: 10½"/26.7 cm.; hand dyed mohair and ultrasuede pads; Collector Ltd. Ed. 20 of 100. *Amanda*: 12"/30.5 cm.; imported caramel color mohair; glass eyes; ribbon of "Williamsburg Rose" color completes this little charmer. Winner of the Golden Teddy Award in 1987. All are fully jointed.
Courtesy Mostly Bears.

Regis **from the MacClassic Collection of Limited Editions: 13"/33 cm.; ⅝" distressed German mohair, medium taupe color; polyfill stuffed; f.j.; medium brown glass eyes; dark brown pearl cotton nose/mouth; four claws; ultrasuede pads; dressed in wool knickers and cap; wood heart buttons; suspenders and trim on cap are leather. The highest quality labels artist Mac Pohlen a perfectionist. Limited to 50.**

***Author's Note*:** **I have seen a Teddy which was sold clearly labeled as an Artist Bear with no attempt at misrepresentation. It was made by an artist in West Germany from vintage mohair and felt obtained from old coats and hats at flea markets. The Teddy has antique style glass eyes, is stuffed with excelsior, is made with traditional techniques, and even "smells right"! He has been expertly "appraised" as a 1920s bear, probably made by Steiff. The use of polyester thread might be the only clue that the bear is contemporary.**

V.
WHEELED ANIMALS

Mechanical Animals

Unique Steiff velveteen dog on cast iron wheels: 5¾"/14.6 cm. high inc. wheels, 6"/15.2 cm. long; firmly cotton stuffed; black glass eyes; brown floss nose/mouth. Extremely rare small size of a wheeled toy, ca. 1910. Courtesy Jeremy Bleecher and Patricia Gallagher.

Bearishly handsome in a life-like stance on cast iron wheels: 24"/61 cm. high, 32"/81 cm. long; FF button; brennessel (like coating material); excelsior stuffed over frame; unjointed; large shoe button eyes; twisted hard, black cotton floss nose/mouth; four stitched claws; felt pads; working pull growler. A great face, ca. 1910. Note the curving line from eye to ear indicative of large Steiff wheeled bears. Mint.
Private Collection.

Decorative goat: 10"/25.4 cm. high without base, 12"/30.5 cm. long; goat hair covers wood and papier mache body; green glass eyes; carved wood mouth; original reins, wide red collar and surcingle to bind a saddle or pack, ca. 1900. Life-like bleating sound when the head is pulled back. There is considerable interest in antique goats as collectibles.
Private Collection.

Some farsighted collectors prefer the choice bears on wheels: 10½"/26.7 cm high, 17"/43.2 cm. long; rich brown mohair; e.s.; unjointed; amber glass eyes; twisted black cotton floss nose/mouth, no claws; the felt pads have settled around the axles; original leather collar. Cast iron wheels were used until 1925. Personality plus bear in mint condition; maker unknown.
Private Collection.

Record Teddy: one of three sizes; 11"/28 cm. high, 9"/23 cm. long; FF button wooden wheels incised "Steiff"; e.s.; f.j.; shoe button eyes; twisted hard, cotton floss nose/mouth on factory clipped snout; three floss claws; felt pads; squeaker. This expressive Teddy on scooter cart is extremely rare and desired by all, especially in this superb condition, ca. 1913.
Courtesy Karen Silverstein.

Intense expression: 6"/15 cm. high, 8½"/21.6 cm. long; brown long pile mohair. Standing bears have a *brown* fur covering more often than the fully jointed models. The pull toy has excelsior stuffing; amber glass eyes; twisted hard, black cotton floss nose/mouth. This style of bear on cast iron wheels spanned a number of years, 1905-1925; possible Steiff, no I.D. Mint.
Private Collection.

Pull toy on stained wooden wheels: 9½"/24 cm. high, 11"/28 cm. long; FF button; worsted wool with nap (brennessel); e.s.; unjointed; shoe button eyes; pearl cotton nose/mouth; four claws; missing leather collar imprinted "Steiff." This wool coat-type fabric held up well from ca. 1913, the first year for wooden wheels. Private Collection.

St. Bernard: 8½"/21.6 cm. high, 9½"/24 cm. long; bushy tail is 4½"/11.4 cm long; FF button; long pile white mohair with inset markings; e.s.; amber glass eyes; "tulip ears" giving a perky look; twisted hard, tan cotton floss nose/mouth, no claws; cast iron wheels painted bronze. Missing leather collar impressed with "Steiff." Steiff made this model in nine sizes from 1905-1913. Mint. Private Collection.

Two who will always love and protect each other shown in studio portrait ca. 1908. The rich, thick, curly mohair of the Steiff St. Bernard (named "Captain") is evident. Vintage photographs of children with toys are eagerly sought.

"Rion": 17"/43 cm. high, 18"/45.5 cm. long; FF button; short gold mohair; natural mohair chin; very long and curly *natural* mohair (tipped in black) for mane, belly and tail ruff; e.s.; steel frame in legs; unjointed; orange glass eyes; pink pearl cotton nose; black mouth and claws disintegrated on touch (early black dyes tended to be harsh); no pads; working pull string growler/metal ring; hardwood wheels (2" diam.) painted red; steel base with pivoting front axles. Note the complex pattern, tight stitching and *lack of extensive airbrushing* ca. 1912. After spending many years near a coal furnace Rion was beautifully cleaned and groomed by Valerie Vann.
Courtesy Vivienne Roche.

The elephant forms the center of interest in the Steiff circus: 7½"/19 cm. high, 9"/23 cm. long; FF button; grey felt on cast iron wheels; e.s.; shoe button eyes with white felt backing (the first Steiff elelphants did not have felt backing); smiling elephant face. The original felt circus blanket is a clue to dating, ca. 1915. Available in ten sizes.
Courtesy Sherilyn Allmond.

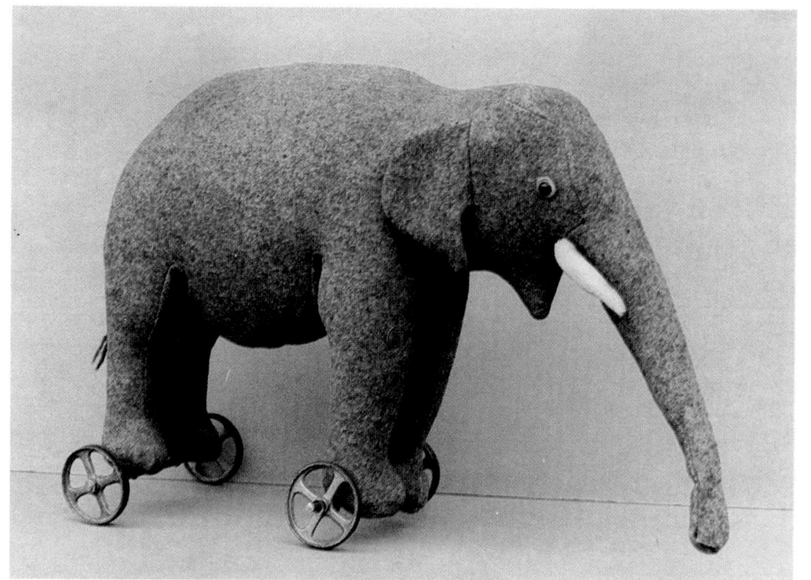

Bing elephant: 10½"/27 cm. high, 16"/41 cm. long (inc. trunk); felt; e.s.; shoe button eyes backed with white felt; felt tusks; stuffed felt (4½") tail with frayed grey yarn ruff; cast iron wheels brushed with gold, ca. 1920. The conformation is similar to the Steiff elephant, however, the ears and mouth are different. Attached to right shoulder is the identifying red metal button the size of a thumbtack. "Made in Bavaria" and the initials "B.W." (Bing Werke) are inside the black outline. "G.B.N." (Gebruder Bing Nurnberg) identified toys until 1920. From 1920-32 "B.W." was used. Bing affixed their mark on bears under the arm or more usually at the wrist or right ear. Bing is noted for their fascinating *mechanical* animals.
Courtesy Dave and Ann Abbott.

Fine lines and detailed design utilizing many pattern pieces of the Steiff donkey pull toy: 8"/20.3 cm. high, 9½"/24 cm. long; FF button; grey wool flannel; e.s.; unjointed; shoe button eyes; original bridle with four blank Steiff buttons, saddle and blanket. Made in nine sizes. The unusual mint condition from 1905-1915 adds to the value.
Private Collection.

"Don' t you dare bark. I'm bigger than you are," said the cat: 9½"/24 cm. high, 11½"/29 cm. long on cast iron wheels. Dog: 8"/20 cm. high, 9"/23 cm. long; stained (earliest) wooden wheels. Both are felt; e.s.; unjointed; have shoe button eyes; cat has light tan stitched nose/mouth, dog's is black; no claws or pads; squeakers; no I.D. but can be documented as Steiff, ca. 1913. Wheeled animals have always held fascination for children. The rarity of early models makes them desirable to collectors today.
Private Collection.

Three micro-mini wool ravens hover above while *Bully* on wheels and *Ball Mopsy* drink from their birdbath. *Bully*: 9"/23 cm. long; FF button; red S.T. (1926-34); mohair and velveteen; e.s.; swivel head; horsehair ruff; eccentric wooden wheels. Sure to capture hearts is *Ball Mopsy:* 6"/15 cm. high, sitting; Dralon; soft stuffed; voice; extremely rare, ca. 1958. Also in the series were *Ball Rabbit Hoppy* and *Ball Cat Sulla.* Steiff ravens are suspended on almost invisible nylon threads; felt wings; sold in a clear plastic cylinder. Seagull, bat and fish mobiles were also made for the nursery ca. 1960s-1970s.
Courtesy Mary Benavente.

Molly mounted on red wooden eccentric wheels that give a hopping action, ca. 1930: 9"/23 cm. high, 9"/23 cm. long; FF button; white mohair frosted with rust color markings; e.s.; swivel head; twisted hard, black cotton floss nose/mouth; three claws; glass eyes to melt your heart. Missing bell. A popular wheeled toy then and now. Other forms of *Molly* have been found with green, purple or orange frosting.
Private Collection.

Fox on eccentric wooden wheels: 9"/23 cm. long; FF button; mohair; e.s.; ca. 1920. Steiff has traditionally made beautiful fox faces. Pull toys are in demand.
Courtesy Michelle Daunton.

Record Peter, coaster pull toy: 11"/28 cm. high; FF button; red, brown and tan felt; e.s.; f.j.; shoe button eyes with a tiny felt backing; painted red mouth and nose; prehensile hands and feet on the elaborately contoured body. Extremely mint with vibrant red felt and like new (stained) wheels; unusual to find these with no wear, ca. 1932.
Courtesy Barbara Baldwin.

Coco Pavian on eccentric wheels: 10"/25 cm. high, RSB, S.T. 1325; grey short mohair body, thicker white mohair frames the felt face; e.s.; swivel head; green glass cat eyes; pink airbrushed nose/mouth; grey felt paws; red felt cap; original pullstring, ca. 1957. Hard to find on wheels.
Courtesy Debbi Anton.

Steiff galloping horse and child's pedal cart: horse, 21"/53.5 cm. high, 25"/63.5 cm. long; mohair; e.s.; unjointed; felt lined ears; brown glass eyes; leather hoofs, felt pads; white horse hair mane and full tail (17") long; original felt blanket; studded leather bridle and fitted harness. Three wheel pedal cart (working); painted blue seat is marked, "Steiff 3999, Made in Germany." Steiff also made a kiddie tractor of similar design without the horse. Purchased in 1953 at FAO Schwarz for a lucky child. *Jocko*, 23½"/60 cm.; RSB; S.T. 5360,2; pet name on *large* C.T. which is proportionate to size of animal. (See *TB & SA, Second Series* pg. 68.) Note, the legs are bent to sit easily. *Larger sizes* of *Jocko* are highly collectible.
Courtesy Barbara Baldwin.

Pull toy with "Steiff" imprinted on eccentric wheels: 6"/15 cm. high, 8"/20.5 cm. long; felt in striking colors; e.s.; velveteen head with shoe button eyes/red felt backing; orange felt bill and feet; waddles as pulled along, ca. 1913. The brightly colored Mallard was popular for many years before and since. In 1988 Steiff made a Museum Collection replica in an issue of 4,000 worldwide; retail, $125.00. Moths and dust have damaged many of the early felt toys. Courtesy Beth Savino, Hobby Center Toys.

Waddling goose: 6¾"/17cm. high, 8½"/21.6 cm. long; No. 6317.2; long white mohair touched with grey; e.s.; black glass eyes backed with red felt; felt bill and feet; wooden eccentric wheels; voice box activated when pulled along. This model was a popular toy from 1930s through 1950s and now is in great demand as a collectible. If store new would be worth 100% more.
Courtesy Dave and Ann Abbott.

Hermann Teddy: 16"/40.5 cm.; beige short pile (¼") mohair; e.s.; f.j.; orangish glass eyes; black floss nose/mouth, three claws; felt pads; loud growler (as most Hermann bears have), ca. 1940-50. Waddling duck on eccentric green wheels squeaks when pulled along: 5½"/14 cm. high; RSB; S.T. 2314,2; vivid multicolored mohair; e.s.; unjointed; black glass eyes; orange felt bill and cutout webbed feet; original blue bow, ca. 1950-60. Duck is more common than goose. Mohair *miniatures* (3¼"-4") were also made on eccentric wheels. These include a rabbit, *Bully*, Dachshund, *Cockie*, Tabby cat and pony.
Courtesy Barbara Baldwin.

Steiff riding Boxer: 20"/50 cm. high; US-Zone tag; mohair over steel frame (strong enough for child or adult); e.s.; glass eyes; twisted hard, black cotton floss nose, black airbrushed snout (faded); three stitched claws; pull growler; missing red leather collar; disc/rubber wheels; "STEIFF 100 x 15" in raised letters on the black rubber tires. (See close-up photo). Breed is hard to find as a wheeled toy, ca. early 1950s.
Courtesy Dana Zastrow.

Patty Playpal (36"/91 cm., ca. 1960) enjoys her toy dog: 13"/33 cm. high, 9"/23 cm. long; tagged, "Hygienic Toys, Made in Britain by Gwentoys Ltd."; woolly synthetic plush; firmly cotton stuffed; unjointed; amber glass eyes; hard plastic nose. Frame and chassis of carrier is steel with plastic/metal wheels and hard rubber tires; ca. 1950s. Designed for vigorous play, push along toys were popular for many years (1935-80) and are usually of English origin. They appear in Chiltern and Merrythought catalogues.
Courtesy Kay Bransky.

Long-haired Dachshund: 7"/18 cm. high, 10½"/ 26.5 cm. long; RSB; S.T. 1317, 10; C.T. *Waldi*: long and short cinnamon mohair; e.s.; unjointed; black plastic button eyes; twisted hard, black cotton floss (vertical) nose with elongated side and center stitches; painted mouth and claws; feet have metal rods with loops around axles; blue painted wheels mounted eccentrically, a Steiff innovation since 1913. Note S.T. is attached to *green* leather collar (also used for *Young Bear*). Original green cotton woven pull cord adds to value. Dachshunds are common, but hard to find on wheels, ca. 1960s.
Courtesy Valerie Vann.

Hobby Horse: 40"/102 cm.; RSB; S.T. 56/150; brown and white felt; red leather bridle; wooden stick body; wooden wheels. The head has brown glass eyes; brown painted nose; open peach felt mouth; black horsehair mane. Made from 1940-60s. Played with, therefore hard to find today. Also available with a less desirable wooden head.
Courtesy Debbi Anton.

Sturdy riding turtle for a child: 13½"/34 cm. high, 18"/43 cm. long; made 1961-76; mohair on a steel frame with hand grip. The turtle's front legs serve as a foot rest; steel rockers were also available for the series (turtle, ladybug and beetle). The solid white tires are marked, "Steiff 100"; the red/white pull string is missing. Limited demand.
Courtesy Chris McWilliams.

Mechanical Animals

Mechanical store display: 40"/102 cm. ca. 1913. The driver is a center seam, originally dressed farmer; FF button; painted face and arms now associated with Steiff display dolls. There are two movements: the donkey rears up and down by action of rod at front leg. The farmer whips donkey; the metal rod to his right arm mechanism acts as his "seat." The wooden wagon has dovetailed corners and large wooden wheels with metal rims. Donkey: 14"/36 cm. high, 14"/36 cm. long; FF button; e.s.; large shoe button eyes; tan felt open mouth; black mohair tail ruff; short horsehair mane. The harness is leather, felt and heavy cotton tape. Two curved metal rods attach wagon to donkey. Courtesy Joy Kelleher, Special Joys Museum.

Grissy donkey and grey plush cat on 18"/46 cm. x 11"/28 cm. platform was once a Christmas store display. As the metal rod beneath the donkey's tail is turned, the basket of gifts on *Grissy's* back falls over; the attached arm of cat pulls it back. The saddle blanket is curved metal covered with burlap on which is glued the basket holding wrapped gifts. These are tied on long ribbons to the basket and spill in and out as basket turns. *Grissy*: 15"/38 cm. long, IB; C.T. pet name; ca. 1960s. He has a metal rod up one back leg connecting mechanism to platform. Cat, 12"/30.5 cm.; no I.D.; the floppy body has a jointed head and wire in one leg to maintain shape. Note extra long arms to allow joining to saddle blanket for movement. Fascinating.
Courtesy Joy Kelleher, Special Joys Museum.

Squeaker toy with spring: 8½"/22 cm.; push down head, dog pops up; unjointed; excelsior stuffed head and arms are sewn on; sparse mohair, brown mohair (poseable) wired ears; blown milk glass eyes with gold threaded pupil. The eyes can be rotated to change expression. Yarn (horizontal) nose/mouth; red felt tongue. A variation of "Tubby" made by Einco, ca. 1915. Cackling Hen: 5"/13 cm.; tin and cardboard, printed Easter scene; turn handle for noise. Stamped, "Made in USA."
Courtesy Diane Hoffman.

Automated Pussy Cat: 12"/30.5 cm.; spring wound with incorporated key marked "RD" molded in oval; papier mache covered with rabbit fur; glass eyes; painted thin line mouth; pink tint to ears. The head, arms and tail are mechanically jointed to imitate natural movements of perhaps sipping and fanning (missing props), Attributed to Roullet & Decamps, France, (1865-1921), ca. 1920.
Courtesy Diane Hoffman.

Steiff bear with internal movement: 8"/20 cm. high, 13"/33 cm. long: FF button; red S.T.; all mohair with inset snout; unjointed limbs; when tail is moved head turns in a circular motion; e.s.; glass eyes; dark brown pearl cotton nose/mouth; four rose/tan stitched claws; felt pads. A rare piece for the connoisseur, ca. 1929.
Courtesy Barbara Baldwin.

Acrobatic Bear, activated by winding the arms *backwards:* 6¼"/15.8 cm.; paper label on bear, metal stand and box all marked, "Modern Toys Made in Japan"; brown plush with knit backing glued to metal frame; wire jointed; paws have a flat metal hook to hang on stand; plastic "stalk" eyes; black metal nose. The 8" stand is made in two parts and represents a tree branch. Hard to find with original (colorful) box. Instructions inside lid. These toys provided happy pastimes for children of the 1930s.
Courtesy Phyllis Blaser.

Key-wind panda: 6"/15 cm.; black and white plush over metal; painted metal mask face; *rubber* hands; original 1950s-type ribbon; wind silver metal key to start yo-yo, head goes to and fro; on/off switch in back. Marked, "Made in Japan." Entertaining addition to a bear collection. Collectors are segmenting themselves into specific fields, one of which is this modern day "automata."
Courtesy Evelyn Thomas.

Dancing Circus bear who performed across Europe with gypsies ca. 1907: 5"/12.7 cm.; flocked papier mache; cardboard soles marked "Germany"; key-wind. Right: pink and white plush covered tin poodle, 4¾"/12 cm.; when the key is wound she spins and wags her tail, ca. 1950s Japan. Of special interest to a camera buff.
Courtesy Dana Zastrow.

The history of the Steiff Co. is replete with innovation and achievement and is characterized by animals of striking originality and beauty such as the mechanical tiger. He sits on a drum 8"/20 cm. high. This houses the electric motor (marked "Made in Germany") that enables the 18"/46 cm. traditional Bengal tiger to have a pawing motion while the body is rotating. The long tail is SOLIDLY stuffed with excelsior (many of the "big cat" family are found with breaks in their tails). The wooden teeth are 1"/2.5. cm. long, the ball is 4"/10 cm. and the total weight is 43 pounds. There was also a mechanical lamb and bear in the series; a special order for a display at a hotel in the Hamptons.
Courtesy Barbara Baldwin.

Steiff Village made in 1955 for the FAO Schwarz Boston toy store. There are 110 animals in the 10ft./3.05 m. by 17 ft./5.18 m. village. The cars (made for Steiff by their own contractors) and backdrop are molded vulcanized rubber over wood. Representing a race track, the animation is run by a single motor beneath the platform. The cars travel around the track and the "people" in the spectator section cheer them on. Townspeople have come out of their houses to view the race. Note the many details throughout, for example, cotton simulating smoke from the exhaust of the red vehicle. The unique and humorous assemblage is one of a kind. Over the years Steiff has created a number of animated displays incorporating their toys.
Courtesy Michelle Daunton.

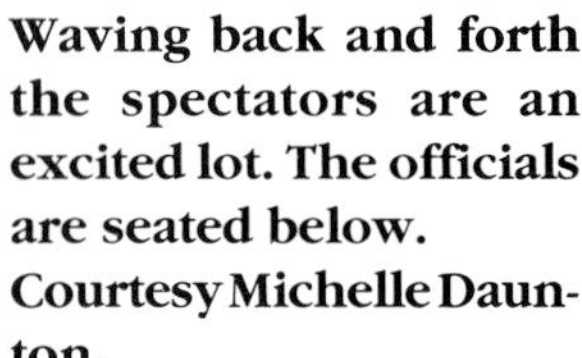

Waving back and forth the spectators are an excited lot. The officials are seated below.
Courtesy Michelle Daunton.

**"Broken Down Car" (27"/69 cm. high) has a separate motor. The man under the car moves his feet. *Jocko* is turning the crank and showing signs of grief over the breakdown. *Lulac* is distressed and moves her head from side to side. The bear with fruit is a pedestrian who happened upon the scene.
Courtesy Michelle Daunton.**

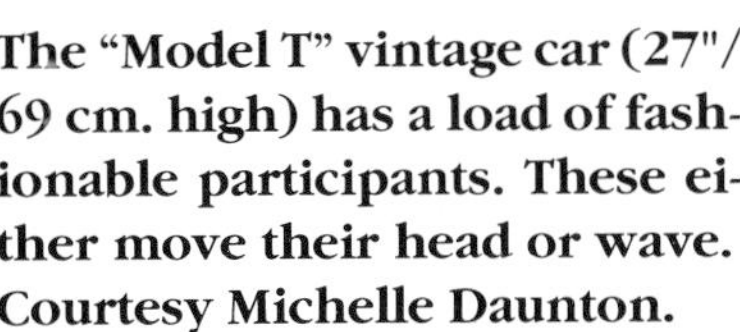

**The "Model T" vintage car (27"/69 cm. high) has a load of fashionable participants. These either move their head or wave.
Courtesy Michelle Daunton.**

VI.
SCHUCO TEDDY BEARS & ANIMALS

Splendid group of Yes/No bears, ca. 1920s. Left and center are Schuco *Messenger Bears* with removable leather pouches. Right is a *Bellhop*. (L-R), 14½"/37 cm.; 11"/28 cm.; 14½"/37 cm.; all are mohair with made-to-body outfits; e.s.; f.j.; have three floss claws; eyes (L-R) are brown glass, shoe buttons and clear glass. Left and center have twisted hard, dark brown cotton floss nose/mouth; *Bellhop* has black. Left and center have *woven cloth pads*; Bellhop's are replaced with felt. Extremely collectible and rare bears, unlike the more common Bellhop monkey.

Pink frosted mohair music bear: 18"/46 cm.; e.s.; f.j.; oversized clear glass eyes; pearl cotton nose, mouth and four claws; felt pads; when tummy is pressed music plays. No I.D.; probably Schuco, ca. 1920s. The "blown out" left paw pad does not alter value of this extremely rare (color) and desirable Teddy.

Clockwise: Schuco violinist, 4½"/11.4 cm.; when wound he spins and bows his violin with two different motions. The 1937 Schuco catalogue shows eight versions of violinist: monkey, pig and six different people. Unusual 1920s bear with yellow cotton head and made-to-body felt clown suit: 7¼"/18.4 cm.; wire jointed arms only. *Bonzo* on trapeze 9¾"/25 cm. inc. frame; painted papier mache face; rabbit fur body; wire jointed limbs; pressure on wire lever activates toy, ca. 1926. Schuco Yes/No Teddy with orange/scarlet tipped mohair: 11"/28 cm.; e.s.; f.j.; silver glass eyes; pearl cotton nose/mouth; cloth pads; squeaker; desirable color, ca. 1930s. Dime store bears purchased by present owner in early 1930s for 10¢-15¢: 4½"/11.4 cm. to 5¾"/14.6 cm.; all are mohair; e.s.; wire jointed limbs; glass "stalk" eyes; yarn nose/mouth. These came in red, gold (most common), blue and pink.

Rare Schuco Yes/No. Parrot from 1926: 6"/15 cm. high, 11"/28 cm. long; green, yellow and red mohair; brown/black glass eyes with white felt backing; red felt beak; tan felt over wire feet; by moving tail, head turns Yes/No. Choice piece. Courtesy Idele Gilbert.

Yes/No Fox: 13"/33 cm.; mohair; e.s.; f.j.; unusual *red* faceted jewel eyes with metal rim; metal glasses fit into head; black floss outlines ears, nose and mouth; muslin pads; no claws; working squeaker, ca. 1920s. Humanized Schuco Yes/No animals are extremely desirable. The popular theme originally came from the ancient fables where the humanized animals have the characteristics and foibles of real people. Courtesy Barbara Baldwin.

Yes/No Bulldog: 7" high; mohair; e.s.; tail moves head Yes/No; unusual tri-color glass eyes; twisted hard, cotton floss nose (similar to Steiff style); sewn mouth; three stitched claws; no pads or voice box; original scarf and metal pipe (essential for full value); ca. 1930s. Shows the ability of Schuco designers to portray personality traits. Courtesy Barbara Baldwin.

Key-wind mechanical: 4½"/12 cm. high; soft mohair over metal frame body; felt covering on face, hands and feet; tiny glass eyes. The mirror and comb are celluloid. When wound, the monkey combs hair and wiggles tail, ca. 1920s. Great amusement value in a very collectible piece attributed to Schuco.
Courtesy Wanda Loukides.

Rare Schuco novelty: Yo-Yo, 5"/13 cm. overall; mohair covered metal head; metal body; pipe cleaner limbs; felt hat, ears, hands and feet. Going through the head is the red/white string tied on the end with a green wooden ball, ca. pre WWII. There will always be great demand for the unusual. The stand was custom made to show the yo-yo effectively.
Courtesy Jim Lambert.

The creativity of Schuco designers. *Blecky:* 3½"/9 cm.; stock #7305/9 from box; tag "Made in Western Germany"; mohair over metal frame; f.j.; cutout felt hands, feet and ears; painted metal baby face; when plunger at base of body is depressed *Blecky* sticks out plastic tongue; twist plunger to rotate head; ca. 1950-60. Novelty items are sought after by Schuco collectors. Original box, tag and mint condition increase value. Perfume bottle monkey in original box showing Deco-style graphic of woman holding monkey; caption, "My Darling, Mein Liebling!" Scarlet mohair; 3½"/9 cm.; paper hang tag "Made in Germany" (indicates pre WWII); molded and flocked metal face; a 1926 novelty for a girl's dresser. *Top:* 2¼"/5.7 cm. (rare tiny size); pink *velveteen* (unusual) over metal frame; molded and painted metal face in style of perfume monkey, ca. 1920-30.
Courtesy Laurie Hix.

Perfume Bottle Bear: 3½"/9 cm.; *bright red* mohair over metal body; jointed limbs; remove head to find perfume tube with cork stopper. Red is the most rare color to have in one's perfume/compact collection. Short black (rare color) mohair; 2¼"/6 cm.; metal body; wood arms; f.j.; black glass bead eyes; brown cotton floss nose/mouth; black felt hands and feet with tiny metal piece inserted so bear will stand; original owner bear, 1938 exactly. The 1930s 2¼" mini Schucos are far more finely crafted than the 2½" ones from the 1950s which do *not* have felt hands and feet. Short pink mohair; 4⅞"/12 cm.; metal form; black metal bead eyes; black pearl cotton nose/mouth; no pads; rare size, color and mint condition.

Miniature monkey with removable head and fitted perfume bottle: 5"/12.5 cm.; brown mohair over metal form; f.j.; painted metal face with inset brown metal eyes; felt ears, hands and feet. This style is shown in Schuco catalogues from 1930-50. Key-wind *Bellhop Bear*: 5¼"/13.3 cm; mohair head and upper body/arms; metal frame; jointed arms and head; black metal eyes; heavy black thread nose/mouth; no paw claws; metal feet without wheels. When (Schuco) key is wound the bear dances in circles. Original felt cap and pants (missing belt). Cute face and size for the well-made mechanical, ca. 1930.
Courtesy Marlene Wendt.

Schuco wind-ups: all 4"/10cm.-5"/12.5 cm.; US-Zone era (1947-53); left to right: mouse holding baby mouse by the arms; felt over metal; when wound he swings baby and dances in circles. (This mechanical mouse is the subject of a children's book, *The Mouse and His Child.* There was also an animated cartoon based on this title.) Elf lifts baby gnome and spins; Scottie with red plaid blanket; boy in felt clothes drinks from stein; monkey lifts baby monkey.
Courtesy Harriet Purtill.

Schuco *Peck-Peck* birds: 2½"/6.5 cm. high, 4½"/11.5 cm. long; mohair over metal form; black metal eyes; tan metal beak; black or tan metal feet. Assorted colors are: black/red/grey; black/green/grey; black/orange/grey; black/grey/dark green and black/yellow/light green. When key (stamped "Schuco") is wound they hop around and peck the ground. In 1929 the company introduced the mechanical *Pecking bird*. Its popularity catapulted them into a position of leadership in the toy industry. The bird remained a staple in the line until the early 1950s. Courtesy Idele Gilbert.

Schuco *Tricky Dwarf* with patented head movement: 10"/25.4 c.; felt, center seam; Yes/No head; jointed limbs; tiny button eyes framed with metal spectacles; mohair beard; brightly painted facial features; made-to-body felt shirt; non-removable velveteen pants; VELVETEEN cap; felt slippers with heavy cardboard soles. This friendly fellow is often found missing cap, belt or slippers, ca. 1950s. The same "Tricky" doll was also sold as *Father Christmas* wearing a removable Santa Claus-type coat and hat. Courtesy Barbara Baldwin.

Steiff Yes/No Gnome: 9"/23 cm.; tiny FF button *behind* left ear; almost identical to the Schuco model. The MOHAIR HAT and RED FELT SPOT (on top of bald head to mark where hat is sewn) define the doll as Steiff. Shown with Steiff: 6½"/17 cm. high mohair rabbit on eccentric wheels, RSB, US-Zone tag, original ribbon with bell; sitting mohair bunnies (adorable and popular), 3¼"/8 cm. and 3½"/9 cm., from the same 1950s period. Private Collection.

"Louise": left, 14"/36 cm.; mohair; e.s.; f.j.; metallic gold glass eyes; floss nose/mouth; three claws; short mohair pads (matching snout) with cardboard innersoles. Note the short body and long heavy legs typifying Schuco. Demand is less for *standard* Schuco bears, ca. 1950s. "Schucie": right, 20"/51 cm.; music box has US-Zone label; curly mohair; e.s.; Yes/No head, disc jointed limbs; extra large (¾"diam.) glass eyes; pearl cotton nose/mouth; four claws; felt pads (no cardboard innersoles); key in back for music box playing German folk tune. Note: hands turn backward and snout turns up like a ski jump. Extremely desirable large musical Schuco with Yes/No function. Shown with *Circus Babies* by Elizabeth Gale; ill. by John Dukes McKee; N.Y. Rand McNally, 1930.

The special preciousness of a tiny *Tricky:* 8"/20 cm.; plastic medallion, "Schuco Tricky//Made in US-Zone Germany"; golden mohair; hard stuffed with excelsior; f.j.; tail turns head; amber glass eyes; black twisted floss nose/mouth; felt pads; three floss claws, ca. 1950. Schuco Yes/No bears are *very* collectible.
Courtesy Barbara Baldwin.

Rolly Bear on roller skates: 8"/20 cm.; mohair; e.s.; jointed limbs; clear glass eyes; floss nose/mouth on clipped snout; three hand claws; felt pads; key wind clockwork movement--as stick is moved bear skates backwards or forwards. Bottom of skates marked "Schuco Rolly, Made in US-Zone, Germany." A clown, monkey and bunny were also made. However, the bear (of any given series) is always the most avidly sought. If a mechanical toy is non-working the value is dramatically decreased. Highly collectible in this super mint condition with original scarf. An earlier 8½" Skating Bear was made by Bing.
Courtesy Barbara Baldwin.

Yes/No Panda: 3½"/9cm.; mohair; metal frame; f.j.; glass eyes; floss nose/mouth. Demand is for the largest (16½") and smallest (3½"). There is less interest in the medium size. Original owner bear. In the 1950s it was the type of miniature toy bought by a grandmother (Dorothy Brenner) for a special grandchild (Karen Silverstein).

A comparison of Schuco and Steiff monkeys. Steiff: 8"/20 cm.; RSB underside left foot; C.T. *Jocko*; mohair; e.s.; f.j.; green glass cat eyes; airbrushed red mouth and triangular nose; felt face, ears and mitten hands with stitched fingers. Below 10" the Steiff chimps have a closed mouth and NO beards. The 6½" and larger *white* is desirable to *Jocko* collectors, ca. 1950s. Schuco: 20"/51 cm.; dense mohair; e.s.; f.j.; felt face, ears and mitten hands with stitched fingers; oversize glass eyes, inset with EYELIDS giving the distinctive Schuco "look"; cheeks and lips are heavily airbrushed with rose; *closed* mouth with white mohair beard, ca. 1960s. Schuco monkeys in large sizes are overlooked. Presently they are not as desirable as (large) Steiff monkeys.
Courtesy Barbara Baldwin.

Noah's Ark **charmers cleverly capturing each animal's characteristics. The miniature series is comprised of 31 animals, ca. 1950-60. Missing here is a grey Scottie, gold and white Tabby cat, black cat, koala and turtle. All are 2"/5 cm. to 3"/7.5 cm.; individually packed in a colored box; made of mohair or wool astrakhan plush; limbs and heads are movable except for the unjointed turtle, penguin, owl, porcupine, finch, crow and ladybug. All have the patented metal frame except the porcupine (hedgehog) and ladybug that are soft stuffed. There is wide use of pipe cleaners for limbs, tails and antennae. (L-R) front: ladybug, porcupine, pig, standing Panda/tail; standing monkey/tail, two rabbits, fox (gold pipe cleaner tail), white Terrier, black Scottie, grey cat. Second row: elephant, tiger, lion, raccoon, monkey (metal face), squirrel, black poodle, Dalmatian puppy,** ***Tramp, Lady*****, white cat. Perch: penguin, owl, bird (Finch), crow. The most rare pictured are: standing Panda/tail ($200.00); standing monkey/tail ($150.00) squirrel ($150.00); Finch ($100.00); Dalmatian ($150.00);** ***Lady*** **($150.00) and** ***Tramp*** **($125.00.). The lion, raccoon, penguin and cats are more common ($100.00 UP). The ladybug is $50.00-75.00. The contemporary wooden ark is made by Artesonia Rinconada.**
Courtesy Idele Gilbert.

Miniatures from ***Noah's Ark:*** **all are mohair except the astrakhan plush poodle with pipe cleaner ears and tail and pompon topknot. All are fully jointed except the squirrel that has pipe cleaner limbs; yarn tuft ears; fluffy yarn tail and holds green pompon nut. Pig: felt ears and snout; curly pipe cleaner tail; original blue cotton ribbon. Raccoon: white felt hands and feet; bushy mohair tail. Box adds value.**
Courtesy Laurie Hix.

Schuco dressed rooster: 12"/30.5 cm.; jointed by bendable wire (wire in plumed tail moves head Yes/No); excelsior stuffed white mohair head; soft stuffed red/white stripe cotton body; glass eyes with painted orange backing; inset red felt face and yellow felt beak; felt comb, waddle and tail; white felt feet and hands; rayon taffeta pants sewn on at waist; removable felt jacket/black felt collar and one round black button; black felt clogs with thick cardboard soles, ca. 1950s. There is great demand for costumed animals.

Schuco from Disney's *Lady and the Tramp:* center, *Lady,* 8"/20.5 cm. high; mohair; e.s.; poseable by bendable wire; plastic googly eyes; felt eyelashes, painted eyebrows; black floss nose/mouth; four claws; original plastic collar; Schuco Hegi era, ca. late 1960s. Left *Lady,* 10"/25 cm. high; same as above except for black plastic button eyes, longer curly mohair ears and plastic nose. *Tramp,* 8"/20.5 high, cloth tag "Schuco" sewn inside of right hind leg; grey, brown and white mohair; e.s.; jointed by bendable wire; red felt lined ears; plastic googly eyes; plastic nose; no claws. Tramp is hardest to find. All are popular as Disney collectibles, therefore value is increased.
Courtesy Barbara Baldwin.

Trip-Trap **animals: 7¼"/18 cm. high, 7½"/19 cm. long. All are mohair; excelsior stuffed over a steel frame; have jointed legs, wide rubber wheels on feet; Spaniels' eyes are plastic, Terrier's glass; black plastic noses/yarn mouths. Left Spaniel has original red plastic collar and plastic tag, 'Schuco Trip-Trap Patent//Patents appld. for in USA-England-Schwiz (etc.)//Made in US-Zone Germany." Also made as a Scottie, Poodle, Airedale, Bulldog, Chow, Dalmatian (caricature), Dachshund and Tabby cat. When led on a leash these animals trot along on all fours, ca. 1950. Other early companies, for example Bing, used a similar walking mechanism.**
Courtesy Idele Gilbert.

Schuco from 1960s. (L-R), bear: 13"/33cm.; tagged, "Original//Schuco//bigo//bello//DEGM"; mohair, soft stuffed; head swivels on metal rod; limbs poseable by bendable wire; glass eyes; floss nose, open felt mouth; felt pads; squeaker. Desirable dressed bear; 15"/38 cm.; mohair;*felt hands;* soft stuffed; poseable by bendable wire; glass eyes; floss nose/mouth; colorful polyester dress/hat. Character known in Europe: 10"/25 cm.; mohair and synthetic plush; soft stuffed; swivel head, limbs and tail poseable by bendable wire; tri-color oval glass eyes; floss nose, velveteen mouth; painted nails on velveteen hands and foot pads (cardboard innersoles). Unusual. Rare in U.S.

VII.
TEDDY BEAR RELATED ITEMS

Fictional Characters
Advertising Animals
and Puppets

Personable Tea Cosey made by Steiff ca. 1913: 15"/38 cm.; dense mohair; excelsior stuffed head, kapok stuffed arms; shoe button eyes; black floss nose/mouth; four claws; felt paw pads; lined with heavy felt for insulation; rare and appealing example.
Courtesy Barbara Baldwin.

Copyright 1892 by McLoughlin Bros., New York; soft cover; 8⅜"/22 cm. by 10⅝"/27 cm.; part of the *Little Kitten Series.* Now reproduced in a slightly altered size by B. Shackman & Co., Inc. Good condition. Collectors are stalking early books related to the Teddy Bear.

Steiff egg warmers before 1926: rooster and hen set, 4½"/11 cm. high; tiny FF buttons; all felt; machine stitched applique; painted beak; shoe button eyes/white felt backing. Velvet chick lined with felt; 4"/10 cm. high; shoe button eyes; airbrushed markings; remnants of WHITE S.T. under FF button. The chick is extremely rare. The cock head was also available as a tea cosey. These two dimensional utilitarian objects were made for the German market, ca. 1912-20. Courtesy Betsy Gottschalk.

Cotton batting bear on tinsel swing: overall 5"/12.7 cm. high, 3½"/9 cm. side; bear is 2½"/6.4 cm. high seated on a 2½" gilded wooden swing; black glitter eyes. The gold wrapped wire is decorated with a sprig of paper greenery. A treasure from Germany, ca. 1900. Bear ornament: 3"/7.6 cm. high; *feather light* German glass; pearlized pale green painting; gold painted claws; paws rest on knees, ca. early 1900s.
Courtesy Nancy Roeder.

***Roosevelt Bear* series of pottery produced by Buffalo Pottery. Choice children's pitcher, 5"/12.5 cm. high; vitrified china; bright multicolor transfer scene and lyric; gilt on handle and rim; reintroduced in 1919 ten years after the demise of Eaton's books. The style is different from the 1906 period, the scene is the same. Marked with a buffalo on a field of grass. Highly collectible by Buffalo Pottery collectors and in this case automobile buffs.**
Courtesy Barbara Baldwin.

Fired color decals on German plate: 6"/15 cm.; stamped "71."

> Silverhair I declare you have broken Bruin's chair!
> When they reach their home (or lair)
> When they see the havoc there
> T'will be more than they can bear

The intruder in the famous story of *The Three Bears* did not become Goldilocks until 1888. "Silverhair" indicates before 1888.
Courtesy Marian Swartz.

Depression Carnival Glass children's plates: 8½"/22 cm. diam.; beaded edging. Left, "Little Bo Peep" surrounded by 16 dancing Roosevelt-type bears. Right, two bruin-type bears with 15 Dutch children dancing around, ca. 1920-40. Uncommon and desirable.
Courtesy Marian Swartz.

Paper items are called ephemera meaning short lived or transitory. Fortunately, a number of vintage Teddy Bear related paper items have survived. Center, Huld's Puzzle Series No. 15a, Copr. 1907 and postmarked 1908 with 1¢ stamps. The four postcards building the figure are to be mailed in sequence. Reproductions are available today. Top left, "Stung by Bee," Copr. 1906 by Natl. Art Co.; below, "Good Night," Copr. 1907 by MT Sheahan, Boston. Of great interest is top right, "Will You Be My Teddy Bear," Copr. 1907 by Up-To-Date Novelty Co.; made of WOOD, decorated with delicate wood burning; faceted (early) plastic eyes are recessed; front is for signature; postmark 1907. Below, "In Mind I Love You Still," 1908 embroidery.
Courtesy Marian Swartz.

Steiff pillow dog, *Jack*: 4"/10 cm. high, 12"/30.5 cm. square; no I.D.; all mohair; excelsior stuffed dog's head; unjointed; brown glass eyes; twisted hard, floss nose/mouth. The novel pillow or pajama bag is also found as a Bully dog and cat, ca. 1932. A rare find at Bermondsey Market, London. Courtesy Jean Ann Smith.

Molly dog as a purse: 6"/15 cm. high, 8"/20 cm. long; FF button; yellow S.T. with *handwritten* No. 85108,1311d; frosted mohair; e.s.; jointed head only; glass eyes; pearl cotton nose/mouth; three stitched claws. A zipper is in puppy's back. The metal closure is marked, "Zipp, DRP Nurnberg." A special pet for a girl to carry, ca. 1927. Rare novelties are in great demand.

Cotton hankie, 1930-40 era; large bear in one corner, a smaller bear in other three. Left: bear cut from a piece of old silk fabric and stuffed. Right: 6"/15 cm. Teddy; gold plushy *corduroy*; wire jointed limbs, rigid head; amber glass stickpin eyes; black thread nose/mouth; squeaker; looking like a football player with high shoulders, ca. 1920s.
Courtesy Wanda Loukides.

No. 3 STEIFF TOYS „Button in Ear" BRAND.
MARGARETE STEIFF Co
INVENTORS OF THE TEDDY-BEAR. NEW YORK 16th STR.

No. 4 STEIFF TOYS „Button in Ear" BRAND.
MARGARETE STEIFF Co
INVENTORS OF THE TEDDY-BEAR. NEW YORK 16th STR.

STEIFF TOYS „Button in Ear" BRAND.
MARGARETE STEIFF Co
INVENTORS OF THE TEDDY-BEAR.
No. 5
NEW-YORK 16th STR.

Rare Steiff advertising stamps from the 1920s: 3"/7.5 cm. high; each says, "Steiff Toys, Button in Ear Brand, Margarete Steiff Co, Inventors of the Teddy-Bear, New York 16th Str." Notably featured are the Dolly Circus Bear, Roly Poly Clown, Golliwog; fully jointed fox and dolls. They are numbered 3-8 (1 and 2 are missing). Rare memorabilia. Mint. Courtesy Debbi Anton.

Gingerbread House is a true rarity: 20"/51 cm. high, 20"/51 cm. wide, 12"/30 cm. deep; Steiff logo on roof; molded vulcanized rubber over wood; probably display piece, ca. 1950s. Shown with 1950s Santa, 7½"/19 cm.; witch hand puppet, 6½", ca. 1971; Halloween cat *(Tom Cat)*, 5½" /14 cm., mohair (no velvet on this size), ca. late 1950s.
Courtesy Michelle Daunton.

Steiff and other animals on a children's record cover ca. 1960 suggest the magic of childhood.

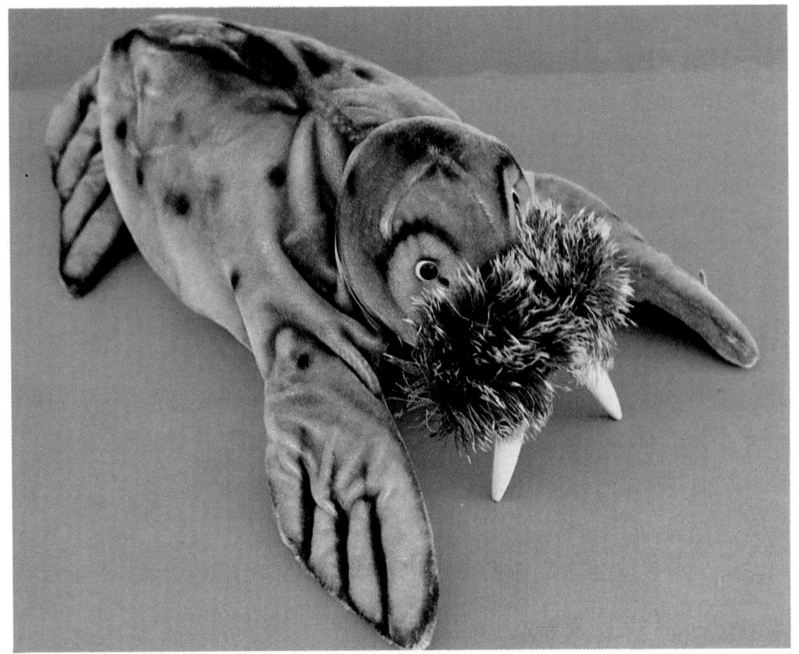

Paddy with expression of total surprise. Pajama Bag: 18"/45 cm. long; RSB; S.T. 2345,00; large C.T. (1⅛" diam.) *Paddy*; short pile mohair spotted with blue; frosted long mohair whiskers; B&W plastic eyes; pink pearl cotton nose with airbrushed nostrils; ivory color plastic tusks (3½" long); stitched flippers; excelsior stuffed head. The zippered bag is lined with navy blue taffeta. Shown in the 1965 FAO Schwarz catalogue. *Paddy* in all forms is popular.

Turtle Pajama Bag: 5"/12 cm. high, 18"/45 cm. long; RSB; S.T. 2334,90; mohair; black glass eyes; black painted nose; peach felt open mouth; four brown felt claws. Zippered pouch for pajamas; can also be used as a large arm puppet. Similar to but larger than the all mohair *Slo*. Other Pajama Pals made ca. 1960s are *Zotty* Bear, Polar Bear and *Paddy* walrus. Hard to find. Courtesy Debbi Anton.

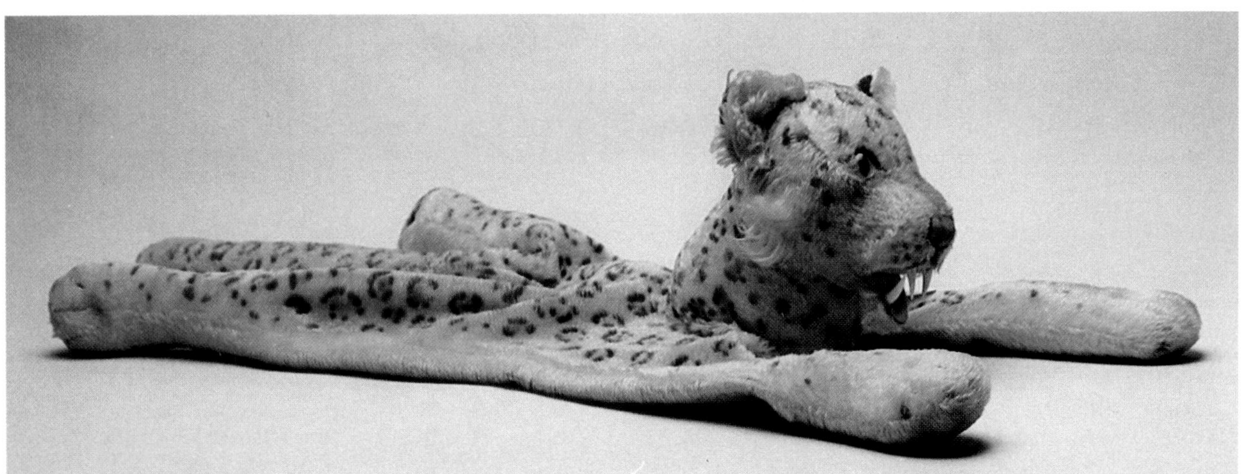

**Steiff Leopard Rug: 7"/18 cm. high, 32"/81 cm. long; unknown stock number. Probably an early 1960s display piece, this unusual rug has excelsior stuffed head, paws and tail; striking green glass eyes; pink floss nose; open peach felt mouth with four teeth; three stitched claws. The body lies flat and is unstuffed; not to be confused with the zippered animals (no zipper or pouch is present). A comforting companion for the fireplace. Rare.
Courtesy Debbi Anton.**

Fictional Characters

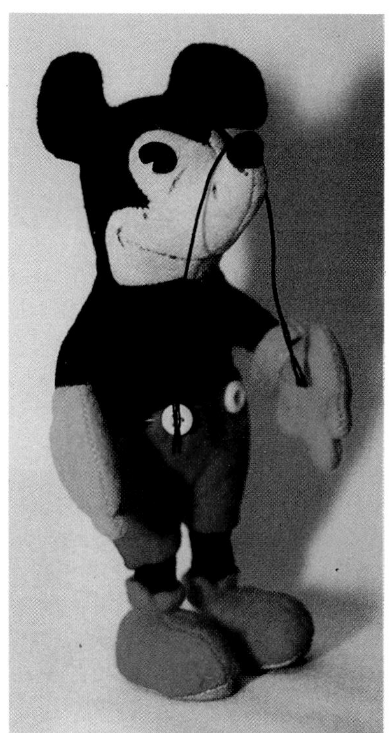

Steiff *Mickey Mouse*, 1931-34: 5"/13 cm.; no button, marked on foot, "Mickey Mouse/Design Patent By Margarete Steiff/New York"; all felt; e.s.; (larger velveteen models are hard stuffed cotton); oil cloth eyes; painted mouth; yarn tail is (often) missing. Note the bright colors throughout. Walt Disney was said to be particularly pleased with this design. The 5" all felt *Minnie* is seen in Vol. I, *TB&SA,* pg. 232. Collectors might do well to concentrate on *Minnie Mouse*. *Mickey* appeared at least five times to *Minnie's* one; the old law of supply and demand. *Mickey* is popular in Japan where he is affectionately called *Miki Kuchi*. He is the little guy coping with great odds in making a place for himself.
Courtesy Jim Lambert.

Schuco *Mickey Mouse*: 10"/25 cm.; mohair body, felt pants; unjointed; plastic eyes and nose; red felt smiling mouth; pipestem legs end in big circular shoes while hands are encased in four-fingered felt gloves, ca. 1950s. On Nov. 28, 1928 *Mickey* opened at New York's Colony Theater in *Steamboat Willie.* The mouse was conceived as a series of easy-to-animate circles. Great demand for *Mickey Mouse* collectibles.
Courtesy Barbara Baldwin.

Winnie the Pooh/Christopher Robin cutout dolls; many costumes and clothes in vivid colors; Whitman Publishing Co. #947, 1935. The cut set is mounted on board and framed. Shown with R. John Wright's first issue of *Christopher Robin*: 20"/51 cm.; felt; f.j.; painted features with the "Little Children" face; blue cotton smock, white cotton hat; typical of the E.H. Shepard drawings. Tag sewn into clothing, "R. John Wright Dolls, Christopher Robin, Winnie the Pooh, 0082/100, Walt Disney Productions"; sold with 8" *Pooh*. *Christopher Robin* II has a mackintosh and umbrella. Choice collector pieces.
Courtesy Rebecca Vaughn Gardner.

Endearing Winnie the Pooh stuffed figures well crafted by Gund and sold at Sears for a short time, ca. 1966. Now collectible: 5"/12.5 cm. to 6"/15 cm.; *Pooh* is velveteen with a knit jersey sweater; *Rabbit, Eeyore, Tigger* and *Kanga* are made of corduroy with glued-on features and accents; *Roo* is felt. All are stuffed with wood chips and tagged, "Gund//Walt Disney Prod.//Made in Japan." *Piglet* is missing from the set and hard to find. *Pooh* is the most common. In 1963 Knickerbocker made a larger set of plush. Pooh wore a turquoise green jacket.
Courtesy Rebecca Vaughn Gardner.

Donald Duck: 17"/43 cm., a significant large size; woolly plush; e.s.; unjointed; plastic-type eyes with painted backs; felt bill and webbed feet; felt cap, knitted sweater; possible Chad Valley, ca. 1930-1940. Uncommon example of a popular Disney character. The original skis increase value markedly. Around 1938, long billed Donald Duck gave way to the now standard version.
Courtesy Dottie Ayers.

Long billed, scowling *Donald Duck*: 16"/41 cm.; tagged, "Kreuger, original *Silly Symphony*" (a series Disney did that included *The Three Pigs* and others); velveteen; kapok stuffed; unjointed; hand painted oilcloth feet/ wood soles and bill over open wooden mouth; rare example of *Donald*; American, ca. 1930s. Shown with personalized Teddy, "T.J." 20"/51 cm.; orangish mohair; excelsior/kapok mix; f.j.; probably glass eyes replaced by the more available shoe buttons; three double strand claws; repadding done long ago adds interest to this bear in "found condition." Unknown maker, ca. 1920.
Courtesy Diane Hoffman.

Fred Flintstone takes a rollicking ride on ***Dino***: 12½"/32 cm. high, 18"/45.5 cm. long; marked "Louis Marx, Inc., 1962"; painted metal body covered with lavender synthetic plush; Fred's body is metal also; both have vinyl heads. Batteries give life: ***Dino's*** head moves from side to side; his mouth opens and legs move on hidden wheels while Fred rocks back and forth in his lithographed Sudan chair; interior spring gives ***Dino's*** tail shape and a jaunty wiggle. Rare.
Courtesy Mary Benavente.

Thumper, Schuco's Yes/No rabbit: 12"/30.5 cm.; plastic tag, "Tricky, US-Zone, Germany" (1947-53); grey, beige and white mohair, pink mohair lined ears; cotton stuffed; swivel Yes/No head and disc jointed arms; large B&W googly glass eyes; applied red plastic nose; red felt mouth and white felt "buck teeth"; felt pads on (long) feet only; three floss claws; no whiskers; non-working squeaker. A smaller (9¼") ***Thumper*** was available with unjointed arms. A crossover collectible of special interest to Disney fans.
Courtesy Barbara Baldwin.

Bonzo: 11"/30 cm.; blond mohair; unjointed; glass eyes inset into felt, hair eyelashes; black floss nose, red felt tongue; felt lined ears; cardboard innersoles under felt foot pads; ***brown*** floss claws on felt mitten hands. Note the airbrushed navel. Replaced ribbon. Unknown maker, ca. 1950. All high quality examples of ***Bonzo*** are collectible.

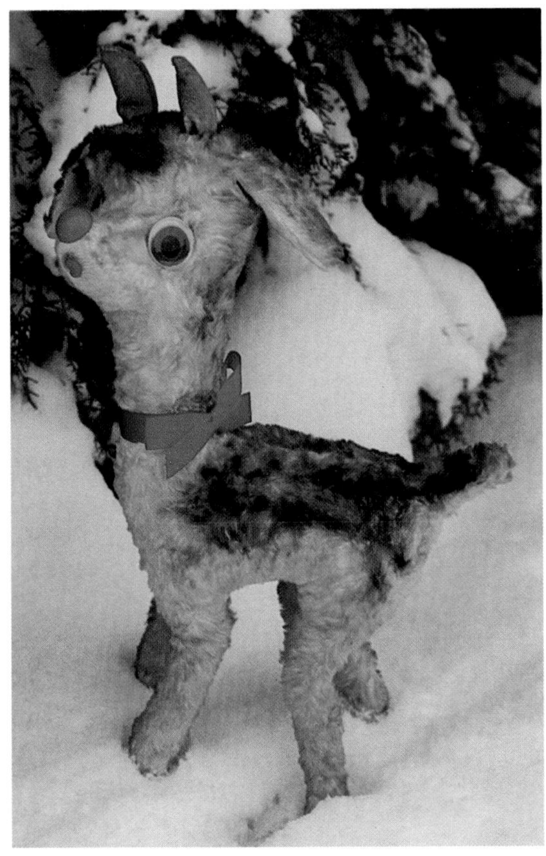

Rudolph, The Red Nosed Reindeer: 15"/38 cm. high, cotton plush with brown markings; e.s.; unjointed; brown and black plastic buttons encased in disc eyes; pink velveteen lined ears; green felt horns; red plastic bulbous nose; red felt tongue; unknown American maker, ca. 1950. Limited demand for cotton plush.

Comic Giraffe: 19"/48 cm.; RSB; Dralon plush (the favorite synthetic fabric of the 1950s and 1960s); cotton hard stuffed; unjointed; plastic eyes accented by long eyelashes; open felt painted mouth. The special creature is too rare to have created demand.
Courtesy Beth Savino, Hobby Center Toys.

Scamp from Disney's *Lady and the Tramp*: 7"/18 cm. high, 8"/20 cm. long; catalogue No. 2051; mohair; soft stuffed; unjointed; eyes of vinyl patches with painted pupils and iris; vinyl nose, open mouth/red felt tongue; innovative lining of ears with *purple*. Tag on foot, "Merrythought, Ironbridge Shops, Made in England." ca. 1958-59; one of the several dozen character animals created by Walt Disney and made by Merrythought Ltd. from 1954-80. The desirable older Merrythought animals are seldom found.
Courtesy Kay Bransky.

Under the banana tree are *Mockie* the Trevira pigmy hippo and his friend *Reinhold das nashorn*, a special order for *Stern* magazine. Mohair rhino-doll with a rakish black mohair crew cut: 8½"/22 cm.; S.T. 4322,05; C.T. with pet name; foam rubber stuffed; jointed head and arms; plastic eyes; felt horn; leatherette pads; four painted claws; one size made 1964 only; retailed for $7.00. Rare today. *Mockie*: 8"/20 cm. long; IB; S.T. 1120/20; C.T. pet name; markings airbrushed on Trevira velvet. Also made in 5½"/14 cm. size, ca. 1975. Trevira velvet animals are becoming scarce.
Courtesy Mary Benavente.

Gogo: 6"/15 cm.; RSB; C.T. pet name; paper tag, "Ask for the picture book *Around the World with Gogo*"; S.T. 4615,00; Dralon; polyester hard stuffed; jointed head only; black plastic eyes; airbrushed and stitched nose/mouth; felt feet and hands; bushy squirrel tail, ca. 1965. Hard to find but limited demand.
Courtesy Elaine Lehn.

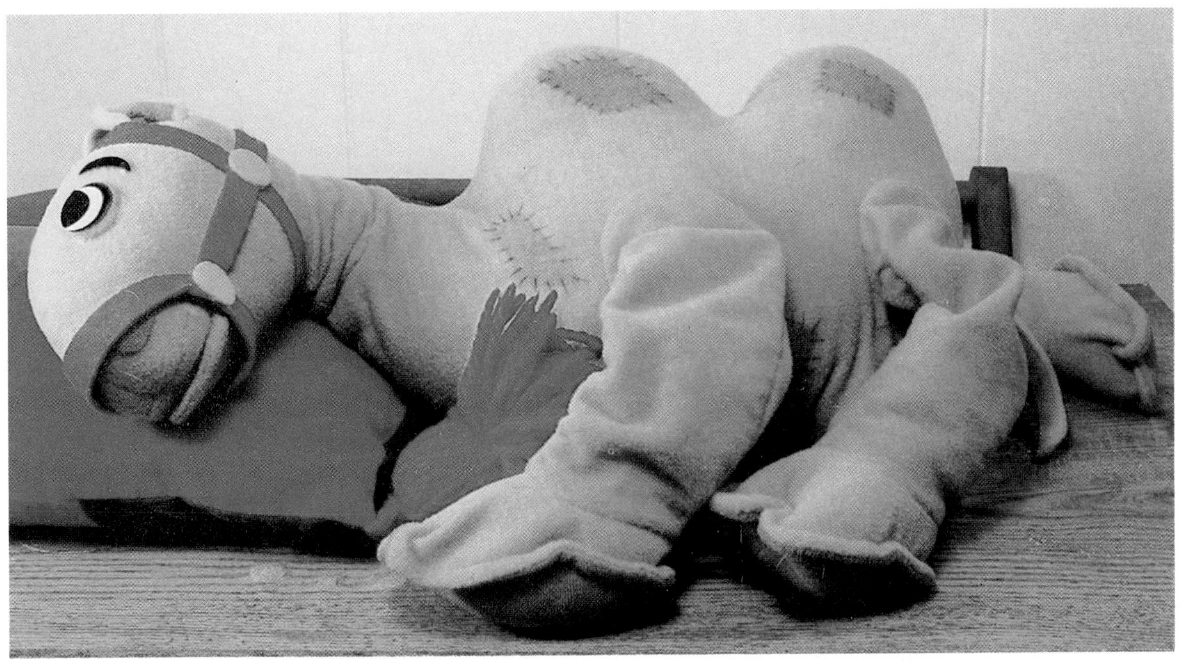

"The Camel with the Wrinkled Knees" rests on his velvet pillow. From the Raggedy Ann and Andy story of the same name. Printed-on patches and purposely wrinkled knees give a well-loved look to this endearing camel: 18"/46 cm.; synthetic flannel body, trim and harness. Knickerbocker, 1976. An earlier version can also be found.
Courtesy Mary Benavente.

Rupert: 13½"/34 cm., tagged "Real Soft Toys, Watford Herts, Made in England," ca. 1987. *Rupert* was and is a British national institution showing the "timelessness" of this white bear head with human hands and body. In 1920, the original artist was Mary Tourtel, followed by Alfred Bestall from 1935-65. Today *Rupert* is drawn by other artists. He appears in *Rupert Bear Annuals* and daily strips in the *Daily Express*, London. In the 1930s and 1940s Samson Low was licensed to publish a series of *Little Yellow Rupert Books. Rupert* is always dressed in a bright red sweater, yellow checked scarf and trousers and white boots. Pedigree Toys produced a 16"/41 cm. model of him in the 1960s. This failed to have the original lovable look.
Courtesy Ruth Nett.

Advertising Animals and Puppets

Albert Ziegler GmbH has been manufacturing fire fighting equipment for over 90 years. The company expanded during this time and has distributed some choice promotional toys made by Steiff. The 1912 Steiff Fire Brigade mechanical display is on permanent exhibit at the Ziegler factory in Giengen. Fireman doll: 18"/46 cm.; RSB with yellow tag, "Made in Germany"; rubber head with pointed nose; felt body; e.s.; jointed limbs; glass eyes; molded hat with leather strap; felt outfit; leather shoes/felt soles; double strap belt, hatchet and rope. 1950s Steiff bear: 14"/36 cm.; RSB; yellow S.T. 5335,03; C.T. "Original Teddy"; rare chocolate brown mohair; same molded hat, belt, hatchet and rope; four silver buttons sewn on chest; felt collar with silver brads. He holds a rubber hose and a leather bucket/rope handle. A tag in the Fireman's chest pocket translates: "Good day, I come from Albert Ziegler Hose and Firefighting Factory, Giengen (Brenz);" reverse, "Ziegler//Hosing//Sent//always//Dependable."

THE GERM: 4"/10 cm. high; watermelon C.T. Peck; egg-shaped head of kelly green mohair; hard stuffed cotton; unjointed; body and limbs are green felt over wire armature; tiny button eyes backed with eye-shaped white leather; red felt mitten hands and slippers. Complete with his pick. This imaginative creature is appropriately called "The Germ." A very limited number were made as an advertising piece for a German drugstore named PECK, ca. late 1940s. Only a few examples are known to have survived.

Advertising animals mirror the products of our everyday lives and chronicle the changes. Premium for Celestial Seasonings "Sleepy Time" Herb Tea. The toy represents Papa Bear from picture on box: 17"/43 cm.; plush; shredded polyurethane stuffed; unjointed; eyes stitched as in sleep; plastic nose, floss mouth; black plush pads; nightshirt with trademark and red night cap. Note bear has legs with *knees* and slouches nicely. Tagged, "Celestial Seasonings, Herb Teas, Collector's Series, SLEEPY BEAR, No. 002140 of 5000." Made by "Trudy, Norwalk, Conn." shown with postcard; tea mug is missing; ca. 1985.
Courtesy Valerie Vann.

Promotional T.R. bear made for the commissioning of the USS Theodore Roosevelt CVN-71: 11"/28 cm.; tagged, "Telemarks Speciality Toys, New Hampshire"; synthetic plush; polyester stuffed; unjointed; plastic eyes; black yarn nose/mouth; no pads; dressed like T.R.; note the anchors on buttons of jacket. He wears "Good Bears of the World" pin that was presented to each sailor at the commissioning. Issue price, $35.00. A rare commemorative Teddy, ca. 1987. Tin lithographed (signed) tray; T.R. as a "Rough Rider."
Courtesy Beth Savino, Hobby Center Toys.

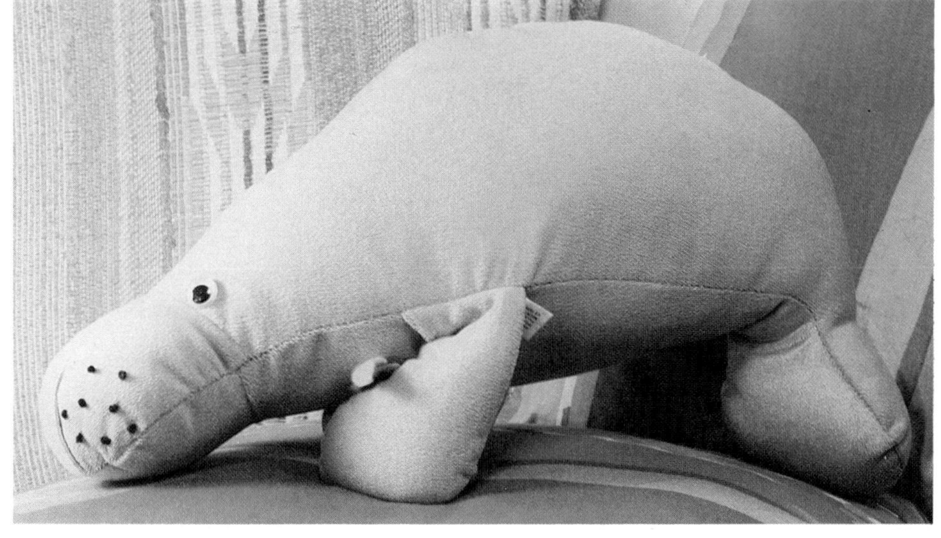

The docile Manatee (Sea Cow) clutches his water hyacinth between Velcro lined flippers: 17"/43 cm. long; luminous grey synthetic velvet. An endangered species distantly related to elephants, Sea Cows spend winter months basking in warm springs along the Florida coast and must be protected from motor boat propellers. Sold by "Whale Gifts" to promote awareness and kindness toward Manatees. Made by Pet Project Inc., Crystal River FL, 1983.
Courtesy Mary Benavente.

Hidy & Howdy were the official mascots of the 1988 Winter Olympics in Calgary, Canada. This was the first time that a *pair* of mascots was chosen. The 8"/20 cm. bear pair sold for $16.00 U.S. and the 14"/35.6 cm. pair sold for $33.00 U.S.; white synthetic plush; polyester stuffed; unjointed; felt noses. *Hidy* has blue eyes; *Howdy* has brown eyes; made by Hasbro, Canada, Inc. and were not exported. They appeared on many of the souvenirs such as Olympic pins and posters. A satisfying tangent of the Teddy Bear hobby would be to collect all the mascots from past Olympics.
Courtesy Sheree Barnes.

Terrier Puppet, left: 8½"/21.5 cm. high; metal tag at front bottom, "Czechoslovakia Kersa"; white mohair; clear/black glass eyes; yarn nose/mouth; three *yarn* claws; felt lined pointed ears. Spaniel, center: 8½"/21.5 cm. high; long pile mohair body, shaved snout; *dark* brown mohair ears; shoe button eyes; shiny thread nose/mouth, five stitched claws; unknown maker, ca. 1920. Note the pink satin lining (Steiff did not line their hand puppets); stitches attach head to cardboard fingerholes (non-Steiff method). Bear: 8½"/21.5 cm.; excelsior stuffed head; brown mohair, beige inset snout; glass eyes; brown *yarn* nose, open felt mouth; peach felt pads. Maker unknown, ca. 1950. Courtesy Idele Gilbert.

Rare white mohair *Jocko* hand puppet: 6"/15 cm.; FF button; excelsior stuffed head; peach felt face, ears and hands; pink mohair beard; green glass cat eyes; ca. 1930. *Tiger Cub:* 6"/15 cm.; no I.D. but self-recognizable; mohair; pearl cotton nose/mouth; three stitched claws; nylon whiskers; desirable puppet. *Gora:* 6¾"/17 cm.; RSB; S.T. 0617,05; C.T.; Dralon; excelsior stuffed head; B&W plastic googly eyes; peach felt ears. Rare Gorilla puppet, ca. 1961. Courtesy Idele Gilbert.

Mimic puppets, front: 6"/15 cm. high, 11"/28 cm. long; RSB; C.T. "Mimic" with pet name; *Dally*, S.T. 150/0328; *Biggie* (Beagle) S.T. 230/0328; *Tessie*, S.T. 470/0328. All are mohair; have excelsior stuffed heads; glass eyes; a black stitched nose, open felt mouth with red felt tongue; three floss claws; tail; pouch underneath; original silver paper tag with instructions for use. Unusually large arm puppets, these were made 1958-59 only, and are one of the few puppets sought after by many collectors. Back: 8"/20.5 cm. "King Charles Spaniel" puppet; FF button; *white* stock tag (1908-1926) #317; mohair; glass eyes; twisted hard, black cotton floss nose and mouth with *red airbrushing*; three floss claws. Rare old time puppet. *Jocko:* 9"/23 cm.; "Watermelon" C.T. only. *Jocko* monkeys and puppets have been a staple throughout Steiff's history; considered common from the 1950s and 1960s; hard to find from the 1930s.
Courtesy Debbi Anton (King Charles Courtesy Of Jean Boyda).

Five RARE hand puppets. All are 8½"/21.5 cm. to 9½"/24cm. high; mohair; have excelsior stuffed heads; glass eyes – the poodle's are humanized; twisted hard, cotton floss noses (except poodle's that is a black button); and three floss claws. Left to right: Terrier; FF button; note one black one orange ear and the black and orange patch under one eye; original blue ribbon with bell attached, ca. pre-1930. Dalmatian; RSB; S.T. 317; C.T. *Dally*; peach velveteen open mouth; original red ribbon. Dally and Snaky are the most rare and desirable of all post WWII hand puppets. King Charles Spaniel; FF button; *red* S.T. 317; watermelon C.T. *Charly*; note the *long* brown ears, ca. 1926-34. Unusual mint condition for this vintage of hand puppet because puppets were playthings. *Beppo* Dachshund; peach felt open mouth with red felt tongue. Grey poodle; rare color. The black *(Snobby)* poodle is more common, ca. 1950s. Courtesy Idele Gilbert.

Puppetry is taken seriously in Europe. Assemblage of hand puppets: all 6"/15 cm. high; RSB; 1950s C.T. on rabbit; mohair; excelsior stuffed heads; unjointed; twisted hard, cotton floss nose/mouth in appropriate colors; three floss claws. Great faces with life-like appearance, texture and coloring. Note the baby look of the rare *Tiger Cub*. Courtesy Barbara Baldwin.

Subtle serpent, *Snaky* hand puppet finds a prize breakfast in the garden: 13"; RSB; C.T. *Snaky;* striking coloration patterns to the mohair mark him as a Cobra. Still cunning but light-headed because the foam rubber and cardboard lining in his head has disappeared; black-rimmed green plastic eyes glow-in-the-dark; orange felt mouth/red felt tongue. Coveted by many; made 1965 only.
Courtesy Mary Benavente.

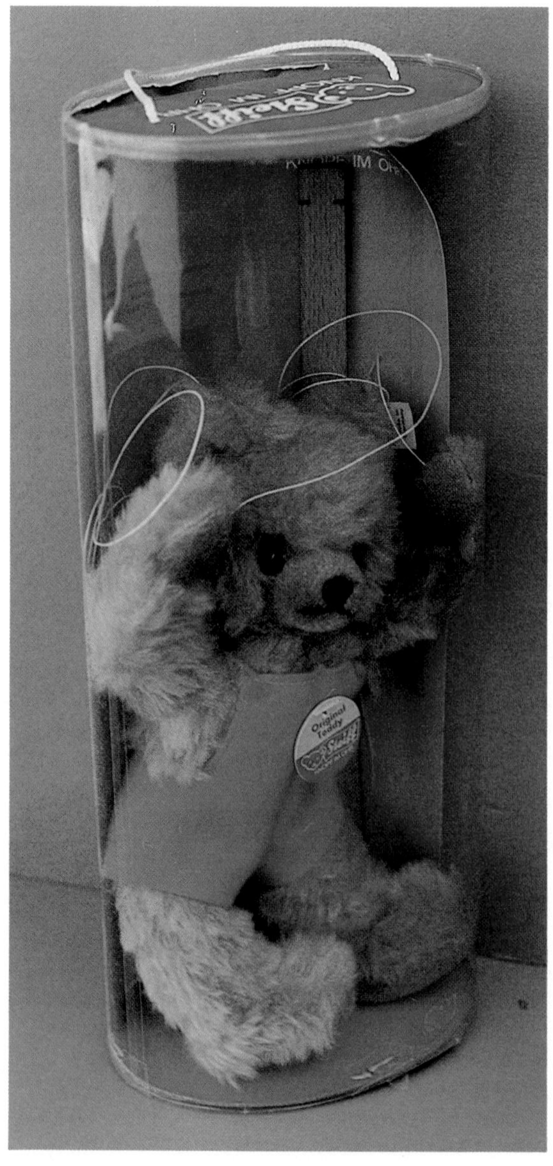

Marionette, an ambassador to the child's world: 9"/23 cm.; IB; S.T. 7726/25; Dralon; unjointed, elbows internally jointed to bend when puppet is exercised; soft stuffed; plastic eyes; stitched nose/mouth; no claws on longish feet; tan Trevira velvet pads; felt overalls with red cord straps sewn to body; waxy strings embedded in paws and at shoulders. These run through the ears. Designed to operate with sticks or rings. A boy, girl and Chimpanzee complete the set. Short production, ca. 1975.
Courtesy Dave and Ann Abbott.

VIII. GOLLIWOGS

The wise collector looking for enjoyment and investment potential should seriously stalk Golliwogs. The key to value is age, condition and uniqueness. Manufacturer's I.D. also adds to value. Size is not a major factor in determining the value of a Golliwog, unless over 24"/61 cm. tall. Chad Valley, Pedigree, Merrythought and Dean's made this size in fairly large numbers.

Handmade Golliwogs must not be discounted. Before mass production began in 1930, practically all Gollys were homemade. Since the Golliwog attained immense popularity immediately after his introduction in 1895, he was made almost exclusively by mothers for their children during the next 35 years. These early dolls are extremely rare and highly prized collector's items today. Homemade examples can also be considered "folk art," thereby having double value for those who covet this traditional symbol of British childhood.

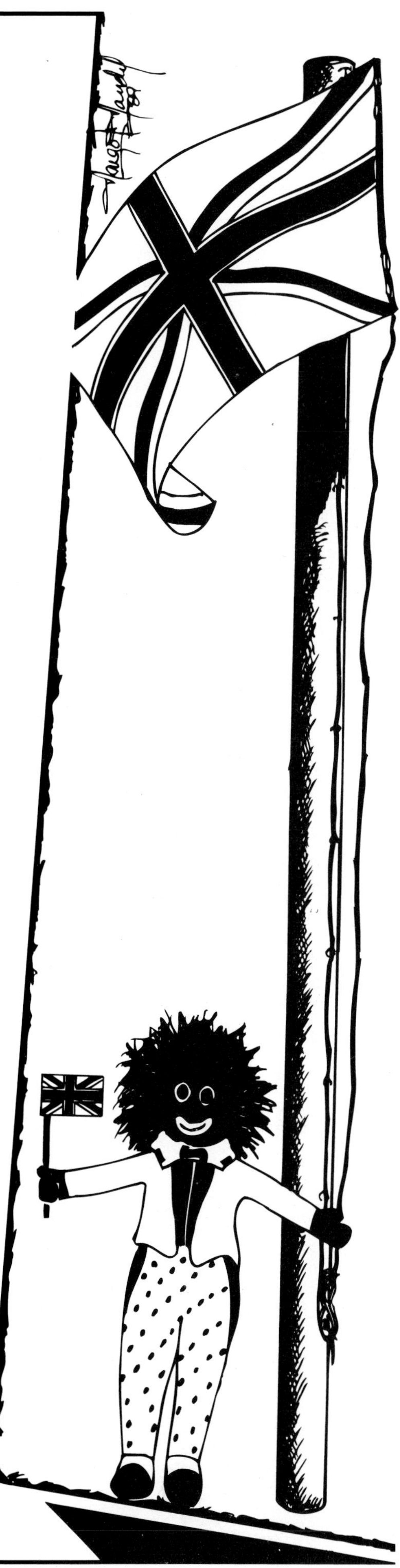

The book that started it all: *The Adventures of Two Dutch Dolls -- and A Golliwogg;* illustrated by Florence Upton; verses by Bertha Upton; published by Longmans, Green and Company of London, England, 1895. Although published in great numbers, the Upton series of Golliwog books are hard to find intact. Unscrupulous dealers dismantle them for the color plates. Complete books with all 32 plates in good condition range from $150.00-200.00. Individual plates sell for $40.00 up. There are 13 books in the series. The 1950s book (right) tells the story of a forgotten Golliwog who finds a new home. A plastic (working) squeaker is contained in the back cover.
Courtesy Kathy Thomas.

Pre-1930 Golliwogs are EXTREMELY hard to find, thus causing a greater leap in value. Early body style, ca. 1910-25: 22"/56 cm.; kapok stuffed; clothes and body are of cotton sateen with *sewn on* foil and raffia trims. Special features: shoe button eyes backed by fabric-covered brass buttons (an early eye treatment); hair made of the same fringe found on lampshades, ca. 1910. Note the unusual three-piece head construction; unknown manufacturer. Left: biscuit tin marked "Hudson Scott & Sons Ltd., Carlisle England." The one-of-a-kind piece is a factory prototype with the lithographer's mark instead of a biscuit maker's. Wheels turn on axles and top lifts off to hold biscuits, ca. 1900-1920. A RARE item for an advanced biscuit tin collector as well. These higher priced, more unusual items have the fastest sales potential. Right, child size glazed china cup: 2"/5 cm. high; decal decorated with the elusive "Girliewog" and friend; father and baby appear on reverse; ca. 1920s when orange and green were popular colors for Golly's clothes; English, no mark.
Courtesy Kathy Thomas.

A French version of the popular Golliwog resulted in a figural perfume bottle filled with "Le Golliwogg" fragrance; made by de Vigny, Paris. Contained in the original satin-lined box: 3"/3¾" high; sealskin hair; a wonderful and easy to find addition to a collection; Deco Period, ca. 1920-30. *Soft Toy Making* by Ouida Pearse, 1932, contained instructions and patterns for 29 toys including a "big and noble" Golliwog. The 20"/51 cm. Golly shown here is similar in proportion and detailing to the one in Pearse's book. He has a velvet face; Persian Lamb hair; felt hands and feet; kapok stuffing; felt and button eyes; felt mouth; satin waistcoat/silk ruffle; satin bow; removable wool jacket; wool pants; satin socks; all show a large amount of detailing for a homemade example, ca. 1930.
Courtesy Kathy Thomas.

Unusual celluloid mask face Golliwog: 15"/38 cm.; wool plush body and hair; excelsior stuffed head; wooden beads inside eyes move freely; kapok stuffed; working squeaker, ca. 1930s. Possible maker: Birkenhead Toy Factory, England. Mohair bear: 17"/43 cm.; e.s.; f.j.; early non-working squeaker; mint; possible Ideal, ca. 1905. Although mainly an English product, Golliwogs were produced in Germany, Australia and Ireland: 15"/38 cm.; cotton clothes; felt face, hands and feet; woolly hair; kapok stuffed; early cardboard squeaker; tag in back of neck, "Pedigree, Made in N. Ireland." Pedigree often used glued-on plastic features, especially a *large* red mouth; ca. 1930s. Tagged, "Chad Valley Chiltern, Hygienic Toys, Made in England": 11"/28 cm.; felt face, hands and shoes; corduroy clothes; plush hair; plastic eyes; felt nose and mouth; stuffed with multicolored shredded foam (popular filling from 1950s-present); ca. 1967. Bear holds china sugar bowl (missing lid) made by Shenango China; decal decorated with Gollys and bears, ca. 1930. In 1983 Lledo, Ltd. (the "Matchbox" of England) made the replica of 1910 delivery truck advertising Robertson's Golden Shred with tiny Golliwog.
Courtesy Kathy Thomas.

Left Golly: 15"/38 cm.; interesting fabric combination looks like that from a mother's scrap basket; cotton body; wool vest/tails; embroidered eyes; mouth is similar to material used by Chad Valley; narrow strip of woolly plush around face; stuffed with an old cut-up wool sweater; unknown maker, ca. 1940s. Steiff Teddy: 12"/30.5 cm.; near mint, ca. 1908. Seated Golly: 18"/46 cm.; felt coat, vest, nose and mouth; celluloid eyes; cotton pants. Unusual features: LARGE FEET; uncarded wool hair; clothes are separate from body but non-removable; unknown maker, ca.1930. He closely resembles those made from 1900-1930 when Gollys were first mass produced. Right, Golly with *blue* glass eyes over felt circles: 15"/38 cm.; pants and hands are cotton; remainder of materials are felt; kapok stuffed; mohair pelt wig; unknown maker, ca.1940s. Paper covered balsa wood block pictures unusual *red* haired Golly. Date and maker unknown. Courtesy Kathy Thomas.

Early Chiltern: 13"/33 cm.; all (thin) cotton; printed face; stuffed with grey waste cotton; woolly hair; unusual lapels (with raw edges) added to an otherwise smooth front. There can be different clothing combinations on several dolls with identically printed faces. He is a fairly common style of Golliwog and lesser quality than Chad Valley. However, this example is earlier than many. The larger number of Gollys found are in the 1950s-60s range; the 1930s-40s period is considered early.

Chad Valley Golliwogs are plentiful and one of the easiest to identify if tag (usually found in side seam under arm) is missing. They often used a woven, paper-like material for the mouth and felt or oilcloth for eyes. Glue deteriorated, features were lost and replaced with various materials. This does not appreciably affect value. It is unusual to find a Chad Valley Golliwog with original features. All Gollys above are all cotton with non-removable clothes and woolly plush hair. (L-R), 24"/61 cm. (not an unusual size for this manufacturer); tag under arm; kapok stuffed; excelsior in head and neck for support. The only completely original Chad Valley in the group, ca. 1930s. PRINTED facial features: 13"/33 cm.; kapok stuffed; remnant of tag, ca. 1940s. American mohair bear: 10"/25 cm.; e.s.; f.j.; ca. 1920s. Kapok stuffed: 16"/41 cm.; missing features were lovingly embroidered creating a unique expression; some hair loss, ca. 1930s. Tagged: 17"/43 cm.; replaced cotton eyes and terry cloth mouth; firmly stuffed with kapok, ca. 1940s. Memorize the multicolored stripe of the pants. This is a signature of Chad Valley.
Courtesy Kathy Thomas.

During the 1950s and 1960s, one of the most popular methods of creating handmade Golliwogs was knitting. Note the varied interpretations and expressions that resulted. Knitted Golly: 18"/46 cm.; felt features; looped yarn hair; satin bow tie; stuffed with stockings (a popular filler for the homemade toys), ca. 1960s. Wool yarn: 14"/36 cm.; embroidered features; applied "tails"; stuffed with yarn scraps, ca. 1940. Looped yarn hair: 21"/53 cm.; embroidered face including eyes looking left, a feature introduced by Robertson's Jam Co. in the late 1950s; jacket is removable but leaves Golly armless! Stuffed with stockings, ca. 1950s. Wool and cotton yarns: 18"/46 cm.; looped hair; embroidered features; stuffed with stockings and wool scraps. This Golliwog wears metal loop earrings, ca. 1960s. A frequent companion of the Golliwog is the early 20th century "Dutch Doll": 12"/30.5 cm.; dressed in stripes of the American flag, as was one of the main characters of the original Florence Upton books. These 19th century dolls are available as good reproductions from the 1950s ($30.00.-50.00). They are being reproduced again today. C.S.P.
Courtesy Kathy Thomas.

Group of modern day Dean's Golliwogs. Since Dean's Childsplay Toys, Ltd. has discontinued the manufacture of soft toys, a marked rise in the value of these toys is expected, making even the inexpensive current Gollys a worthwhile addition to a beginning collection. Left: 15"/38 cm.; all felt with plush hair; celluloid googly eyes; polyester stuffed. Center: 13"/33 cm.; "Mr. Golly," printed cotton; applied plush hair; available in a cutout sheet (a long standing Dean's product) as well as a made up version; replica of an early 1900s Dean's Golliwog. Right: 17"/43 cm.; printed cloth body; plush hair; removable felt jacket; shredded foam stuffed. This style of Golly has been in Dean's line for over 20 years. Earlier versions had lock-in black button eyes and are the most commonly found Golliwog today.
Courtesy Kathy Thomas.

Flat teddy from 1960 exactly: 17"/43 cm.; long mohair; hard stuffed cotton; unjointed; eyes replaced by wonderful yellow plastic faceted buttons; black yarn small nose; remnants of red felt tongue; velveteen pads; no squeaker. Inexpensive pieces have value too, both real and potential. Friend: 13"/33 cm.; hard stuffed cotton; non-removable clothes; mohair hair; reinforcing ring-type eyes of white oil cloth glued onto black cotton face. Paper tag reverse side, "By appointment to HM Queen Elizabeth the Queen Mother Toymakers." Cloth tag in left seam, "Hygienic Toys Made in England by Chad Valley Co. Ltd." Chad Valley made this style of Golly from 1950s-70s.

**Merrythought: 19"/48 cm.; Limited Edition for 1986 (one year production but no numbering); Merrythought's version of a Golliwog from 1895, the year of the first Upton book. He is made of velveteen and cotton and is quite fancy for a Golliwog and especially for Merrythought. In 1986 he sold for $59.50. Since then, he has more than doubled in price due to great demand. Shown with 16"/41 cm. mohair traditional Teddy with (sensible) leather pads; tagged "Big Softies, Ilkey Yorkshire England," ca. 1986.
Courtesy Rosemary Moran.**

R. John Wright's midsized Pooh: 14"/35.5 cm.; English mohair; polyester hard stuffed; jointed limbs only; handmade felt bee in ear; no costume; tag sewn into back of right foot; Bennington Potters "Hunny" Pot (not shown). The first 500 pots had a paper sticker, "Hunny." The remainder had "Hunny" in the glaze; 1988 edition of 5,000, retail $165.00. Small Golly: 8½"/22 cm. velveteen head, hands and feet; glass paperweight-type eyes; shoe button nose; made-to-body clothes. Merrythought's special 1988 edition of an early design; issue price, $35.00. Both have investment potential.
Courtesy Rebecca Vaughn Gardner.

As well as being a "soft" toy, Golliwogs are found in various metal versions. (L-R), 6½"/16.5 cm.; cast iron still bank has only traces of original paint (red pants, tie and mouth; blue coat). Highly prized and considered rare by bank collectors. Double value if found with original paint, ca. 1910-25. Child tends to her doll as Golliwog looks on. This tin originally held Riley's toffee, giving credence to the theory that Golliwogs can be found on almost ANYTHING. Date unknown. The Golliwog as a trapeze toy - can also be removed to somersault on the floor; winding arms creates motion; hand-painted tin; unknown German maker, ca. 1910. *Rare piece.*
Courtesy Kathy Thomas.

Robertson's store displays: left, 15"/38 cm.; enamel over metal sign with early style Robertson's Golliwog advertising marmalade; probably once displayed in stores selling this product; ca. before 1955 (when Robertson's changed the style of their Golliwog.) A Golliwog of magnificent proportions: 30"/76 cm. electrified store display; a rare example of early Robertson's advertising. Made of hand-laid plaster; the inner bulb lights his eyes and the jar of marmalade; ca. 1930s.
Courtesy Kathy Thomas.

When Golliwog dolls become hard to find, colorful ephemera is an inexpensive way to round out a collection. Paper valentine shows two different styles of Golliwogs; printed in Brazil, ca. 1926. Golliwog decorates a match box (date unknown). Center, metal doll furniture set in original box shows the ever popular duo Teddy and Golly sharing a table, ca. pre-war 1940s. A Grace Drayton paper doll holds a basket of toys. Far right, lithographed cardboard squeak toy features Golliwog "motoring" (a popular Golliwog activity). Press front of car to activate squeaker, ca. 1930s.
Courtesy Kathy Thomas.

In addition to being a toy in itself, the Golliwog was a popular decoration for many other toys. Tin clickers: 4"/10 cm. high; left shows position when "Clicker" in back is depressed; right depicts action when released. Marked, "Made in Germany, US-Zone." Fairly easy to find toy. Center, tin sandpail: 3½"/9 cm. high; copper bail; scene shows Gollys in various poses playing ball; marked, "Happynak Seaside Pail no. 4, Made in England," ca. 1950s. Easy to find.
Courtesy Kathy Thomas.

The Robertson's Jam Co. adopted the Golliwog as an advertising symbol in 1930; its use continues today. Robertson's premiums are perhaps the most plentiful Golliwog items available. (L-R), the start of the cycle - the jar of jam. Token is removed and put aside until enough are collected to obtain the premium of your choice. Paper bag advertising Robertson's marmalade; the collected tokens are attached to the back. Sender then checks off desired pin style and mails in ; ca. late 1950s. All cloth Golly in marmalade jar was once offered as a premium: 6"/15 cm.; marked, "Made in England - Anne Wilkenson Designs Ltd. under License to James Robertson & Sons, 1980." Another choice might have been this Golliwog story which credits him to North America; ca. 1981.
Courtesy Kathy Thomas.

According to Robertson's, more than 20 million Golliwog pins have been given out to children collecting the tokens. This makes these pins (1¼"/3.2 cm.) among the easiest item to find, as well as being relatively inexpensive. Three distinct styles exist. Top Row: the original Robertson's Golliwog; smooth style, round head, centered pupils and "Golden Shred" on his vest, ca. 1930-55. Center: skaters; style was changed to make him appear more friendly; differences are "bumps" indicating hair on top half of face, eyes looking left, "watermelon mouth" and absence of "Golden Shred," ca, 1956 on. Bottom: pins available today. Similar to late 1950s style, these pins feature Golly in modern occupations (older styles generally centered around sports). They have a "painted" appearance, as opposed to transparent enameling found on earlier models. The heads are smaller and have "ears." Current pins have "C. James Robertson and Sons PM Ltd." engraved on back. Earlier pins are either blank or have name of pin manufacturer (which varies) in raised letters. Courtesy Kathy Thomas.

Mr. Gollywog designed and handmade by the superb artist Maria Schmidt: 22"/56 cm.; tagged on coat tail, "The Charlestowne Bear//Created By//Maria Schmidt"; all felt; f.j.; hard stuffed; shoe button eyes. Note the intricate pattern, long nose (found on Steiff's 1913 Golly) and pronounced knees. A sold out limited edition of 12, ca. 1987. Issue price $350.00. Now in great demand; an important piece by an important artist. Shown with Upton book; copyrighted 1898, published by Longmans, Green & Co., London. Courtesy Beth Savino, Hobby Center Toys.

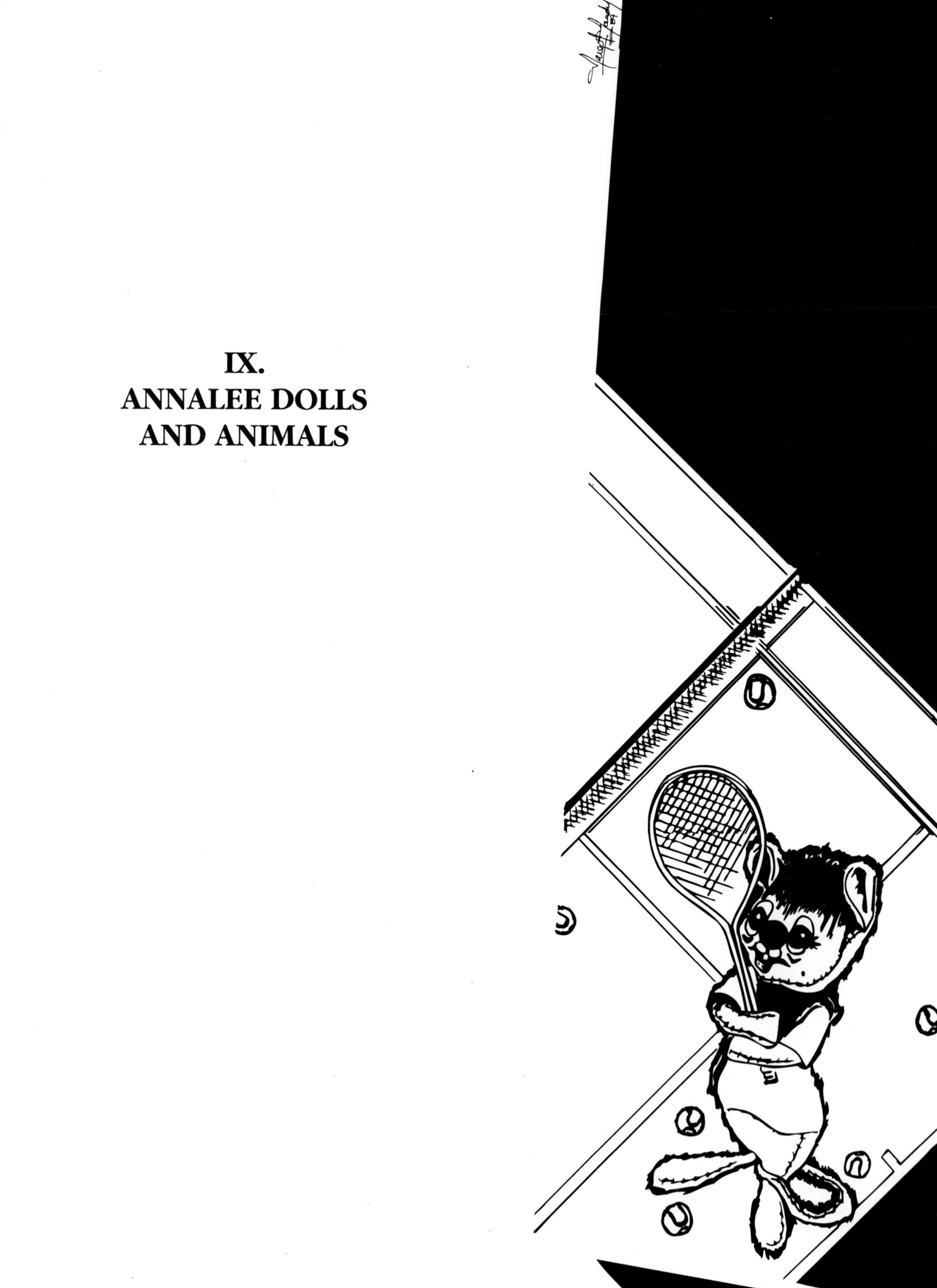

IX.
ANNALEE DOLLS AND ANIMALS

Country or Garden Girl: 10"/25 cm.; 1954; individually made by Annalee who handpainted the sunny face and stitched the clothes from scraps of fabric. It is possible but not probable that there are other dolls identically dressed. Extremely rare. Courtesy Annalee Mobilitee Dolls, Inc.

Bathing Beauty: 10"/25 cm.; 1956; the bescarfed beauty was totally handmade and painted by Annalee; stuffed with string and cotton batten; poseable by bendable wire. Extremely rare and important example of the artist's work. Courtesy Annalee Mobilitee Dolls, Inc.

Girl Water Skier: 10"/25 cm.; 1957; all handmade and painted by Annalee; stuffed with string and cotton batting; poseable by bendable wire armature. The skis were hand crafted by the artist's husband, Chip, and signed by Annalee. A crucial example pertinent to the evolution of the company as well as an outstanding and rare model to excite the Annalee collector. Boy and girl water skiers (in much poorer condition) sold at the 1989 Annalee auction at $700.00 for the pair. Courtesy Annalee Mobilitee Dolls, Inc.

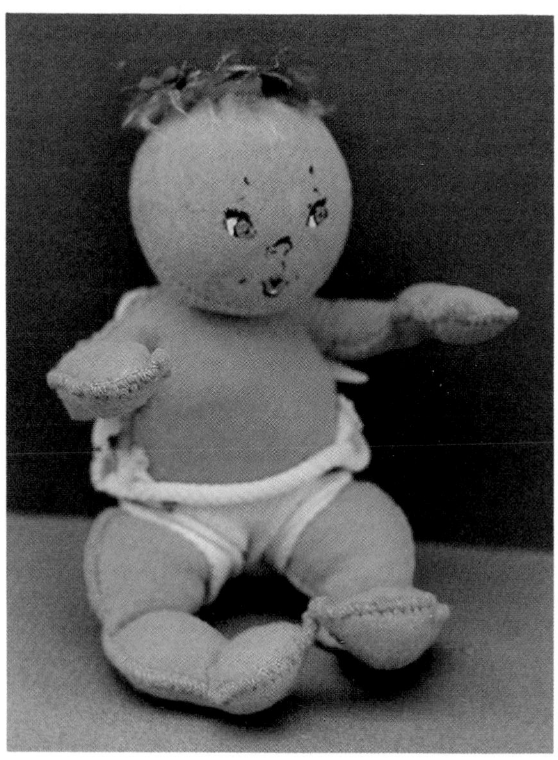

Baby Angel**: 7"/18 cm.; 1964; small white felt wings on back of beige felt body; white feather hair; wreath on head is made of green paper leaves and tiny red berries; wears a cotton knit diaper. Extremely rare and desirable early Annalee.**
Courtesy Bette Todd.

Wee-Ski: **7"/18 cm.; 1960; issue price $3.95; embroidered tag; white felt (also made in red and green); tinsel scarf; no hair; glued to wooden skis; wire poles. A similar doll, *Imp-Ski*, was made the same year. This and the *Wee-Ski* could have either a felt or tinsel scarf. In the early years trimmings were sometimes interchanged. Note the fine body contouring and the starburst hands. A wonderful older piece; a treasure for any collector.**
Courtesy Bette Todd.

(L-R), *Gnome:* **12"/30 cm.; 1978. This chubby gnome came in four colors: red, kelly green, white and mint green. Some came with scarves; possibly some did not. Cute, desirable and hard to find. *Gnome:*** **7"/18 cm.; 1980. Gnomes tend to have beards and a chubby build, whereas elves are skinny and beardless.**
Courtesy Bette Todd.

Fishing Boy: 7"/18 cm.; 1983; carries a wooden (dowel) fishing pole with a vinyl frog on the end; red hair; burlap hat. *Country Girl with Basket:* 7"/18 cm.; 1983; carries a straw basket; sold separately from *Fishing Boy*, but they are generally considered a pair. These charming and desirable examples were made 1983-84 only; issue price was $16.95 in 1984.
Courtesy Bette Todd.

A sign of the times. *Aerobic Dancers:* 10"/25 cm.; 1984; these redheaded beauties were made 1984-1985 in a total issue of 4,785. They came in several color combinations; nylon leotards; terry cloth leg warmers. In 1984 a more rare 18" size was available. These poseable dancers continue to escalate in value.
Courtesy Bette Todd.

Monk with Jug: 8"/20 cm.; 1984; body is hollow, fabric wraps around a wire base; carries pottery jug. Over the years monks have come in various sizes with different accessories. The older monks are hard to find. *Cupid:* 7"/18 cm.; 1984; white felt wings; plastic quiver on back holds two wood and felt arrows; wire bow/string. Made in 1984-85. When the Valentine figures were discontinued *Cupid* became popular. *Indian Boy:* 7"/18 cm.; 1987 only (2,700 made); the small feather is important. Destined to be valuable.
Courtesy Bette Todd.

Ghost Kid with Pumpkin: 7"/18 cm.; 1987-1989; a cute example from Annalee's rapidly expanding Halloween line. *Scarecrow:* 10"/25 cm.; 1984; scarecrows have been manufactured periodically and are extremely collectible. Also available in an 18" size. Some years scarecrows were as large as 42"/ 107 cm.
Courtesy Tiffany Todd.

Mrs. Santa with Skis and Poles: 7"/18 cm.; 1969 (made 1969-72); flannel body with flannel cape and hood; carries orange wooden skis and aluminum wire poles. *Mr. Santa with Skis and Poles:* 7"/18 cm.; 1973 (made 1965-77); red flannel suit and cap; both have Styrofoam™ balls in their bodies which is characteristic of many small Annalees made before 1981. Hard to find complete and in excellent condition. Many people first buy Annalees for Christmas and then become avid collectors.
Courtesy Bette Todd.

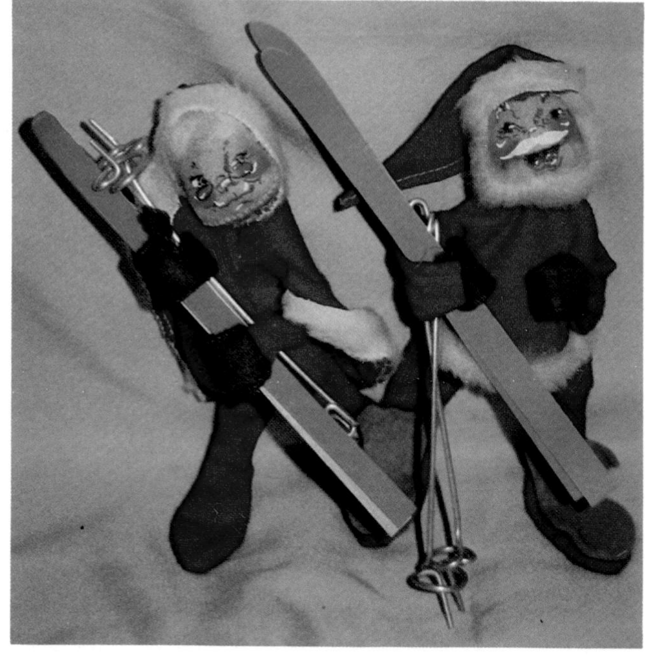

(L-R), top, *Mrs. Santas with Cardholder Skirt:* 18"/46 cm.; 1971 (issue of 1,563), 1972 (issue of 4,072), 1978 (issue of 6,590); all have flannel bodies, felt head and hands. The wires in skirt hems allow adjustment to hold Christmas cards. All skirts are made from the Christmas fabric of that year. However, the stripe is also found in 1972, 1973 and 1975. Bottom, *Mr. and Mrs. Santa:* 7"/18 cm.; 1977 (Mrs. issue of 5,193, Mr. issue of 3,656); clothing shows the Christmas fabric of 1977. *Mrs. Santa:* 7"/18 cm.; 1973 (issue of 3,513); white polished cotton apron and dust cap. Older pieces made from the Christmas prints tend to be collectible.
Courtesy Bette Todd.

(L-R), *Mr. Santa Mouse:* 7"/18 cm.; 1976; issue of 4,018; *white* head and tail; carries burlap sack. Small *white* Santa mice were made from 1971-79; accessories and clothing details changed frequently. Santa Mice of the 1980s are grey. *Nightshirt Boy Mouse*, 12"/30 cm.; 1979; issue of 5,739; *white* felt; carries a candle with base made from the Christmas fabric of the year. Also made were a Caroler, Santa/Sack and Mrs. Santa/Muff. Christmas mice (12") have been made for many years but were *white* only in 1979. White mice are among the most desirable Christmas mice.
Courtesy Bette Todd.

(Top), *Jack Frost Elf:* 22"/56 cm.; 1977 only (2,600 made); adhesive tape-type tag; holding two 10"/25 cm. *Jack Frost Elves* (did not come as a set); coal black hair. Similar elves with a felt snowflake were made in 1981 and 1982. (Bottom), *Christmas Elves:* 10"/25 cm.; 1983 (8,861 made in 1983 alone); paper-type tag; came in green, red and white. These have been produced for several years; also available in spring colors which are called *Spring Elves.*
Courtesy Bette Todd.

Workshop Elves: 10"/25 cm.; 10"/25 cm.; 1981-1983. These busy elves came in four colors: lime green, dark green, white and red. The 1980s *Workshop Elves* carried a plastic tool: screwdriver, hammer, file, level or saw. Cute and desirable. The clothes can distinguish elves from leprechauns. Leprechauns are always made of green felt. The same character from the same year can each have a different face due to the hand painting. *Santa with Fur Trimmed suit:* 7"/18 cm.; 1978. He is more decorative than collectible. A 10" size Santa (known as the "Collector's Santa") was not made until 1988.
Courtesy Cheryl Todd.

Candy Boy and Girl: 18"/46 cm.; 1984; wear made-to-body flannel p.j.'s and hold felt lollipops. The lollipops came in various colors; face, hands and toes are felt; issue price $28.95. The same dolls were made in 1983 without the lollipops and were called *P.J. Kids.* Desirable.
Courtesy Bette Todd.

Gingerbread Boy: 10"/25 cm.; 1984 (4,615 made.) The 10" size was issued only one year; also available in an 18" size; darling addition to any collection; hard to find. *Gingerbread Boy Ornament:* 5"/13 cm.; 1983. This little fellow was issued from 1983-86. Note the fine gold hanging thread present only on ornaments. Annalee began making Christmas ornaments in 1982.
Courtesy Bette Todd.

(L-R), *Reindeer with Saddle Bag:* 18"/46 cm.; 1985; brown felt antlers; black pompon nose (before 1979 they had red pompon noses). Clowns, reindeer, rabbits and mice have pompon noses. Blanket is from the 1985 Christmas fabric. *Doe*: 36"/91 cm.; 1983-84; total issue of 319; separately formed legs; rare. This leg construction is also found on earlier reindeer. *Fawn:* 18"/46 cm.; 1983-84; painted white spots; poseable by bendable wire to lie or stand; hard to find. *Reindeer with Saddle Bag:* 18"/46 cm.; 1987; one year only in this blanket fabric; felt antlers (some reindeer prior to 1985 had pipe cleaner antlers). The above have synthetic plush tail linings, chest plates and topknots.
Courtesy Bette Todd.

Bear with Bumblebee: 7"/18 cm.; 1973. This little brown bear is one of the first Annalee bears. Two brown bears were made in 1973. The other was 18"/46 cm. and has a butterfly on his nose. These were the only brown bears made by Annalee until they were reintroduced in 1984. Desirable. Courtesy Bette Todd.

Star of the Show, *Ballerina Bear:* 18"/46 cm.; 1985; one of the more scarce Annalee bears as only 918 were made during its one year of production; issue price $40.00. She wears a full net tutu with satin straps, satin ballet shoes, a bow in her hair and pink flowers (missing) at her waist. An important bear. Courtesy Bette Todd.

Valentine Bear: 18"/46 cm.; 1985; made only 1985-86 in a total issue of 2,439; the special shirt is important for full value. Annalee had made Valentine dolls of various types over the years, but in 1988 and 1989 no Valentine figures were produced. There is a good future for the older Valentine Annalees. Courtesy Bette Todd.

(L-R), *Valentine Panda:* 10"/25 cm.; 1986 only; issue of 1,940; retail, $19.95; white felt pads; dress is printed with hearts; hair bow; holds a felt heart trimmed in lace; a striking and desirable Panda. *Christmas Panda with Toy Bag:* 10"/25 cm.; 1985; made 1985-86 in a total issue of 10,417; white felt vest; felt scarf, mittens and hat; carries a burlap sack; a desirable Christmas Annalee; also made in an 18" size. Other Christmas Pandas were produced in 1973. They came in 7" and 18" sizes; the vests and hats were different than those of 1985. Courtesy Bette Todd.

***Fishing Bear:* 10"/25 cm.; 1986; light brown felt; dark brown pads; carries a metal pail and wooden fishing pole with a frog on the end. There were 2,817 *Fishing Bears* made in 1986. Issued only one year he is considered one of the cutest and most desirable Annalee Bears. Courtesy Bette Todd.**

(L-R), *Baby Bear with Bee:* 10"/25 cm.; 1985; made 1985-86 in a total issue of 6,496; dark brown glued on felt pads; white hair; red and black bee on nose. Note the small head which was present only on the 1985 *Baby Bear*. The 1986 *Baby Bear* has a larger head similar to the 1986 *Girl Bear* on the right. *Girl Bear:* 10"/25 cm.; 1986; made 1986-87 in a total issue of 6,218; light brown hair with pink hair bow; holds bouquet of pink flowers; a real cutie. Courtesy Bette Todd.

Bear with Sled: 10"/25 cm.; 1986; one of the many Christmas animals made over the years. He has felt mittens; a knit scarf and rides a Flexible Flyer sled. Common but cute. *Eskimo Bear:* 10"/25 cm.; 1988; *red* hair; wearing a green felt parka trimmed with synthetic fur; felt mittens and boots. A colorful and enjoyable example of a Christmas Annalee with investment potential. Both were produced in 1989. The 10" *Bear with Sled* was discontinued in 1990.
Courtesy Bette Todd.

Tennis Boy Mouse: 7"/18 cm.; 1972; holding aluminum racket. Boy and girl tennis mice were made for a number of years. The trim on the boy's shirt changed regularly; girls always have pink trim; some years they wear hats. After 1978 the tennis rackets were white plastic. Note the chunky square face characteristic of the early 1970s mice. Tennis mice are common, but early ones are desirable.
Courtesy Bette Todd.

(L-R), *Hunter Mouse:* 7"/18 cm.; 1973; felt body and tail. Made only three years, he is hard to find. In 1975 he had a red bird on the gun barrel. *Jogger Mouse:* 7"/18 cm.; 1980; red felt body; grey felt head and bias tape tail. The dark lines on pants are drawn on. Produced in 1979 in a blue jogging suit and in 1981 in a green suit. *Skateboard Mouse*: 7"/18 cm.; 1979; an issue of 1,821; retail $7.95. He rides a green skateboard with wooden wheels; also made in 1978 with red mittens.
Courtesy Bette Todd.

Bicycle Boy Mouse: **7"/18 cm.; 1977; rides a wire bicycle; red flag on tail. Boy and girl bicycle mice were made for a number of years. The clothes and bicycle construction have changed frequently.** ***Boating Mouse:*** **7"/18 cm.; 1986; holds a red wooden sailboat; one of the last grey sporting mice produced in the 1980s. Except for six brown Limited Edition mice made in 1989, Annalee produced only grey Christmas mice in 1988 and 1989. Courtesy Bette Todd.**

(L-R), ***Bowling Mouse:*** **7"/18 cm.; 1984; holds a plastic bowling ball; the only bowling mouse of the 1980s. Bowling Mice from 1972-74 wear white shirts.** ***Iceskater Mouse:*** **7"/18 cm.; 1980; wears silver ice skates made from heavy paper. A desirable mouse. Made in 1974-75 and again in 1980-81. The 1975 model wears a red jacket.** ***Cheerleader Mouse:*** **7"/18 cm.; 1982; carries a plastic megaphone and a yarn pompon. In 1983 the sweater had blue trim at the neck and the "NH" was absent. Two year production. Some people collect primarily mice. The total number of mice produced from 1965-1989 exceeds 1,800,770.**
Courtesy Bette Todd.

Cowboy and Cowgirl Mouse: 7"/18 cm.; made in 1982 and 1983; (total boys made -- 3,776; total girls made -- 3,116). He wears white synthetic fur chaps; both carry rope lariats; issue price ea. $12.95. Expecially cute and popular. Slightly different versions of the 7" Cowboy and Cowgirl Mice were made in 1974.
Courtesy Bette Todd.

Retired Grandpa Mice: 7"/18 cm.; (left) 1974; (right) 1984; both hold a newspaper and wooden pipe; note the white beards. The bias tape tail on the 1974 mouse is characteristic of mice between 1974 and 1983. Before 1974 the tails were generally made of felt. Between 1983 and 1987 the tails were usually made of grey flannel. In 1987 felt tails reappeared. Popular theme.
Courtesy Bette Todd.

Yum Yum Bunnies: 7"/18 cm.; 1966; all felt; raw cotton tails. They are among the very early bunnies produced by Annalee and are noted for their fat, brown faces. *Yum Yum Bunnies* also came with an orange body and yellow jacket; issue price $3.95. These extremely desirable bunnies were also made in an 18" size. Lucky is the collector who finds one of either size.
Courtesy Bette Todd.

(Front), *Country Boy and Girl Bunny with Bushel Basket:* 7"/18 cm.; 1984; paper-type tag; beige felt; wear Easter fabric from 1984; sold as a pair with basket and eggs. (Back), *Girl and Boy Bunny:* 7"/18 cm.; 1978; adhesive tape-type tag; red hair (red hair is desirable on all Annalees); white felt; wearing Easter fabric from 1978. Note, 1970s rabbits were usually made of white felt; small rabbits are usually made of beige felt; larger 1980s rabbits are usually made of beige flannel.
Courtesy Bette Todd.

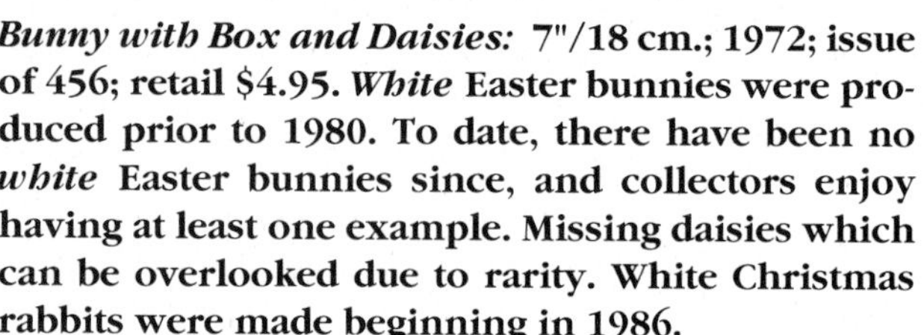

Bunny with Box and Daisies: 7"/18 cm.; 1972; issue of 456; retail $4.95. *White* Easter bunnies were produced prior to 1980. To date, there have been no *white* Easter bunnies since, and collectors enjoy having at least one example. Missing daisies which can be overlooked due to rarity. White Christmas rabbits were made beginning in 1986.

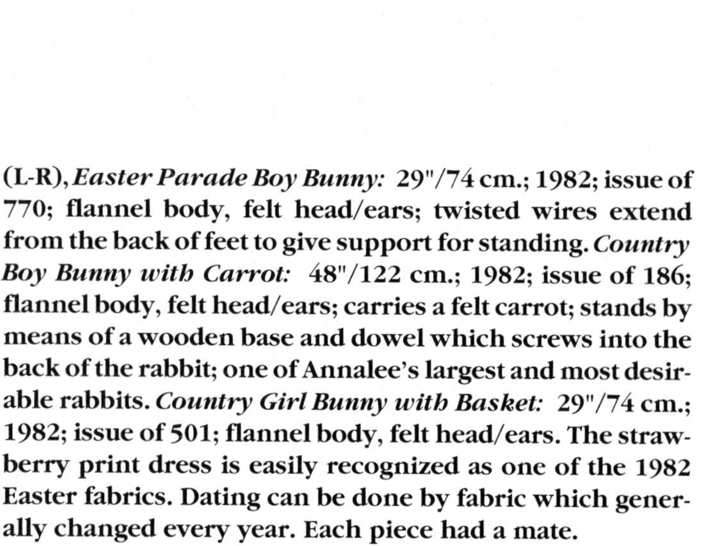

(L-R), *Easter Parade Boy Bunny:* 29"/74 cm.; 1982; issue of 770; flannel body, felt head/ears; twisted wires extend from the back of feet to give support for standing. *Country Boy Bunny with Carrot:* 48"/122 cm.; 1982; issue of 186; flannel body, felt head/ears; carries a felt carrot; stands by means of a wooden base and dowel which screws into the back of the rabbit; one of Annalee's largest and most desirable rabbits. *Country Girl Bunny with Basket:* 29"/74 cm.; 1982; issue of 501; flannel body, felt head/ears. The strawberry print dress is easily recognized as one of the 1982 Easter fabrics. Dating can be done by fabric which generally changed every year. Each piece had a mate.
Courtesy Bette Todd.

Victorian Country Girl and Boy Bunnies: 18"/46 cm.; 1987; tan flannel (not felt) bodies with felt heads and ears; Victorian floral print fabric; salmon color felt hats, vests, shoes and spats. She carries an umbrella; he carries a wooden cane. They are the only pair of Victorian bunnies produced to date and are already collectible. Girl was an issue of 1,492; boy's issue was 1,394. However, with luck, the pair may still be found in a retail store for $100.00.
Courtesy Bette Todd.

(L-R), *Boy Frog:* 10"/25 cm.; 1979; adhesive tape-type tag; note the contouring of the head and eyes and the unique painting of the facial features. Also made in 18" and 42" sizes. *Boy Frog*: 18"/46 cm.; 1980; paper-type tag; girl frogs were also produced. Although frogs have been manufactured periodically over the years, they remain popular with collectors.
Courtesy Bette Todd.

(L-R), *Willie Wog Goin' Fishin':* 10"/25 cm.; 1974 only; issue of 909; both frogs are bright green with a yellow belly and have satin ribbon tags. He wears blue checked pants (characteristic of Willie Wog) and carries a stick fishing pole; also made in 18" and 42" sizes. The larger sizes are even more rare; all are extremely desirable. *Polly Frog Spring Cleaning*: 10"/25 cm.; 1974 only; issue of 580; also made in an 18" size; carries a mop. The original accessories are necessary for full value.
Courtesy Bette Todd.

Santa Fox with Bag: 18"/46 cm.; 1981; wears a red felt jacket trimmed with synthetic plush; holds a sack trimmed with holly; made 1981 and 1982 (1,499 made in 1982); also available in a 7" size. This unusual fox is one of the most sought after Christmas animals.
Courtesy Bette Todd.

Girl Monkey with Banana Trapeze: 12"/30 cm.; 1981; blue bow in hair; came with an unattached felt banana trapeze. If this is missing, reduce value by half. Produced one year only in an issue of 857; retail $23.95. A 12" boy monkey was also available in 1981. He did not have a hair bow. The pair was also made in a 7"/18 cm. size. Other monkeys were produced by Annalee during the 1970s; some had white, chartreuse, bristol blue and hot pink felt bodies. They came in 7", 10", 12" and 22" sizes and in various costumes. Rare and desirable.
Courtesy Bette Todd.

Dragon and Bushbeater: 14"/36 cm.; 1981, (the first dragons are from the early 1980s); one of the most popular Annalee animals. This size came with a 7"/18 cm. *Bushbeater* dressed in leopard skin fabric; dragon holds daisies; issue price $28.95. Also made in a 5" and 29" size; all are uncommon; the 29" is the most rare and in 1987 sold for $1,050.00. Innovative and appealing design. Dragons were reissued in 1990.
Courtesy Bette Todd.

Ballerina Pig with Umbrella: 8"/20 cm.; 1982; issue price $12.95; *flesh* color felt; carries a blue felt umbrella. Made only two years, 1981-82; a popular and cute pig. Other pigs were made over the years -- some were white. Note the difference in eye painting between the two pigs. (Center), *Ballerina Bunny:* 7"/18 cm.; 1980; made 1980-83; issue price $8.95. The wire stands come attached to many Annalee Dolls. Courtesy Bette Todd.

A duck for every occasion. (L-R), top, *Pilot Duck,* 5"/13 cm.; 1984; popular duck. (Center), *Easter Parade Girl Duck,* 5"/13 cm.; 1985. *Easter Parade Boy Duckling*, 5"/13 cm.; 1984. *Duckling,* 5"/13 cm.;1984. *Sailor Duck,* 5"/13 cm.; 1989. (Bottom), *Duckling with Santa Hat,* 5"/13 cm.; 1983. *Duckling in Santa Hat,* 5"/13 cm.; 1983. Only a few special ducks are collectible. Easter Parade ducks and rabbits were made for several years. All wear fancy outfits and Easter bonnets. The color of the hat ribbon changed from year to year.
Courtesy Cheryl and Tiffany Todd.

(L-R), *Skunk with Snowball:* 12"/30 cm.; 1982; felt hat and boots; holds a fluffy snowball defining Christmas theme; issue price $28.95. *Boy Skunk:* 12"/30 cm.; 1982; carries a red Valentine box; has the same synthetic plush skunk's tail; issue price $27.95. Note the painted faces that are unique to Annalee skunks. There was also a girl skunk made in 1982. These are the only three skunks produced to date. They are striking examples and avidly sought after by most collectors.
Courtesy Bette Todd.

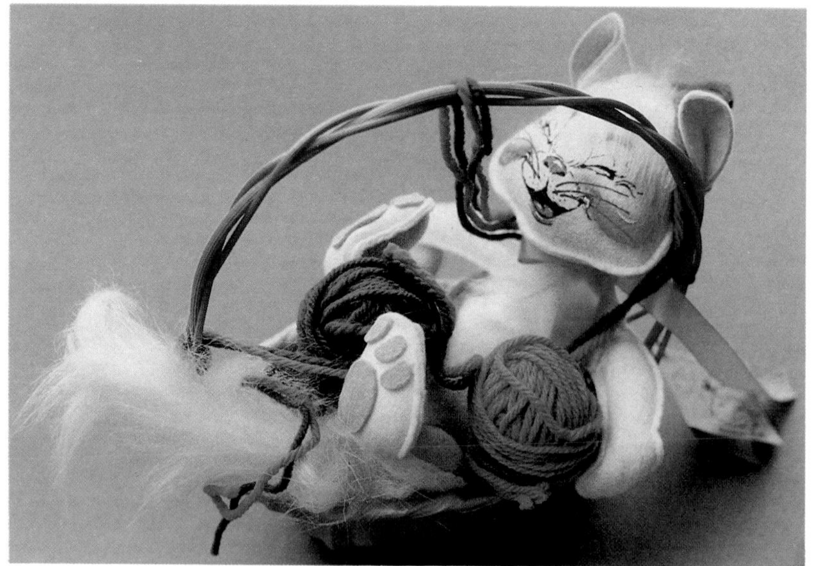

Kitten with Yarn and Basket: 10"/25 cm.; 1987; came in a basket with yarn. Annalee made many cats in the 1960s. Some had brightly colored bodies such as yellow and hot pink. No cats were made from 1973-1984.

(L-R), *Clown:* 18"/46 cm.; 1978; white daisy in black felt hat; wonderfully painted face. Also came in 10" and 42" sizes and in other colors. *Clown:* 10"/25 cm.; 1980; has a brown body which appeared on the clowns of 1980 and 1981; pants are of the same fabric that was used on 1978 Christmas dolls; also made in 18" and 42" sizes. *Clown:* 18"/46 cm.; 1985; also made in a 10" size and in yellow and blue. Cheerful. Clowns give variety to a collection. Generally the design of clowns has changed each year.
Courtesy Bette Todd.

(L-R), *Clown:* 10"/25 cm.; 1977; suit of mattress ticking; felt heads, hands, feet and ruff; also made in 18" and 42" sizes. Additionally, there is a polka dot fabric on some clowns from 1977. *Clown:* 10"/25 cm.; 1981; red hair; wears dotted pants and white felt bow tie; *flannel* body, felt head, hands and feet; also made in 18" and 42" sizes. The larger sizes have suspenders. *Clown:* 10"/25 cm.; 1984; wears polished cotton suit; also available in pink and white and orange and white as well as an 18" and 30" size. *Clown:* 10"/25 cm.; 1987; felt head, hands and feet; wears a pastel cotton suit. This clown came only in this size and color combination and was the last clown issued by Annalee in the 1980s. Recent but hard to find.
Courtesy Bette Todd.

X.
STEIFF DOLLS

Store new (tissue mint) pair: 13½"/34 cm.; TINY FF buttons; remnants of white S.T.; all felt; e.s.; f.j.; inset mohair *full wigs*; boy has tiny black button eyes, girl's are blue/black glass; both use the favored center seam "Character" mold with painted nostrils and mouth. Note the impeccable detailing of original outfits. *Boy's:* cotton; felt with leather buttons; black leather shoes; carrying knapsack trimmed with leather. *Girl's:* cotton dress/apron; finely knit sweater; leather soles on black wool shoes tied with green twisted floss; carrying linen-type umbrella with metal workings and bamboo handle. Steiff dolls are seldom found in this immaculate condition. There will always be collectors wanting such examples.

John Fazendin's German Village lives on (see *TB&SA* Second Series, pg. 137-143). Steiff character child with her pet Pomeranian: one of four sizes available in sitting position, ca. 1913; FF button; white mohair with felt face and front legs; collar and chain. The original dog house and water bucket are charming accessories in the Steiff Village. Courtesy John Fazendin.

Ida Gutsell *center seam* doll (16"/41 cm.;) patented in 1893. Ida's invention was designed in six sections to be cut and sewn from a printed pattern that included a printed garment section. Interesting early American doll in original clothes. In a few years Steiff dolls appeared utilizing a similar principle of Ida's center seam design to give a three-dimensional appearance. Pull toy horse, ca. 1910: 10"/25.4 cm.; high; mohair over hollow papier mache body; cast iron spoked wheels. Steiff *Molly* dog, 4"/10 cm high; original ribbon and bell increase value. Courtesy Tammie Depew.

Their shy beauty enhances the rare LARGE Steiff dolls. Dutchwoman, *Alida*: 20"/50 cm.; all felt; e.s.; f.j.; deep blue glass eyes; pink felt *inset* mouth (unusual and only found on the larger dolls); inset blond mohair wig; well defined fingers. For the most part dolls with the center front seamed faces were developed between 1908-1913, after which time only the costumes were changed. She wears a wool flannel dress; layers of undergarments consisting of cotton bloomers and attached slip, cotton petticoat as well as a wool flannel petticoat; black knee high cotton socks; Dutch style felt shoes. The cotton cap and apron complete her costume. The Hunter, *Hubertus,* same as above; dressed in wool sweater; wool flannel pants with leather belt. Of particular interest are his felt-flannel spats each with six FF buttons; black felt slipper-type shoes. His hunting hat is felt with braid and pompons. Also made in 11", 14", 17" and 23½" size. Both are mint and totally original, ca. 1912. Private Collection.

French Soldier: 12"/30 cm.; no I.D.; excelsior stuffed (as are all Steiff dolls); f.j.; shoe button eyes; painted facial features and mustache; black mohair inset wig under cap; removable khaki uniform, red and gold trim with four blank buttons; leather belt; handmade leather boots of exquisite workmanship, ca. 1915. Steiff made a variety of soldiers: American, Austrian, Belgian, Dutch, English, French, German, Italian and others. Showing attention to detail, these were sold with or without original accessories such as gun and knapsack. However, these gadgets are usually lost by today. Doll is in unplayed with condition.
Courtesy Barbara Baldwin.

Soulmates, ca. 1910-20. Wistful goat on cast iron wheels: 24"/61 cm. high, 22"/56 cm. long; FF button; long curly mohair; e.s.; unjointed; beautiful yellow hand painted glass eyes; leather horns; felt pads on bifurcated hoofs; ca. 1910-20. Shown with Steiff friend: 21"/54 cm.; center seam felt child doll; constructed to have all (original) clothing removable.

Missis **and *Captain* Katzenjammer. Both: FF buttons; jointed arms only; white felt circles back the shoe button eyes; painted facial features; fanned hands. They do not have the conventional center seam. Modeling is aided by a lateral to a cheek seam. *Missis* is a tea cosey: 16"/41 cm.; excelsior stuffed head and arms only. Insulation is provided by the double thickness of green felt skirt and red felt torso; cotton apron; hair-do is a sewn-on cone of cotton cloth. *Captain:* 14"35 cm.; stoutly stuffed with excelsior; grey/black cotton fringe for beard and two clumps of hair in back that protrude from under his felt cap; felt made-to-body suit and shoes. These comic dolls are especially popular in Germany.**
Courtesy Joy Kelleher, Special Joys Museum.

***C omic Farmer Doll*: 12"/30.5 cm.; Steiff FF button in *each ear*; all felt; e.s.; f.j.; inset mohair wig; shoe button eyes; painted facial features; bulbous nose formed by a horizontal seam in center; separate fingers on *large* hands. Most Steiff dolls have mitten hands with stitched fingers; only a few have separately formed fingers. Wearing made-to-body dark blue suit; decorated with *nine* FF buttons. The red felt vest is part of his chest; white collar is sewn to body; fez-type hat; leather boots with *felt* soles, ca. 1910.**
Courtesy Barbara Baldwin.

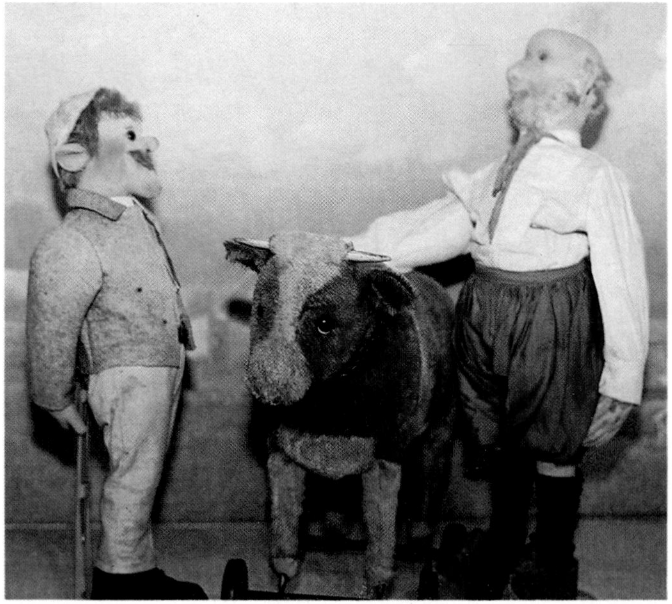

Down on the 1913 farm, the mohair cow (12"/30.5 cm. high, 15"/38 cm. long) on iron wheels is enjoying the sunshine with two center seam, f.j., farmer friends. Left, Farmer: 16½"/42 cm.; brown glass eyes; inset mohair mustache and wig; factory *painted* face with *enlarged* chin and *long* nose, typical of display pieces. His large ears were painted flesh color *over* the FF button. The hands are sewn together behind his back; original clothes. Right, Gentleman Farmer with an interesting face: 19"/48 cm.; clever mouth with *inset wide felt lips*; nose flares at the base and has a bump on the bridge; grey mohair is inserted as a balding head fringe; mutton chop-type mohair whiskers; *flat ears* hold FF button. The original cotton clothing and green knit stockings with wooden shoes are simple and European. Both farmers have only heads and hands of felt; arms, legs and bodies are cotton.
Courtesy Joy Kelleher, Special Joys Museum.

Soldier asking directions from the village artisans. Soldier: 13½"/34 cm.; FF button; center seam; f.j.; small brown glass eyes; *painted* black mustache and hair. He is outfitted with full gear, including canteen and metal sword. From his leather helmet to his wooden cartridge belt, to his high leather boots (each studded with eight FF buttons) he is all business! The accessories enhance value dramatically. *Schneid*-type, the Tailor, left: 14"/35.6 cm.; inset mohair wig; original outfit. His face and arms have been painted flesh-tone; cheeks, lips and nose-tip painted pink; arms are blushed. Often dolls used in store displays were painted to create more color. He had nail holes through both feet, ca. 1913. *Schus:* the Shoemaker, 14"/35.6 cm.; FF button; f.j.; mohair mustache and inset wig; original cotton clothes; long black leather shoes stitched onto legs as feet. Steiff Driver Bear: 5½"/14 cm.; mohair, ca. 1950s. In 1913 these three dolls cost $2.50 each.
Courtesy Joy Kelleher, Special Joys Museum.

It's circus time! *Bully:* 21"/53 cm. high; 32"/81 cm. long; FF button; mohair; e.s. over steel frame; jointed head; painted wooden-ball eyes give a comic expression; felt upper lip and pink-orange mouth with two wooden lower teeth; nose tightly stitched with shiny twisted cotton/silk floss; three floss claws and four painted toes; heavy cardboard reinforces mohair pads; silver nail studs on red leather collar with a 4" hemp fringe, ca. 1930. Directing the act is, left, the *Ringmaster Clown:* 12"/30 cm.; FF button; f.j.; brown painted clown make-up; made-to-body black felt suit/tails and white felt vest. White spats over black leather shoes complete the outfit on this fine fellow. Center, *Happy Hooligan:* 14½"/37 cm.; blank button; f.j.; comic eyes of shoe buttons backed with white felt; painted mouth and mustache; hair is sparse black cotton twist; hat sewn to head; made-to-body red/green felt suit; long leather shoes are also the feet. *Coloro:* 16½"/42 cm.; large ears with FF button; f.j.; blue stars painted around shoe button eyes; original velveteen clown suit, missing ruff, ca. 1911.
Courtesy Joy Kelleher, Special Joys Museum.

Rooster from the book, *Animal Children* published in 1912: 11"/28 cm.; black and rust *long* mohair; e.s.; jointed arms and legs; glass eyes in the celluloid doll's face; felt comb and feet; squeaker; unknown German maker. It would seem that girls are divided into two groups - they are either doll lovers or stuffed animal lovers - seldom both. This unique piece could appeal to both.
Courtesy Dottie Ayers.

Snik, the gnome showing humor and originality: 12"/30 cm.; FF button; red tag, "SNIK 35/ Made in Germany"; felt; e.s.; f.j.; green glass inset eyes making him quite unusual. The inset felt mouth, outlined in red, shows detailed craftmanship. His bright red hair, long full beard (often found shortened by play or deterioration) and eyebrows are sewn-on mohair. Under the oversize clogs are extra-large feet with stitched toes; removable original clothes and leather belt (missing pouch). Also made in an 8½" size. His partner gnome *Snak* came in a big 17" size as well. The gnomes were popular throughout Eastern Europe. Made 1911-1930. Long production period.
Courtesy Beth Savino, Hobby Center Toys.

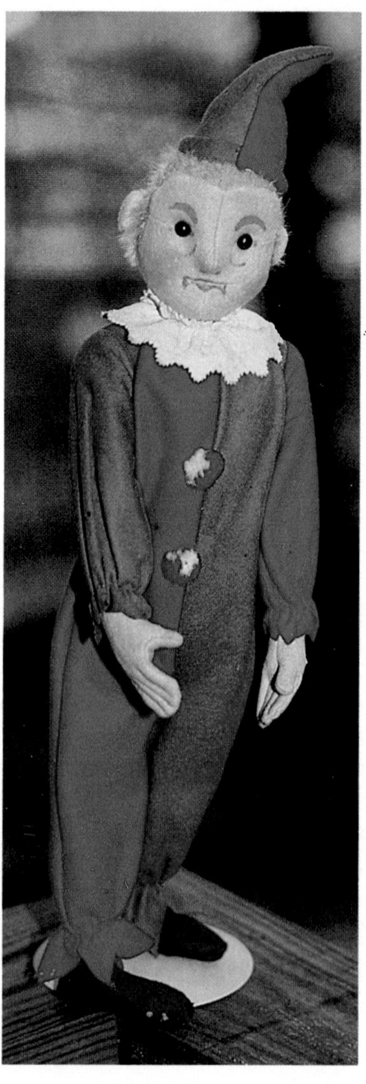

Clown doll for the circus scene: 17"/43 cm.; 19"/48 cm. inc. hat; all felt e.s.; f.j.; blond mohair inset wig; shoe button eyes; heavily painted eyebrows. Note the unusual painted mouth treatment. The blushed cheeks and hands remain vivid, as does the felt clown suit and the sewn-on brown felt slipper shoes. With original box which is extraordinary. One of seven different sizes (1904-1928).
Courtesy Barbara Baldwin.

Children call *Mecki* "The German Mickey Mouse": 25"/64 cm.; molded plastic face/painted features; jersey body and limbs stuffed with foam pellets; unjointed; stapled on mohair wig; inset mohair chest plate; original clothes. Patent infringement from the 1970s. The elephant joined the Steiff Floppy Sleeping Animals ca. 1968: 7"/17 cm. long; C.T. *Floppy Ele*; mohair; foam rubber stuffed; unjointed; eyes embroidered as in sleep; double weight white felt tusks; pink mohair lined ears; removable felt circus blanket. Note nicely curved trunk. Also made in 11"/28 cm. size. Interest in the Floppy Sleeping family remains at a plateau. The Floppy Panda and *Raudi* are the most desirable. Courtesy Diane Hoffman.

Primitive Men: 5"/13 cm. and 7½"/19 cm.; both have RSB and S.T. (on bracelet of large); C.T. *Neander*; small has vinyl head and body with flexible arms; large has vinyl head with felt body and limbs; e.s.; jointed head and arms. Both have hair of rust color mohair; brown mohair plush garment and necklace with plastic tooth (often missing), ca. late 1960s. Limited demand. Collectors enjoy accessorizing their dinosaurs with the *Neanders.* However, dinosaurs were not contemporary with cave men. Courtesy Idele Gilbert.

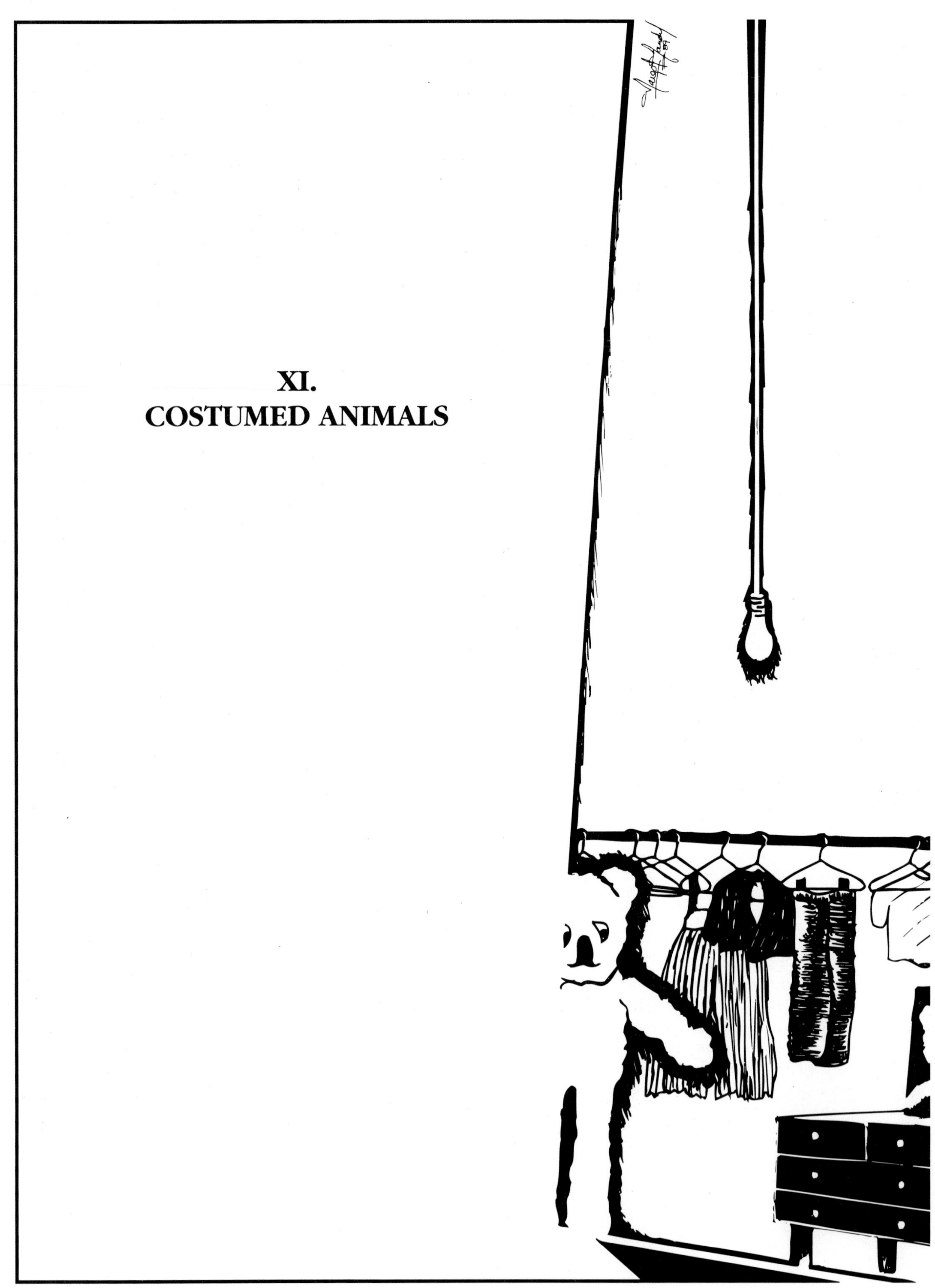

XI.
COSTUMED ANIMALS

"Benham": 25"/64 cm.; medium pile mohair head, lower arms and lower legs with feet; remainder is grey cotton; crushed *cork* stuffed head, excelsior stuffed body/limbs; rigid head; limbs jointed with exterior metal discs; shoe button eyes; black twill nose; thick floss mouth; felt pads. ORIGINAL pink and white one piece shirt/trouser set; pink linen jacket; belt and tie are added. The fabric does not cover the lower body, leaving exposed baled excelsior held together with heavy white thread. The unknown American maker cut every corner to make him as cheaply as possible, ca. 1915. *Rare* Bear Doll today. Shown with bird: 10½"/27 cm.; velveteen and felt; e.s.; metal feet; when wound he dances in a circle; unknown maker, ca. 1915. Dog: 9"/23 cm. long; olive green velveteen; e.s.; legs jointed by bendable wire; ca. 1915. Honey crate toy wagon is a pleasing and useful related toy.

Goose dressed like "Jemima Puddleduck": 10½"/26.5 cm. high, 12"/30.5 cm long; white mohair; e.s.; swivel head only; shoe button eyes; orange felt bill and webbed feet. This was an unusual subject for Steiff, ca. 1910. No I.D.; worth more with I.D. Rare and desirable.
Courtesy Barbara Baldwin.

Original bib attached to Teddy at time of manufacture: 3½"/9 cm.; Steiff FF button; mohair; e.s.; f.j.; black bead eyes; *long* feet; ca. before 1950. The original bib can double value.
Courtesy Gwen Daniel.

Humanized *(Bazi)* Dachshund dressed as a Tyrolean pair: 9"/23 cm.; RSB; S.T. 325; US-Zone tag; mohair heads, hands and feet; flannel bodies; e.s.; jointed heads only; glass eyes; pearl cotton nose/mouth; three painted claws; squeakers. Costumed in cotton and felt. Girl's hat has Edelweiss trim at back; boy's has a white "brush." Boy has orange (Steiff) ribbon scarf and leather button; wooden rifle missing; short production 1954-57. Value is increased for matched pair. Rare and cute; almost as desirable as the dressed foxes (see *TB & SA, Second Series*, pg. 144).
Courtesy Laurie Hix.

Rare and coveted mascot animals: *Navy Goat,* 6"/15 cm. high, 6"/15 cm. long (smallest size); mohair; unjointed; same *green* character eyes as *Brosus, Shere Kahn* and the *Princeton Tiger;* brown stitched nose/mouth; ruled felt horns stiffened with wire; distributed by FAO Schwarz. *Yale Bulldog:* 11"/28 cm. high, 11"/28 cm. long plus 2" tail; RSB; S.T. 3328,2; US-Zone tag; mohair; swivel head; same blue character eyes as *Lulac*; black glass large bead nose; widely painted black mouth on velveteen snout; three floss claws; squeaker; original red leather collar. One ear is sewn down, the other is in "alert position." *A Princeton Tiger, Army Mule* and *Navy Goat* have also been made (limited numbers) in the same large size, sitting position and with a swivel head. *Princeton Tiger*: 4"/10 cm. high, 6"/15 cm. long plus 5" tail; mohair; unjointed; green character eyes; pink floss nose. All are excelsior stuffed and have their original felt blankets.
Courtesy Debbi Anton.

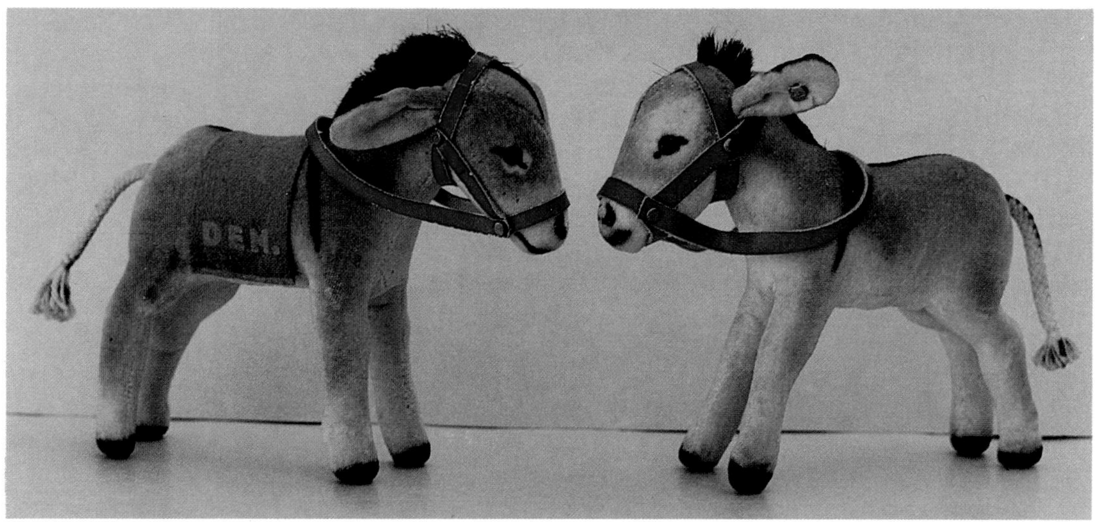

Donkey: 5"/12.7 cm. high, 5½"/14 cm. long; RSB; No. 24/1412,0; grey/ white velveteen; e.s.; unjointed; black glass eyes; painted facial features; bristle mane of horsehair; braided tail; red leather bridle. Left, a mascot for the Democratic Party; girth of white cotton seam binding anchoring the blue felt blanket, securely sewn from the inside with no visible stitches. The "DEM." is stenciled in off-white. He is a dual collectible and highly prized, ca. early 1950s. Courtesy Dave and Ann Abbott.

Steiff *Army Mule:* 6½"/16.5 cm. high, 5½"/14 cm. long; RSB; grey mohair; e.s.; B&W googly glass eyes (the 10" *Army Mule* has BLUE character eyes and open mouth); painted nose/mouth; black horsehair mane; grey rope tail; red thread halter; black felt blanket (missing "A"). The *Army Mule* is more rare than the *Navy Goat.*
Courtesy Idele Gilbert.

Alpine donkey to serenade you: 5"/12.7 cm., grey mohair; e.s.; unjointed; googly glass eyes, embroidered eyelashes; open felt mouth; painted nostrils; original felt hat and blanket. Probably German, ca. 1950-60.
Courtesy Kay Bransky.

Blend of many textures: 11"/28 cm.; mohair head; felt face with airbrushed markings; inset chin from upholstery mohair; hard stuffed cotton; unjointed; plastic eyes/felt eyelids; painted nose; felt ears; cotton plush hands and feet/cardboard innersoles; made-to-body check shirt; felt vest; removable chaps of rabbit fur; red rayon scarf and felt hat. Sewn in left ear is a rayon tag, "Designed by Character, So. Norwalk, Conn," ca. 1950s. Fine quality; limited demand.
Courtesy Diane Hoffman.

Steiff Polar Bear: 5"/12.5 cm. high; no I.D.; mohair; swivel head; glass eyes; stitched nose and mouth; felt pads. Wearing straw hat with artificial flowers; loops of imitation pearls form earrings; light pink taffeta dress is fastened with rhinestones. Dress has sewn-in label, "Helen Ratkai is My Couturiere." There is a Steiff donkey, elephant and two Poodles dressed in a similar fashion and tagged Helen Ratkai, ca. 1950-60. Over-all effect is very pleasant.
Courtesy Kirk Stines.

FAO Schwarz exclusive *City Mouse House:* 13"/33 cm.x7"/18 cm.x4¾"/12 cm.; red bricks painted on outside of wooden house; grey window frames labeled "City Mouse." *Mrs. City Mouse* (3½"/9 cm.; Steiff RSB; S.T. 4308,04) wears a satin dress, rosette hat and rhinestone necklace. The apartment includes two chairs/table; an ornate loveseat; four poster bed/canopy and spread; gilded frame mirror over velvet vanity; candelabra and framed picture. The rug is missing; ca. 1960s. Easier to find than the Country Mouse House.

Pippy, dressed formally in a red felt coat with tails, sings while a 1985 Texas Sesquicentennial armadillo mascot plays the piano. Dressed mouse: 5"/12 cm.; RSB; S.T. 712; C.T. *Pippy*; grey velvet jointed head; flexible rubber arms/legs; glass bead eyes; black felt pants; missing green neck bow. Note: his white gloves are reminiscent of Mickey Mouse. Ca. 1953-58.
Courtesy Mary Benavente.

Lix and *Lixie*, Puss 'N Boots-type pirates: 5"/12 cm.; RSB; S.T. 313B and 313M; C.T. pet name; Tabby striped mohair heads, bushy tails and chest plate; bendable rubber limbs with the usual age hardening; swivel head; green glass cat eyes; pink floss nose/mouth. *Lix* has black felt pants/red trim and lime green cummerbund; *Lixie* wears a red cotton skirt with black cummerbund; both have green felt vests over white cotton shirts, ca. 1957. Popularity is waning because hard to find mint.

Steiff "Original Teddy", dressed by FAO Schwarz in 1969: 13½"/35 cm.; beige mohair; e.s.; f.j.; plastic eyes. The greatest interest in the exclusively dressed bears is in the pre-1965 models. Undressed, he is valued the same as the regular line.

XII.
RABBITS

Steiff velveteen bunnies. Right is a baby's rattle; both are 2½"/6.4 cm. high; left is 5"/12 cm. long; right is 4½"/11.4 cm. long; pre-button era; hard stuffed cotton; unjointed; shoe button eyes; pink stitched nose/mouth, ca. early 1900s. The rattle feature is popular. Attached to the left bunny is a velveteen carrot with green floss leaves. This adds charm and value.

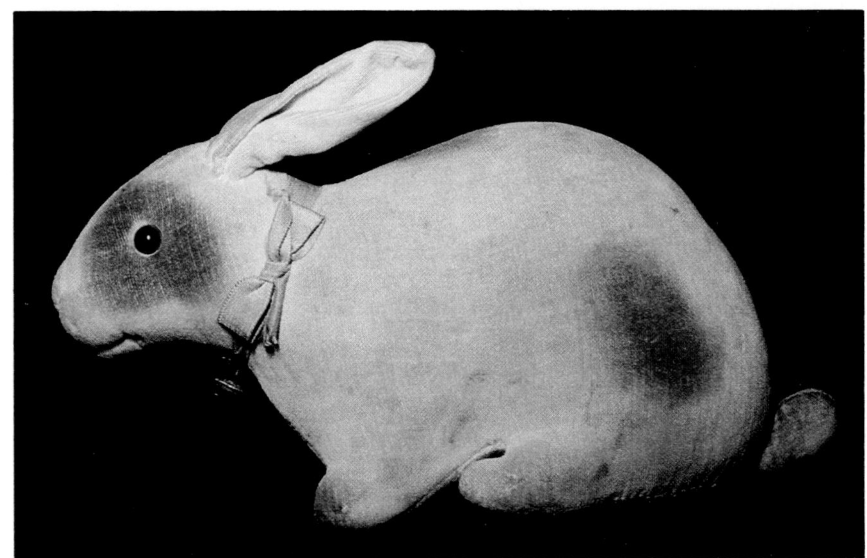

Baby's rattle as a crouching rabbit: 4"/10.2 cm. high, 7½"/19 cm. long plus ¾"/1.9 cm. tail; Steiff, no I.D.; velveteen; cotton stuffed; glass eyes backed with red circles; silk thread nose/mouth; original silk ribbon and brass bell. Uncommon, ca. 1910. Collectors with limited space could focus on these charming velveteen animals from the turn of the century.
Courtesy Jeremy Bleecher and Patricia Gallagher.

Hollander Rabbits, seven times jointed: 12½"/32 cm. inc. (jointed) ears; FF buttons; remnants of white stock tag. Left, two-toned (white and mauve) mohair; right, white mohair with pink mohair lined ears. Both are e.s.; have pink/red glass eyes; pinkish beige twisted floss nose/mouth; no claws or pads; side squeaker, ca. 1911. Top end rabbits in great demand. Shown with 1988 Dutch Rabbit Replica; 6½"/17 cm.; limited to 4,000 worldwide; retail $145.00 with investment potential.

Peter Rabbit: 10"/25 cm.; Steiff logo is *stamped* on the leather sole of slipper; velveteen; e.s.; unjointed; *black glass* eyes with pink felt backing; thin twisted brown floss nose/mouth; no claws or pads. Note the elegant simplicity of the blue felt jacket/pocket and red felt slippers highlighted by yellow stitching, ca. 1905-13. Found in Portobello Market, London.
Courtesy Jean Ann Smith.

Early Steiff *Jack Rabbit* dressed as a human: 12"/30.5 cm.; FF button; grey and brown mohair head, hands and tail; e.s.; jointed at head and arms only; oversize glass eyes; twisted hard, rose color cotton floss nose; red felt tongue; three black floss claws on hands; whiskers; non-removable purple velvet jacket (two brass buttons); velvet striped shirt and socks; orange velvet made-to-body pants; leather belt and shoes. A very sought after larger rabbit in rare mint condition, ca. 1927-1931.
Courtesy Barbara Baldwin.

Woodland rabbits: front, 9"/23 cm.; Steiff tiny FF button; wool coat fabric (brennessel); e.s.; unjointed; shoe button eyes/red felt backing; felt lining in ears attached to covering by blanket stitch at the factory (this is not a repair); tan floss nose/mouth in outline style; no whiskers, ca. 1918. Shown with artist Rosemary Volpi's outstanding original designs: rabbit family, 6"/15 cm. to 9"/23 cm.; wool coat fabric; jointed limbs; glass eyes; impeccably costumed in vintage fabrics. The grandparents are on the bridge; the farmer's wife is in the garden gathering carrots in her apron; a visiting aunt caring for a baby is at the door; the children are in the window.
Courtesy Debbie Masters.

The wonderful charm of a Schuco Yes/No rabbit for communication as well as cuddling: 9"/23 cm. not inc. ears; remnant of Schuco paper tag on chest; long mohair; e.s.; f.j.; pink faceted jewel eyes; floss nose/mouth; no claws; felt pads; voice box; ca. 1920s. Rare and desirable. Courtesy Jeremy Bleecher and Patricia Gallagher.

Rabbit with body like a Teddy Bear: 16"/41 cm.; mohair; velveteen lined ears; stuffed with excelsior and cotton mix; f.j.; glass eyes; no whiskers; twisted hard, tan cotton floss nose/mouth; five claws; felt pads; squeaker; unknown maker. Because of paw curve and shape of pads, he probably dates from late teens-early 1920s. Great rabbit!

Unusual colors from 1920-30: all have Steiff FF buttons; are mohair; e.s.; have jointed heads only; glass eyes; twisted floss nose/mouth; squeakers; no claws or pads. Left, 6½"/16 cm. high not inc. ears, 8"/20 cm. long; burnt orange fur; long feet; no whiskers; crouching postion. Center, 11"/28 cm. high inc. (wired) ears, 8"/20 cm. long; sitting; *pink* body, white ear linings and tummy; oversized eyes; no whiskers; long skinny feet and large head. Right, 9"/23 cm. high inc. (wired) ears; bright orange fur; oversized eyes (typical of Steiff rabbits); long skinny feet; whiskers. Great demand.

Large hopping rabbits with popular "folk art" appeal to set them apart from the "cutesy" bunnies. Felt: 6"/15 cm. high, 12"/30.5 cm. long; *tiny* FF button; remnant of *white* S.T. (1908-26); unjointed; shoe button eyes/ red felt backing; pink floss nose/ mouth; natural wood eccentric wheels imprinted "Steiff/Made in Germany"; original bell attached to neck, ca. 1914. Right, size same as above; beige mohair; FF button, *red* S.T. (1926-34); brown glass eyes; pink floss nose outlined with black; painted wood eccentric wheels, ca. late 1920s. Both rabbits are excelsior stuffed; have whiskers, no claws, and *weights in ears.*

Schuco acrobat: 5"/13 cm.; mohair over metal form; rigid head; jointed legs; wind arms to activate the clockwork (tumbling) mechanism; button eyes; pink floss nose/mouth; felt pads on hands only; no whiskers; pink linen-type fabric lines the ears dating him in 1920s. Rare and desirable; appealing to rabbit, Schuco and/or mechanical collectors.

Manni from 1926-34: 23"/58.5 cm. plus 10"/25 cm. ears; FF button; remnant of *red* S.T.; tipped white mohair (like "Petsy" from the same time period); e.s.; jointed head only; oversize glass eyes; pink twisted floss nose outlined with black floss that forms mouth; no whiskers; three pink-beige floss claws; no pads; squeaker; large brass bell around neck. Note the long (10") feet on this exceptional early rabbit equal in desirability to a fine vintage Teddy.

American rabbit: 15"/38 cm. inc. ears; mohair; pink velveteen ear linings; kapok stuffed; swivel head; arms jointed by bendable wire, stitch jointed legs; pink glass eyes; pink pearl cotton nose, black mouth; horsehair whiskers; squeaker; original silk satin bow; high quality rabbit from 1930-40; unknown maker. Shown with 6"/15 cm. Kiwi bird from New Zealand.

Madame Alexander *Bunny Belle* variation: 13½"/34 cm.; pink muslin firmly stuffed with cotton; stitch jointed arms; painted and molded muslin mask face; yarn hair; pink-lined yellow felt ears; mitten hands; pin-striped stuffed legs; non-removable felt shoes; dotted swiss dress trimmed with felt flowers; attached organdy petticoat, matching undies. Missing hat. The body is not tagged; the dress is tagged, "Madame Alexander New York USA" in blue block letters. Only her rabbit ears distinguish her as an animal and not a person, ca. 1939-40. A rabbit collection should include the wonderful Madame Alexander dressed rabbits.
Courtesy Diane Hoffman.

Dottie Dumbunnie, Madame Alexander rabbit: 16"/40.5 cm.; unjointed; unbleached muslin body; yellow velveteen head; tan suede cloth ear linings; shoe button eyes; pearl cotton nostrils and mouth; lt. green cotton dress with sewn-on apron; plaid neckerchief; fancy hat of floral print dimity, silk ribbon ruffles brim; hemstitched yellow organdy tie; organdy pantaloons and buckram petticoat; sewn-on black felt shoes; two chicks in basket; arm is tacked to dress which is tagged at neck, "Madame Alexander, New York" (red print), ca. 1938. *Desirable rabbit*. Alexander "Posey Pet" *bear:* 17"/43 cm.; unbleached muslin body, rayon plush head, paws and feet; stitch jointed limbs; eyes are violet (poseys) with black bead centers; nose is a black velveteen flower; flowers trim felt hat; cotton dress tagged at neck, "Posey Pet, Madame Alexander" (blue print), ca. 1940s. These special creations *must* have their original clothes for value. Courtesy Rebecca Vaughn Gardner.

Affectionately referred to as "Grandpa" rabbit due to his age and worn look: 5"/12.5 cm. high; printed STEIFF button, not underlined. During the war years when materials were scarce, Steiff experimented with various coverings including *cotton plush*, an unpopular fabric which did not endure; e.s.; swivel head; orange glass eyes; red floss outlines nose/mouth; felt ear linings; painted claws, ca. 1940s. Note the unusual curling of tail that is not seen in later rabbits. Rare, but demand is for the 1950s mohair. Posed with plastic bunnies and candy box, ca. 1950.
Courtesy Mary Benavente.

"Little Man": 20"/51 cm. not inc. ears; metal tag on left foot, "KERSA, Made in Germany"; wool plush head and felt lined ears; flesh color felt body and hands, white wool tail; e.s.; jointed head only; glass eyes; dark brown twisted floss nose/mouth; nylon whiskers; felt coat, vest and shoes (cardboard soles typical of all KERSA dressed animals). Plaid pants complete his country gentleman attire, pre WWII. Desirable.

Charming rabbits for a collection. (L-R), first three are 12"/30 cm. inc. ears; "Painter Rabbit" is 8"/20 cm.; all are tagged, "KERSA, Made in Germany"; have wool plush heads, felt lined ears, felt arms and body; e.s.; jointed head only; first, second and fourth have black glass teardrop eyes, third has black plastic eyes; all have dark brown twisted floss nose/mouth and whiskers; brightly colored original clothes of cotton, taffeta, felt and wool, ca. 1940-50s. The girl is missing slippers.

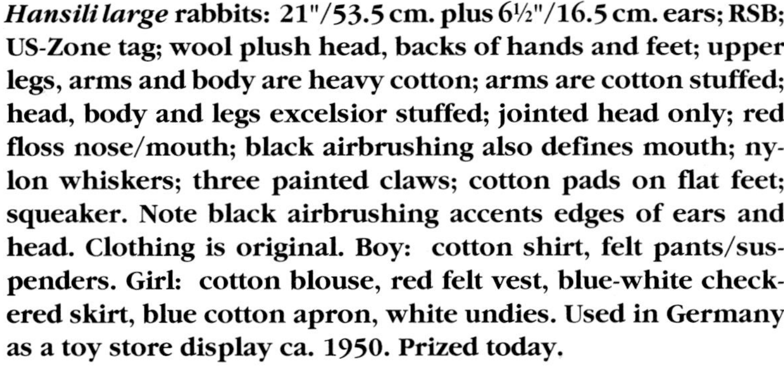

Hansili large rabbits: 21"/53.5 cm. plus 6½"/16.5 cm. ears; RSB; US-Zone tag; wool plush head, backs of hands and feet; upper legs, arms and body are heavy cotton; arms are cotton stuffed; head, body and legs excelsior stuffed; jointed head only; red floss nose/mouth; black airbrushing also defines mouth; nylon whiskers; three painted claws; cotton pads on flat feet; squeaker. Note black airbrushing accents edges of ears and head. Clothing is original. Boy: cotton shirt, felt pants/suspenders. Girl: cotton blouse, red felt vest, blue-white checkered skirt, blue cotton apron, white undies. Used in Germany as a toy store display ca. 1950. Prized today.

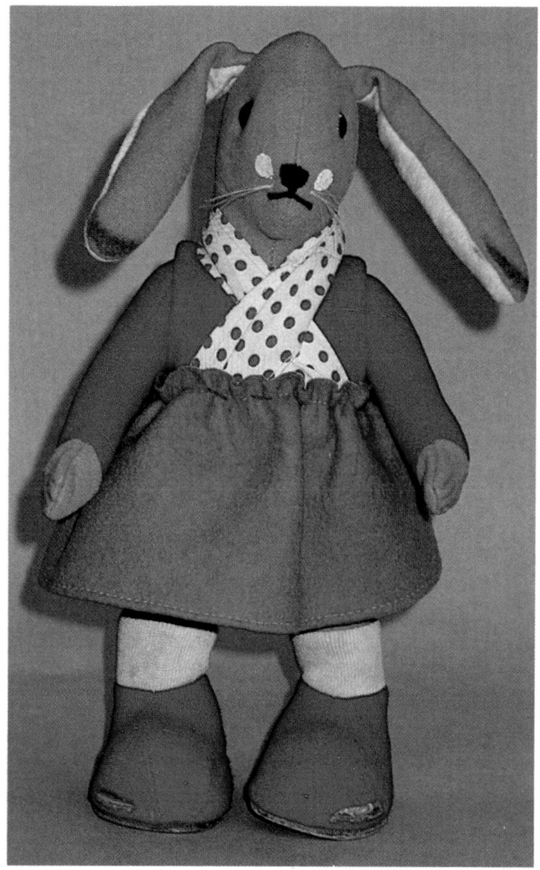

Unusual rabbit: 10"/25 cm.; metal tag on cardboard sole of left shoe, "KERSA, Made in Germany"; felt; e.s.; jointed arms only; black plastic eyes; twisted floss nose/mouth; white painted circles to spotlight whiskers; three airbrushed claws each hand. Colorfully dressed in felt with made-to-body blouse; cotton scarf; white knit socks (missing apron); colors and print can vary, ca. 1948. Kersa also made similar dressed human figures.

Schuco mini rabbits. All are 5"/12.7 cm.; f.j.; have brown/black glass eyes; red twisted floss nose/mouth; felt lined ears, ca. 1950s. Left, light beige synthetic plush over metal; original pink ribbon sewn to chest. Center, gold mohair over metal. Right, Yes/No mechanism; beige mohiar over metal; original green ribbon sewn to chest. Large sizes, color variants and Yes/No function increase the value.

Schuco mini "Thumper" rabbit: 3¼"/8.2 cm. not inc. ears; short (¼") mohair over metal form; white pompon tail; f.j.; glass bead eyes; floss nose/mouth; felt lined ears; specially designed back legs with round hips and large rabbit feet to stand erect, ca. 1950. With rough handling the feet could become detached. No ribbon; note in the 1930s Schuco advertised trimmings of "Silk Ribbon," matte (not satin) finish. Schuco *Noah's Ark* raccoon described in Schuco Section.
Courtesy Valerie Vann.

Due to the many variations, rabbits are avidly sought after by collectors. Made in several sizes and positions: standing, running, sitting, begging, lying, jointed and unjointed, most Steiff rabbits from the 1950s and 1960s are in great demand today. One could concentrate on a rabbit collection alone. After each rabbit, rarity is assigned by a numeral in parenthesis. The scale is 1-10 with 10 the most rare (applies to this group only). Front: 6½" *Vario* (6); 3¼" Running Rabbit (3); 6" *Pummy* (1); 3½" Sitting Rabbit (5); 5" *Bibbie* and *Bib* (9); 4" *Manni* (2); 3½" Lying Rabbit (4); 5" Lying Rabbit (4+); 10" *Vario* (6+). Back: 6½" US-Zone Begging Rabbit, note closed mouth, (7); 10" Easter Rabbit (10); 16" Easter Rabbit (10+); 10" Easter Rabbit (10); 10" male and female *Nikili* (8).
Courtesy Debbi Anton.

Bib and Bibbie: 5"/12.5 cm. inc. ears; *tiny* RSB; C.T. pet name; mohair head, velveteen lined ears (airbrushed); rubber body/limbs; white wool pompon tail; unjointed; glass eyes; twisted pink floss nose/mouth; nylon whiskers; original clothes are felt and cotton, ca. 1950-60. Limited supply (few have survived).

Lulac rabbits: small, 13"/33 cm. plus 4"/10 cm. ears; RSB; S.T. 7343,1; large, 20"/51 cm. plus 6"/15 cm. ears; S.T. unknown; short and long pile mohair; soft stuffed; f.j.; BLUE and black humanized character eyes; pink floss nose, open peach felt mouth; long dangling arms and legs; long mohair on hands and feet; peach felt foot pads. A popular rabbit with huge floppy ears. The smaller *Lulac* enjoyed a long production in the 1950s and 1960s, while the larger size is rarely seen. An even larger size is known to have been made.
Courtesy Debbi Anton.

Fully jointed running rabbit: 6½"/16.5 cm. high; 6½"/16.5 cm. long; RSB; stock number unknown; mohair; e.s.; brown glass eyes; pink floss outlines nose/mouth; three pink painted claws; peach felt ear lining (indicating late 1950s); black airbrushing on ears and tail; squeaker; original blue ribbon. This *standing* fully jointed rabbit is rarer than the well known, fully jointed *Niki*; not to be confused with *Vario* that has a swivel head and jointed rear legs only.

"Town Crier," mechanical, 18"/46 cm.; mohair *Lulac* and friends out on a sunny day. Most of the Steiff store display pieces were designed to work off a main belt-line, as is this piece. A lever beneath the box moves the bell-arm up and down. One leg has a metal rod through it, up body, branching out to the arm mechanism with attached bell handle; ca. early 1970s. *Nikili* (seen elsewhere) is holding his favorite toy, a rust color velveteen elephant: 3½"/9 cm.; FF button; brown glass eyes and bone tusks, ca. 1908. *Quaggy* (duck) and *Kiki* (chicken): 4½"/12 cm.; RSB; C.T pet name; original clothing, he -- felt sailor suit; she -- cotton stripe; rubber body/legs; mohair arms and head; he -- orange felt bill; she -- plastic beak. *Quaggy* has glued-on orange felt webbed feet, ca. 1950s. Mother rabbit (11"/28 cm.) with her celluloid carriage is from 1939-40; RSB; e.s.; jointed head; cotton plush with tan cotton body; original dress/cape; rare. Baby rabbit: 6¾"/17 cm.; inc. ears; RSB; unjointed; mohair with blue cotton upper torso, felt lower body; check cotton skirt, ca. 1951. Right, 9" girl fox (see *TB & SA, Second Series*, pg. 144.) Schuco mini bears, ca. late 1960s.
Courtesy Joy Kelleher, Special Joys Museum.

Nikili rabbits: 10"/25 cm.; RSB; S.T. 725; 1950s C.T.; US-Zone tags; grey mohair; e.s.; jointed head and arms; glass eyes; twisted hard, pale pink cotton floss nose, open mouth with painted tongue; nylon whiskers; three painted claws. One of the signs of mintness are the pink airbrushed ear linings. Boy has made-to-body felt pants, girl a matching top. Note boy has a hankie matching girl's checked skirt. Both have rust color felt shoes and straw baskets. Also made in a 13½" size. There is great demand for this hard to find pair, ca. 1957. The following year Steiff changed the costume design but retained the pet name. Matched pair enhances value.
Courtesy Barbara Baldwin.

Many Teddy Bear people are now collecting rabbits. The extra large begging rabbit is a prize: 25½"/65 cm. (without ears), the largest of five sizes; RSB; S.T. 4365,2; mohair; e.s.; jointed head and arms; brown glass eyes; pink cotton floss outlines nose and (closed) mouth; FURRY NOSE as in nature; no pads; squeaker, ca. 1950s.
Courtesy Dot Franklin.

Beloved *Niki* rabbits. (L-R), 8½"/22 cm., brass button, yellow cloth S.T. 0134/22, 1952 replica made in 1985 (issue price $60.00); -- 6½"/17 cm., S.T. 5317; -- 11"/28 cm., S.T. 5328.2 -- 13½"/34 cm., S.T. 5335,2 -- 8½"/22 cm., S.T. 5322; -- replica, 11"/28 cm., S.T. 0134/28 (issue price $75.00 in 1985); -- 5½"/14 cm., S.T. 5314. All are mohair; made in either (earlier) grey and white or (later) light brown and white; excelsior stuffed and *fully jointed.* The smallest and largest are hardest to find.
Courtesy Debbi Anton.

Dressed rabbits, *Nikili:* 10"/25 cm.; RSB; S.T. 726; beige mohair with beige felt torso; e.s.; jointed head and arms; glass eyes; rose color pearl cotton nose; open felt mouth airbrushed pink; three painted claws; nylon whiskers. Girl's skirt is cotton with a separate printed scarf. Boy has the same pattern on his tie; felt vest and black felt pants; both have felt shoes and flowers at the waist. Also made in a 13½" size, ca. 1958. Rare and desirable *coordinated pair.* Courtesy Barbara Baldwin.

***Yello* and *Yella*: 8"/20.5 cm. (one size only); RSB; S.T. 8720,70 and 8720,80; C.T. with pet name; *yellow* mohair (whence name is derived); e.s.; f.j.; oversize glass eyes; floss nose/mouth; nylon whiskers. Coordinating outfits are often found on Steiff rabbits. Note the striped bow tie matching *Yella's* skirt, blue cotton top. *Yello's* pants are felt with red suspenders. As with all dressed rabbits, it is difficult to find a matched pair, ca. 1967. Mint. Courtesy Barbara Baldwin.**

Steiff Easter Rabbit with original woven basket: 10"/25 cm.; RSB; S.T. 4325; white mohair airbrushed tan and cream color, black accents on ears and at base of tail; e.s.; jointed head and arms; *oversize* brown glass eyes; twisted hard, pink cotton floss outlines nose and mouth; no claws; extra long flat feet to stand; whiskers; buckram stiffens ears. Note the *flat* back to rest the basket (green dyed trim). Shown on cover of 1967 Easter catalogue; also made in a 16" size. Extremely desirable rabbit often missing basket. Courtesy Barbara Baldwin.

Left: 18"/45.5 cm. Schuco rabbit; tan and white mohair head, long arms and feet; red/white striped cotton body; soft stuffed; jointed by bendable wire; glass eyes; pink floss nose/mouth; attached pants, ca. late 1950s. Steiff *Ango* rabbit: 18"/45 cm.; IB; S.T. 3135/45; grey and white fur imitation; soft stuffed; unjointed; brown plastic eyes; brown pearl cotton nose/mouth in outline form. Short production ca. 1977 to be replaced with other similar rabbits for children. Wicker stroller, ca. 1910.
Courtesy Laura Lee Croucher.

Wool mini bunnies - Steiff and pretenders. Four of the five long running species of Steiff are shown with three Asian counterparts, which may be distinguished by either felt or sequin bead eyes and manner of leg and tail attachment. Asian - circumferential (outside loop) stitch; Steiff invisibly tacked on. Steiff eyes are amber with black pupils except for white which has pink with red pupils. Left front: 2½"/6.5 cm. chocolate rabbit, Asian. Steiff never made all chocolate brown. Steiff Dutch rabbits, mother 3½"/9 cm.; and child 2½"/6.5 cm. Back, white Steiff child with pink eyes; grey and white Steiff mother with amber eyes; white bunny, 3"/7.5 cm., bright pink felt ears, black sequin bead eyes, painted nose, Asian. Beige and white are Steiff except 2nd from right is 3"/7.5 cm. Asian. He has felt eyes; and *bright* pink-orange felt ears. Additionally, Steiff made golden brown bunnies and in the mid 1970s fantasy colors (blue, red and yellow "Dutch" style) were available. Condition, I.D. and age affect value.
Courtesy Mary Benavente.

XIII.
ANIMALS
1910-Present

Cats & Dogs

Domestic Animals

Birds

Wild Animals

Cats and Dogs

Siamy: **4"/10 cm.; RSB; mohair; e.s.; swivel head; unique blue glass eyes (glass eyes have more depth than plastic); felt ears; twisted hard, brown cotton floss nose/mouth; three red floss claws; whiskers, ca. early 1950s. Fewer Steiff cat designs were made than dogs. Of those the most rare and desirable 1950s-60s models (in descending order) are: Siamese; Hoppel-Katze; Kalac; Snurry; Fiffy; Kitty-Cat; Tapsy; Gussy; Susi; Lizzy and Tabby (most common).**
Courtesy Barbara Baldwin.

Hoppel-Katze: **8"/20 cm. high, 11"/28 cm. long; RSB; C.T. pet name; mohair; e.s.; unjointed; because of hollow-like tummy, cat jumps up and down when pulled along; green glass cat eyes; rose floss nose/mouth; four claws; whiskers. The Velcro pads are easily detached from metal plates on axles, ca. 1968-69. This uncommon cat was sold with or without wheel frame. The canine counterpart is seen in the 1930-40 bear section. A Dralon hopping rabbit was also made.**
Courtesy Barbara Baldwin.

Collective cats come in a variety of sizes, shapes and breeds. All of the above are mohair. (L-R) front: Steiff *Kalac*; 14"/ 36 cm.; RSB; white Dralon inner ears and pads; f.j. *bright orange* plastic cat eyes. Hardest to find of the 1965 humanized series. Steiff *Kitty-Cat:* 9½"/24 cm. long; US-Zone tag; e.s.; f.j.; green enamel backed cat eyes; squeaker. Note the longer, leaner body and face and *solid Tabby marks* down back. Fechter (Austria): 5"/12 cm. long; hard stuffed; swivel head; amber glass Teddy Bear eyes; felt ears; ca. 1970. Steiff *Fluffy*: 6½"/16 cm. high; RSB; light *blue* and white fur; e.s.; swivel head; beautiful two-tone green enamel backed cat eyes; squeaker; hard to find; ca. 1950. Schuco: 8"/20 cm. high; black; unknown hard stuffed; jointed by bendable wire; green glass cat eyes; ca. 1960s. Back, Schuco Siamese: 9"/23 cm. high inc. tail; deep blue glass eyes; ca. 1950s. Steiff musical and mechanical: 7½"/19 cm. high; RSB; e.s.; swivel head; pale green glass eyes. *Brahm's Lullaby* plays when music box is wound by key inside the base of tail. As it plays, the tail rotates; extremely rare and desirable, ca. 1950s. Schuco Skier: 10"/25 cm.; poseable by bendable wire in limbs *and* tail; B&W googly glass eyes; felt tongue; original ski poles and finely crafted wooden skis (12½"), each marked with a red and gold round seal in German. Similar skis were used for the Steiff rabbit *Rico*. The tail is tied in a knot like the popular German TV cat *Koko*, ca. 1960s. English: 5½"/14 cm. long; e.s.; swivel head; external wire joints each leg; *rose* glass eyes; felt ears; squeaker. Note the comic design with spherical head and broad smile, ca. 1930s. Kersa: 10½"/26 cm. standing; boots are bright coral felt; hard stuffed; f.j.; emerald green glass googly eyes; ca. 1960s. This model is more common in black.

The wonderful face and pick-me-up look of Tabby cat: 7½"/19 cm. high, 9"/ 23 cm. long (plus 5" tail); FF button; white (1908-26) S.T. 5322; lovely shades of pale grey and cream color mohair; e.s.; fully jointed including *jointed tail*; yellow-green glass cat eyes; twisted hard, dark pink cotton floss nose/mouth; *four* claws; no pads; working squeaker. A cat with a *white* stock tag is *rare.* Mint.
Private Collection.

Stylized cat: 8½"/21.6 cm. high, 10"/25.4 cm. long (without tail); long blond mohair; swivel head; unusual black INSET eyes; painted nose/mouth on sculpted snout; velveteen lined ears; pre-WWII tag on belly, "Merrythought Hygienic Toys Made in England."

FAO Schwarz exclusive, attached cats on a 24" felt blanket: Mama *Fiffy* cat, 12"/30.5 cm. long, RSB, swivel head with her non-jointed Tabby Kittens; (L-R), lying outstretched, 3"/7.6 cm., RSB; *curled* (highly unusual position), 2¾"/7 cm., RSB and standing, 2¾"/7 cm., RSB. The outstretched and curled pets are not available individually. Rare set made in limited numbers, ca. 1950s.
Courtesy Barbara Baldwin.

Trio made by Schenker, Austria. Cat: 10½"/27 cm. long not inc. tail; tagged; squirrel fur body; hard stuffed wool; f.j.; green glass cat eyes; pink floss nose/mouth; horsehair whiskers (what one calls nylon filament whiskers often are horsehair); buckskin pads; cute cat, ca. 1950s. Bear of brown caracul fur: 16"/40.6 cm.; ear tag; f.j.; amber glass eyes; floss nose; open red leather mouth and tongue; leather pads; growler, ca. 1950s. Spaniel puppy of goat fur with sheepskin ears: 8"/20 cm. high; unjointed; brown glass eyes; molded plastic nose; open felt mouth and tongue; red plastic collar, ca. 1970s. Limited demand for toys made from real fur.

Dachshund: 5"/13 cm. high, 12"/30 cm., long; FF button; *white* S.T. 6217; mohair coat-type fabric (brennessel) covering; striking black markings; e.s.; f.j.; shoe button eyes; twisted hard, cotton floss nose/mouth; no claws or pads. Rare Dachshund example. Courtesy Carolyn McMaster.

Steiff felt puppy: 7"/18 cm.; FF button; e.s.; unjointed; shoe button eyes; twisted hard, black cotton floss nose/mouth. This pearl cotton has not changed over the years. Note the complex patterning of the inquisitive pup, ca. 1913. The supply of early felt toys in *excellent condition* can never equal the demand. Courtesy Harriet Purtill.

Old Pug: 9½"/24 cm. high, 13"/33 cm. long; FF button; coat-type fabric (brennessel); long mohair on chest and forepaws only; e.s.; f.j.; shoe button eyes; pearl cotton nose/mouth and three claws; original collar. Also sold with leather muzzle and/or blanket, ca. 1908-20. Note the proper pug wrinkles painted on the wistful face; desirable. "Mama's Little Doggy": 6"/15 cm. seated; e.s.; wag tail to move head from side to side (180°); off-white short bristle mohair with silky long brown mohair tail and felt lined ears; e.s.; glass eyes; pearl cotton nose/mouth. Unknown maker, ca. 1925. Courtesy Mary Benavente.

King Charles Spaniel: 8½"/22 cm. high, 11"/28 cm. long; FF button; long pile curly mohair; e.s.; f.j.; glass eyes; rust color, twisted hard cotton floss nose/mouth; three claws. Also made in 6½" and 11½" high sizes and with black markings. This Spaniel is a popularly depicted breed of the late Victorian era often sculpted in porcelain and seen in Victorian paintings of dogs. The *desirable full jointing* enables a playful stance resembling a real dog. Mint and rare, ca. 1913. Private Collection.

Treff, Steiff Blood Hounds: left, 6"/15cm.; center, 12"/30.5 cm.; right, 4"/10 cm.; FF buttons; red S.T.; 6" has watermelon mouth C.T. with pet name; all are tan mohair; e.s.; have swivel heads; brown glass eyes attached beneath slits in fur covering; twisted hard, black cotton floss nose/sewn closed mouth; three floss claws. The largest has *oversize* convex eyes giving a great face to this *very rare* size. Though made in a number of sizes and positions from 1928-1938, all are elusive models to collectors of early dogs. *Treff* was designed to compete with the English *Dismal Desmond*.
Courtesy Barbara Baldwin.

Rare character dog, left: 4½"/12 cm. high; FF button; greyish mohair; e.s.; swivel head; B&W googly glass eyes; pearl cotton nose in downward points; felt mouth; three stitched claws, ca. 1920-30. *Rattler*, center: 4"/10 cm. high; cream color mohair; e.s.; internally jointed by wire, tail moves head in a circular motion; humanized brown glass eyes; stitched nose/mouth; no claws. No I.D. but self-recognizable as *Rattler* with the whiskers unique to this rare and appealing dog. Made in eight sizes, ca. 1932. *Foxy* with the BLACK markings found only before 1940: 4"/10 cm. high; watermelon C.T. with pet name; mohair; e.s.; swivel head; amber glass eyes; stitched nose/mouth, no claws; original bell, ca. 1930s. Desirable.
Courtesy Barbara Baldwin.

Steiff *grey* Scotty: 8"/20 cm. high, 12"/30 cm. long; FF button; dense mohair with a tweed-like appearance; e.s.; swivel head; *large* amber glass eyes; twisted hard, black cotton floss nose/mouth; three rose color floss claws; working squeaker. Two FF buttons rivet the unusual white leather collar with a cutout design; original bell, ca. 1930s. Rare color and desirable animal.
Courtesy Barbara Baldwin.

Watermelon C.T. with "Scotty" in red (brown) ink with unusual inscription, "Int. Pat. appld. for," pre-1950 (1934-50). The woolly plush used on the 3"/8 cm. dog indicates 1940s when this fur covering is most often found. A woolly Scotty is a rarity. This miniature's C.T. is a tad frayed. Those skilled in the techniques of library work and bookbinding can easily repair frayed, torn and soiled paper tags.
Courtesy Laurie Hix.

Steiff Terrier: 10"/25 cm. long; FF button; brown tipped medium pile (½") mohair body. The snout, ears and feet are solid brown mohair; e.s.; swivel head only; amber glass eyes; twisted hard, black cotton floss nose/mouth; squeaker; black leather collar; near mint, ca. 1930. Pre-1940 animals are in great demand.

Clockwise: Peky: 5½"/14 cm. high, 7"/18 cm. long; RSB; C.T. *Peky*; mohair coat in vivid colors; e.s.; swivel head; common but beautiful, ca. 1950s. The homemade collar embroidered "Rags" suits the 7½"/19 cm. high, 11"/28 cm. long mutt; FF button; mohair; unjointed; pre-1940. Airedale Terrier on wooden wheels: 14"/36 cm. high, 17"/43 cm. long; FF button; mohair; great face, ca. 1939-40. *Tessie* Schnauzer: 10½"/27 cm. high, 13½"/34 cm. long; mohair e.s. swivel head; humanized oval eyes; rare large size, but less demand for the breed, ca. 1958-on. *Biggie*: 7"/18 cm. high *sitting*; IB; S.T. 4090/18; C.T. pet name; mohair; e.s.; swivel head; round glass eyes; original collar; also made in a 4"/10 cm. size ca. 1965-71.
Courtesy Cynthia's Country Store.

Posey Pet dog: 8"/20 cm. high, 11½"/29 cm. long; cotton plush; soft stuffed; unjointed; black plastic eyes, black felt "petal" eyelashes; brown felt sewn-on nose/ decorative brown tail in a cluster of felt posy petals sewn together; tagged, "*Posey Pet*, Madame Alexander, New York USA," ca. 1942-43. *Posey Pet* is the popular name for Alexander stuffed animals. They can be found without posies. Madame also made oilcloth animals, ca. 1942. These are almost always found without tags and must be identified from catalogues. A horse, lamb and cat are the most common.
Courtesy Nan C. Moorehead.

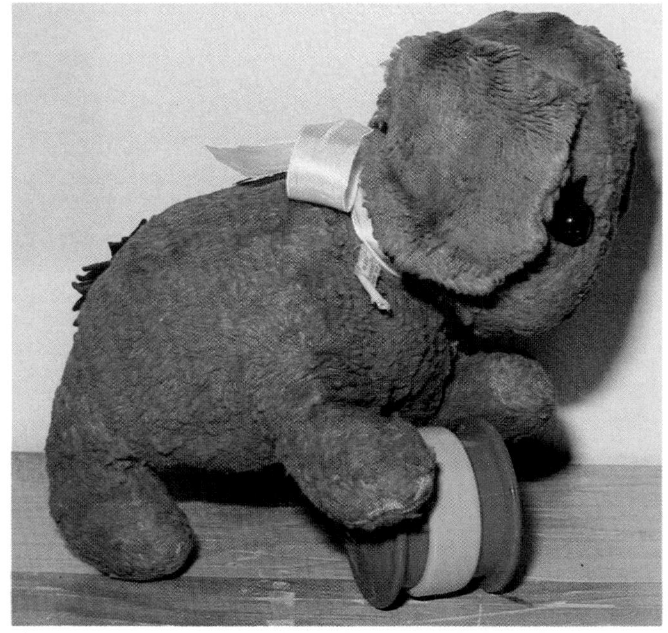

STUDIO mohair *Arco*: 34"/86 cm. high, 37"/94 cm. long; oversize RSB; e.s.; swivel head; glass eyes; twisted hard, heavy floss nose; open felt mouth with painted teeth; long felt tongue; three stitched claws. Handsome and mint, ca. 1950s. *Snobby-Lac* is 36"/91 cm.; large RSB; *handwritten* stock tag number (often found in early 1950s); all mohair with poodle cut pompons on head, paws and tail; e.s.; f.j.; large glass eyes; leather nose; no claws. Rare color and size.
Courtesy Barbara Baldwin.

Dogs in the park. All are mohair; e.s.; unjointed; have glass eyes; pearl cotton nose/mouth. Front, *Fellow*: 8½"/22 cm. high; FF button; white S.T.; watermelon C.T. pet name; original leather collar. The first Airedales were called *Fellow*. In the 1940s the pet name was changed to *Terry*. Left rear, *Terry*: 13½"/35 cm. high; FF button; yellow S.T. 1334,02; US-Zone tag; squeaker. Center, 11"/28 cm. high; no button; C.T. *Terry*; US-Zone tag. The two rarest and largest of six sizes. Right, *Foxy*: 13½"/35 cm.; *Foxy* and *Terry* share the same pattern in different colors. Private Collection.

Chows: left, standing: 4¾"/12 cm. high, 5"/13 cm. long; buff color (maize). Right, sitting: 4"/10 cm. high; white. Both have RSB; S.T. 1512 and 3510; C.T. *Chow*; bushy wool plush; e.s.; unjointed; brown glass eyes; stitched nose/mouth (painted red highlight); three painted red claws; no pads; velvet ears tinted pink; velvet faces; curled tails; ca. 1956. The original pink bow is stitched to side of white dog (also catalogued as *Pomeranian*). The standing buff Chow is more common than the white, which is rare.
Courtesy Elaine Lehn.

Hermann Chow or Husky: a solid little dog, 4½"/11 cm. high, 3½"/9 cm. long; bristly wool plush with a peach cast; airbrushed *felt* snout; *felt* ears. His removable harness (with buckle) is red plastic with chrome studs; C.T. "Hermann Teddy Original." The Steiff Chow is more slender. Purchased in 1961 by owner at the Hermann Exhibit at the Chicago Trade Fair.
Courtesy Mary Benavente.

Cockie: 11"/28 cm. high, 13"/33 cm. long; RSB; S.T. 1328,0; luxurious long pile cream color mohair with brown markings, short pile mohair snout; glass eyes; twisted hard, black cotton floss nose in contoured downward points; three stitched claws; squeaker. Also made in 4½" and 6½"size, ca. 1951-57. This largest size is hard to find, but demand is limited.
Courtesy Dave and Ann Abbott.

Butch, the Cover Dog: 6"/15 cm. high, 7½"/19 cm. long; no button or S.T.; C.T., "Butch, the Cover Dog, Copyright by Albert Staehle," signed by the artist. Butch was a *Saturday Evening Post* cover dog, appearing quite a few times, drawn by Albert Staehle before 1956. He is mohair; has a swivel head; doleful bulbous glass eyes; no voice box; a variant of the *Cockie* mold but elevated to celebrity status by his chest tag.
Courtesy Chris Irons.

Maidy: 12"/30.5 cm. high, 10"/25 cm. long plus 2"/5 cm. tail; RSB; S.T. 1330,06; C.T. with pet name; curly Persian wool plush; e.s.; *unjointed*; brown and white glass humanized eyes; twisted hard, black cotton floss nose, pink floss mouth and three claws; no pads. Short production, 1959 *only*; also made in 10" size; both are hard to find. The jointed *Snobby* mohair poodle was heavily produced.
Courtesy Debbi Anton.

German Shepherd: 4"/9 cm. high, 5"/13 cm. long; RSB; RED CHEST TAG (*Arco* in red printing); brown mohair and velveteen face, felt ears; e.s.; unjointed; tiny glass eyes; twisted floss nose/mouth. Closely resembles a wolf cub, ca. 1953-57. Value is enhanced by the "Red Chest Tag." The rarest *Arcos* are standing (any size) *without* the tongue; second rarest is this 4" with velveteen snout. Brown is more rare than grey in a velvet nose. Lying *Arcos* are the most common. Extremely rare sitting *Arcos* were made, ca. 1930.
Courtesy Elaine Lehn.

Sitting Boxers: 4"/10 cm. and 5½"/14 cm.; *small*, RSB, S.T. 3310, C.T. *Sarras* in *desirable* RED PRINT (often found in conjunction with US-Zone tag); *large*, US-Zone tag. Both are mohair; e.s.; have swivel head; glass eyes; floss noses; three painted claws. Large has mohair jowls with black velveteen chin and mohair ears lined with velveteen; small has velveteen jowls/chin and felt ears; detailed faces. Boxers are plentiful. Collectors find them early in their collecting career. The sitting position is harder to find than standing.
Courtesy Elaine Lehn.

St. Bernards: standing, 4"/10 cm. high (1950s) and sitting 5"/13 cm. high (1960s); RSB; S.T. 1310 and 3312; C.T. standing "St. Bernard" (if present); C.T. sitting *Bernie*. Both are mohair; e.s.; unjointed; have glass eyes; three painted claws; no pads; black floss noses; standing -- floss mouth; sitting -- painted mouth. Note the huge eyes framed with black airbrushing giving *Bernie* a sweet expression. The 1950s 5½" and 8½" standing (not shown) are extremely rare. Even *Bernie* with keg is easier to find. The 1960s sitting model was also made in a more rare 8½" size. This 4" standing is easiest to find, but none are common and ALL are desirable. The lying St. Bernard Racker animal is a true rarity.
Courtesy Elaine Lehn.

Foxy: sitting, 4"/10 cm. and 5½"/14 cm. high; standing, 6½"/16 cm. high, 7"/18 cm. long; all have RSB; large sitting has US-Zone tag; all are mohair (small sitting has felt ears); e.s.; unjointed; have brown glass eyes; twisted hard, black cotton floss nose/mouth accented by pink airbrushing; standing has three stitched claws; sitting have three painted claws; standing has a squeaker; all have ears sewn down; small has pink ribbon; other two have collars; sitting (1945-52) are scarce; standing (1958-on) is common. Any pedigree Steiff toy under $100.00 is desirable.
Courtesy Elaine Lehn.

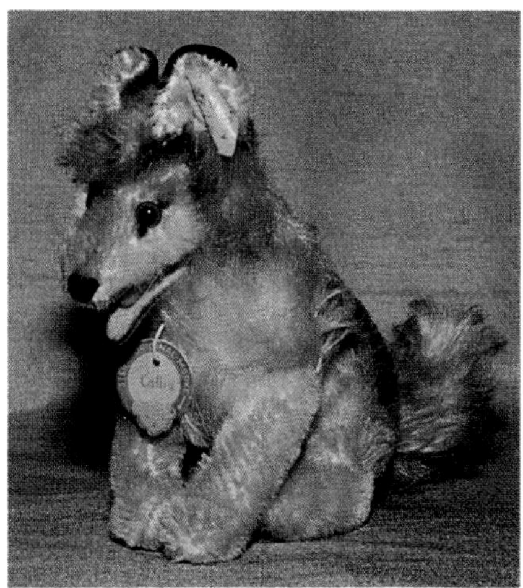

**Sitting Collie: 4"/10 cm. high; RSB; S.T. 3312; C.T. *Collie*; mohair with black velveteen backed ears; e.s.; unjointed; glass eyes; black *felt* nose; felt open mouth and tongue; no claws or pads, ca. 1960s. Lying Collies are common, especially the small one. Sitting Collies are harder to find; small sitting is the most desirable. Generally, the smallest size of any given animal is the most popular.
Courtesy Elaine Lehn.**

**Beagles: small, 4"/10 cm. high, 4½"/11.4 cm. long; medium, 6½"/17 cm. high, 7½"/19 cm. long; RSB; S.T. 1317 and 1310; C.T. *Biggie* and *Beagle Biggie* attached to red leather collars; both are mohair; e.s.; unjointed; have *humanized glass eyes*; floss nose/mouth; small, three painted claws; medium, three stitched claws; medium has squeaker, ca. 1958-60. Also made in 10" size. The 4" Beagle sold for $2.25 in 1960. Should be popular with Snoopy fans.
Courtesy Elaine Lehn.**

**Basset Hounds: 8½"/22 cm.; 6"/15 cm.; 5"/12.5 cm.; mohair; e.s.; largest and smallest have swivel heads; medium is unjointed; plastic googly eyes (smallest's are sparkly); floss noses, painted mouths; the largest has stitched claws; smallest two have painted claws; only large has squeaker; 1961-69. The 5" size is the most desirable followed by the 6" size. Although he has a wonderful expression, the 8½" size is not as popular.
Courtesy Elaine Lehn.**

***Rolly* Dalmatian: 4"/10 cm. high, 5"/12.5 cm. long; RSB; C.T. "Rolly, Cop. Walt Disney Productions," made for *101 Dalmatians;* mohair; e.s.; unjointed; plastic googly eyes; floss nose; painted mouth; three painted claws; red leather collar; silly expression; also made in 7" size, ca. 1960s. Some of the most rare and desirable 1950-60s dogs (in descending order) are: *Rolly* (very rare); Sealyham; *Hoppel-dackel*; *Sulac*; *Laika* spacedog; 5½" and 8½" standing St. Bernard; sitting *Foxy*; 10" *Molly*; *Maidy*; Scotty (especially larger sizes); *Bernie* with keg; *Corso*; standing *Arco* without tongue; 4" velvet nosed *Arco*; and sitting white Pomeranian.
Courtesy Elaine Lehn.**

Doby Doberman standing proud and tall: 23"/58 cm.; finest synthetic plush; hard stuffed with shredded polyurethane; plastic eyes and nose; choke chain; sure to win "Best of Show." Lifelike and high quality; short production by Dakin. 1984-85; issue price, $40.00. Certain Dakin animals from this period should not be ignored.

Dismal Desmond: 9½"/23 cm. high, 10"/25 cm. long (not inc. tail); printed with Dean's trademark (a bulldog and terrier tugging at a rag book) on back of neck; hand tag, "I'm Dismal Desmond// a Howling Success//First Produced in 1926; (reverse) Dean's Dismal Desmond//he became a household name// A faithful reproduction of the most famous soft toy of his time. First produced in 1926 -- the creation of Richard Ellett//Dean's Tag Book Co. Ltd.//Rye, Sussex, England." Printed cotton flannel, red felt tongue; originally made in volumes and in various sizes (both sitting and standing) for ten years. This reproduction was issued in 1987 at $22.00 retail. In 1988 Dean's was bought out. The old stock is interesting and collectible.

Domestic Animals

Pig: 10"/25 cm. high, 14"/35.5 cm. long; *tiny* FF button; white mohair; e.s.; unjointed; blue glass eyes; flesh color *mesh* nose; felt pads. The bellows voice box produces an "oinker" sound, ca. 1924. Desirable.
Courtesy Barbara Baldwin.

Holstein cow with great appeal creating demand: 25½"/65 cm. high, 37"/94 cm. long; RSB; S.T. 520/1365,90; black and white mohair; excelsior stuffed over steel frame; unjointed; blown milk glass eyes/brown pupil; leather horns and hoofs; felt udder. Original leather collar with cow bell shows European influence. A 12" high baby with open mouth completed the set, ca. 1955. Steiff made no other mohair Holstein cows in smaller sizes.
Courtesy Michelle Daunton.

Oxy: 8½"/22 cm. high, 11"/28 cm. long; RSB; S.T. 1322,02; silky tan mohair; unjointed; B&W googly glass eyes; light tan velveteen nose and mouth; airbrushed hoofs; squeaker (found in the larger sizes of any given Steiff animal); sold without ribbon and bell which have been added. Limited production ca. 1958. Also available in 4" (with braided rope tail) and 5½" high sizes. This largest is extremely rare.
Courtesy Beth Savino, Hobby Center Toys.

Tassel-ended tail looks ready to switch through the air. European comic character cow: 15"/38 cm. x 15"/38 cm.; tan and white mohair over wood composition; f.j.; brown felt horns; *pie-shaped* felt eyes; formed nostrils; open mouth/red felt tongue; pink felt hoofs and udder. Unknown maker, ca. 1940-50.
Courtesy Nan C. Moorehead.

Purists want the old Steiff from the 1950s heyday such as lying *Lamby*: 3½"/9 cm. high, 4½"/11 cm. long; RSB; C.T. pet name; woolly plush; e.s.; unjointed; green glass cat eyes; floss nose/mouth; no claws; original pink ribbon and bell; sweet baby face. Extremely rare only in this smallest lying size.
Courtesy Elaine Lehn.

Lying *Zicky* goats are among the most rare Steiff animals: left, 4½"/11 cm. high, 5½"/14 cm. long; right, 3½"/9 cm. high, 4"/10 cm. long; RSB; S.T. 2314 and 2310; both are mohair; e.s.; unjointed; have green glass cat eyes; brown floss nose/red airbrushing; floss mouth; felt under tail. Large has felt lined mohair ears; tiny wood horns. Small has felt ears; no horns. Short production, ca early 1950s. Standing *Zicky* is easily found; only the largest (9" and 14") are scarce.
Courtesy Elaine Lehn.

Flock: Left, *Lamby*, 8½"/21.6 cm. high; RSB; S.T. 6522,04; wool plush; airbrushed with yellow (especially fugitive) and brown; e.s.; metal armature in legs; green plastic eyes; red twisted floss nose/mouth; the middle of five sizes, ca. 1960s; missing bell and blue ribbon (the largest size, 13½"/35 cm. had a pink ribbon). Center: *Cosy Lamb*, 8½"/21.6 cm; S.T. 5140/22; long and short Dralon with yellow markings; stuffed with synthetic fiber; green plastic eyes; pink velveteen ear linings and open mouth/painted tongue; made 1969-77. Right: *Locky*, 8½"/21.6 cm.; incised brass button; S.T. 3450/22; washable acrylic, ca. 1980-82.
Courtesy Dave and Ann Abbott.

STUDIO Baby Boar: 12"/30 cm. high, 24"/61 cm. long; RSB; mohair with spotting done by a resist method; e.s.; unjointed; brown glass eyes; snout is 6" long; tan felt nose, painted nostrils; peach felt open mouth, brown mohair lower jaw; ca. 1960s. Most STUDIO animals are costly, although demand is limited. Mohair Baby Boar: 5½"/14 cm. long; blue eyes; tan felt ears and nose; ca. 1970.

The sweet face of Steiff's desirable MOHAIR donkey: 8½"/22 cm. high, 10½"/27 cm. long; RSB; S.T. 1322,0; e.s.; black glass eyes; painted nose/mouth; short black horsehair mane; black mohair ruff on tail; leather bridle; also made in 5" and 11" size, ca. 1958. The open pink felt mouth and life-like contouring, usually found only on STUDIO animals, set this horse apart: 8½"/22 cm. high, 9"/23 cm. long; RSB; S.T. 1322,0; C.T. "Original Steiff," mohair; amber glass eyes; painted nose and hoofs; gold horsehair mane and tail; also made in 11" and 13½" size, ca. 1958. New pattern for Panda: 5½"/14 cm.; mohair with inset chest plate; f.j.; amber plastic eyes/black felt backing; stitched nose/mouth; *white cloth* S.T. 0218/14, L.ED. 1,000 pcs; hand numbered C.T. in Steiff colors, "Hobby Center Toys 1988 Mohair Panda." Sold out immediately at $60.00. It was the lowest number of a small Steiff piece ever done until the 9"/23 cm. black mohair bear (320 made) for the 1989 UFDC Convention in St. Louis.

Velveteen colt: 5½"/14 cm. high, 6"/15 cm. long; RSB; C.T. "Original Steiff"; e.s.; unjointed; glass eyes; painted nose and mouth; white felt ears tinted pink; mohair mane and tail. An 11" mohair colt was also made, ca. 1957. Hard to find in excellent condition but limited demand.
Courtesy Elaine Lehn.

The full spectrum of mohair *Flossy* from the 1960s and early 1970s: lengths, 5"/12.5 cm.; 11"/28 cm.; 26"/66 cm.; C.T. with pet name; (see *TB & SA*, pg. 255 for description). Only the large fish has excelsior (mixed with soft stuffing). Of special interest is the yellow and brown *tiger striped* fish discontinued at an early date, rare in all sizes. The smallest size of the orange and blue fish (scale pattern) is the most common. Earlier *Flossies* had a rounder head, later ones are more triangular (narrow) with eyes set lower and wider to give a surprised expression. Later orange fish can be almost red. The only mohair *Flossy* missing from group is the elusive 30" long blue Riding Fish, ca. 1971.
Courtesy Idele Gilbert.

Cosy Flossy and small wood fish lurk in the crevices of a fossil grotto. Grouper: 10"/25 cm. high; brass button; cloth S.T. 5285/25; pea green plush; felt fins; yellow plastic eyes. Also made in royal blue as well as a 6¼"/16 cm. size, ca. 1982. The wool minis come in two sizes. The earlier (1967) Coral Fish are 2"/5 cm.; have plastic fins; *amber* plastic eyes; made in five colors (green not shown). The larger Angel Fish are 4½/10 cm.; have thick brown felt fins; *yellow* plastic eyes; came in five colors (red not shown) ca. 1977. They are less compact than the 1960s model.
Courtesy Mary Benevente

Flora Cow, with impeccable Holstein markings, rolls her plastic eyes in surprise: 7¾"/20 cm. high, 11"/28 cm. long; IB; S.T. 3916/20. Trevira velvet; polyurethane foam stuffed; soft felt horns; Dralon topknot, ear linings and tail ruff; bell and leather collar. Made 1978 only; these artistic Trevira velvet animals should not be overlooked; already rare. In 1982 another Flora Cow appeared: 10"; tan woven fur and box-like frame.
Courtesy Mary Benavente.

Birds

Parrot with jointed legs: 9"/23 cm. high, 14"/35.5 cm. long; mohair; e.s.; white felt accents the black shoe button eyes; beige felt beak and feet/wire armature; original bell with remnant of turquoise ribbon sewn to chest. The high quality maker is unknown, ca. 1920. Demand is surging for fine stuffed toys from the pre 1930s era.
Courtesy Idele Gilbert.

"Bug in Trouble." Left, 9½"/24 cm. high; rose mohair; Gund-type eyes (metal backing with amber celluloid over movable black discs); felt bill and tops of feet; ca. 1930s. Chicken: 10½"/26 cm.; wool pile; soft stuffed; black glass eyes; felt comb and beak; green felt boots and hat/red feather, ca. 1950s. Wind-up baby chick; yellow mohair; metal beak and legs; key is imprinted "Schuco"; when wound he hops around and pecks the ground. Shown in 1937 catalogue. Mechanism works sluggishly; if in perfect working order, double price. If non-working, a mechanical is almost worthless. Duckling: 5"/12 cm.; Steiff IB on left wing; short mohair; black plastic eyes; felt bill and feet; brown felt tail, ca. late 1960s. Schuco Lady Bug: 1¾"/4 cm.; mohair and felt; pipe cleaner legs and feelers; no eyes, ca. 1950-60.

Larger sizes of known models. Of special interest is the FAO Schwarz Special: 7"/17 cm. high seated Cockie; RSB; C.T. *Revue Susi*; S.T. 3317.06; B&W mohair; swivel head; B&W glass eyes; pearl cotton nose; squeaker; Schwarz wooden tag. Original to dog, the flowers in hair are tied with a pink satin bow to a staple; in great demand. Peggy penguin: 20"/51 cm.; mohair; swivel head; brown glass eyes; The beak is red felt with yellow felt accents (found on the larger sizes); squeaker; beautiful penguin markings. Unusual size but little demand. Bessy: 10"/25 cm. high, 12"/30 cm. long; RSB; S.T. 1325,0; leather collar; cow bell. These trimmings are important for full value. Also made in a 5" and 6½" size. This rare largest size shows off her great cow belly, ca. 1958. Childhood toys of Candice Feldstein.

Steiff mohair birds with movable wings: 4"/10 cm. high; RSB; C.T. "Original Steiff." Left, Finch; S.T. 622/6310,03; red face, black head, lt. tan chest, brown back. Right, Bluebonnet; S.T. 622/6310,04; yellow chest, blue and green wings and back. Both have black glass eyes; plastic covered wire legs that when moved rotate the opposite (horsehair) wing. In 1957-59 also available in a Bullfinch with black wings and a red chest. Hard to find and desirable.
Courtesy Idele Gilbert.

Mohair birds with pink plastic feet and beaks; velveteen wings and tails: 4"/10 cm. high. Left to right: Sparrow, RSB, S.T. 2540/10; brown/black glass eyes; Goldfinch, RSB, S.T. 2546/10; black plastic eyes; Titmouse, S.T. 2542/10; black plastic eyes; Bullfinch, RSB; S.T. 2544/10; pink Dralon chest, black and grey mohair back and head; black plastic eyes. The complete set from 1969.
Courtesy Idele Gilbert.

Ballbody chickens: 4"/10 cm. and 6½"/17 cm. high; RSB; S.T. 3310/3314; mohair; supersoft stuffing; unjointed; black glass bead eyes; yellow plastic beak; orange felt legs/feet and combs; squeakers, ca. 1957-61. A popular Easter toy, common in the standing position, much harder to find in this sitting posture. Wooden Birdhouse; RSB; S.T. 7807,40; perch and opening for a wool mini bird; ca. late 1950s, early 1960s. In 1971 Steiff made the more common birdhouse *bank*.
Courtesy Debbi Anton.

Wool plush duckling: 5½"/14 cm.; RSB; S.T. 6514; yellow with dark grey highlights; e.s.; unjointed; black bead eyes/red felt backing; felt beak and webbed feet. Steiff used this woolly plush on several animals during the late 1940s, early 1950s. Uncommon but limited demand.
Courtesy Elaine Lehn.

STUDIO Macaw, a regal bird with blue and gold feather design. A wonderful display piece for any decor; larger than life size: 12"/30.5 cm. high, 36"/90 cm. long; RSB; S.T. 1345;90; mohair; e.s.; green plastic eyes rimmed in black; rubber beak; felt feet with wire armature; the mohair wings and tail cover a cardboard form, ca. early 1960s. Rare.
Courtesy Debbi Anton.

STUDIO Turkey: 30"/76 cm.; RSB; tail is all multicolored mohair; head is molded out of soft rubber (not PVC). There is no mohair on the head and it is removable; e.s.; glass eyes; felt feet, ca. 1967. Rare pieces are always in demand. Turkeys are popular with topical collectors.
Courtesy Michelle Daunton.

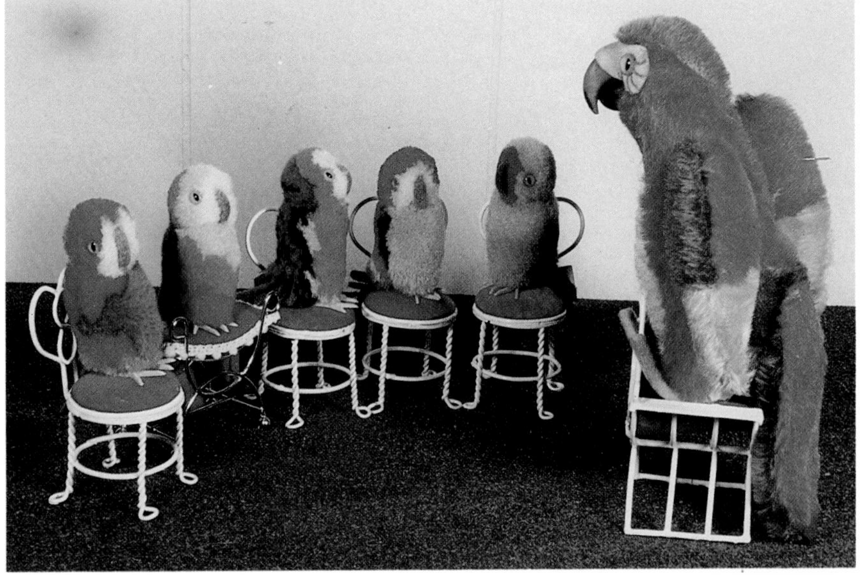

***Lora* directs a symphony of color and song (*Lora* is a female parrot in Spanish). The directress is 5"/12.7 cm. high and mohair. The *perricos* are 2½"/6.4 cm. high; have green plastic cat eyes; thick felt beaks and tails; two-toed plastic feet. This is the complete set of wool minis, ca. 1975. A wool parrot mobile was also made.**
Courtesy Mary Benavente.

***Valentine Bird* and her court, Steiff *Cheerup Birds.* She reigns on her special day surrounded by blue and yellow Cardinals. All are 3½"/9 cm.; S.T. 1509; wool; have glass eyes; felt beak, combs and *plumed* tail; plastic feet (giving poor balance). Small (1½") birds are more scarce, however, this model is never common. The red is most abundant; a *green Cheerup Bird* is the most elusive; ca. late 1950s; discontinued ca. 1967. Posed with tiny Steiff ladybugs and Flower Fairies card from Norcross, 1955.**
Courtesy Mary Benavente.

The rarest of the Steiff wool miniature *Cheerup Birds* in his malachite bathtub. The green mini has come to be called the *St. Patrick's Bird:* 3½"/9 cm.; distinguishing plumed tail; metal feet (one of the earliest), ca. 1958.
Courtesy Mary Benavente.

Pigeon and spring peeps on a park bench. Hard to find wool Pigeon: 2½"/6 cm.; RSB; S.T. 892/506,40; blue felt fanned tail; plastic feet (earlier versions had white metal feet allowing them to stand securely); ca. 1958-1977. Yellow green birds (bottom): 3¼"/ 8 cm.; less dense body and brighter colors (1970s) and 1½"/4 cm. from 1960s. Atop lamp post: 3¼"/8 cm. older version, compact pompon body in muted colors; metal feet. Yellow/blue birds are shown in the large 3¼" size with metal feet having the 1950s compact body and again in 1½" baby with plastic feet, ca. 1960s.
Courtesy Mary Benavente.

Sporting frilly wings and black felt feet, the wool swans appeared in the 1964 Easter catalogue: 3¼"/ 8 cm.; RSB; S.T. 899/4508, 46; same series as wool miniature duck and goose; discontinued 1969. Rare. Hallmark lacy Valentines from 1955-56.
Courtesy Mary Benavente.

A vision in pink. Angel winged STUDIO *Starli* Cockatoo guards her egg: 18"/ 45.5 cm. long inc. tail; incised brass button; S.T. 2545/30; red STUDIO C.T; Dralon delicately airbrushed with pink; Pellon crest. Limited demand for this hard to find bird from 1981-84. Personal name: "Ofelia" - likes to wear her owner's jewelry and has her own pink taffeta skirt.
Courtesy Mary Benavente.

Wild Animals

Steiff elephant: 12"/30.5 cm. high; blank button; *white* S.T. 5217; short pile grey mohair; e.s.; f.j.; shoe button eyes; felt tusks; smaller, full cut ears as found on the Asian elephant; twisted hard, black cotton floss sewn around base of feet to denote toes (important to an elephant because they walk on their toes), ca. 1908. Animals before 1912 bring premium prices.
Courtesy Barbara Baldwin.

Sly Fox: 7"/18 cm. high, 10"/25 cm. long plus 5"/13 cm. tail; FF button; luxurious mohair; e.s.; f.j.; glass eyes; stitched nose/mouth (note: downward points were also made by other companies); three claws; no pads; squeaker; one of three sizes, ca. 1910-25. Mint, fully jointed animals from the early period are scarce. In 1989, Steiff issued this forest creature as a Museum Replica (4¾" high) limited to 4,000 worldwide; retail, $150.00.

Fully jointed Steiff squirrel from the 1920s: 7½"/19 cm.; orange and white mohair; e.s.; glass eyes; twisted hard, black cotton floss nose/mouth; three black floss claws; squeaker. Note the *long* feet and bushy tail. Rare animal to find fully jointed. The color, jointing, age and mint condition create great demand.
Courtesy Beth Savino, Hobby Center Toys.

Steiff *Snake*: 10ft./3.05 m. long; mohair; contains a wire armature (can be posed to stand in "attack position" or to lie flat); glass eyes; open felt mouth with two bone teeth. The colors differ from *Snaky* puppet which is primarily done in greens. The *Snake* is airbrushed in oranges, coral, purples and rose. The *Snake* was costly to produce. Records show only a few were made, ca. late 1950s.
Courtesy Barbara Baldwin.

Rare striped monkey, *Jocko* type: 11"/28 cm.; FF button; RED S.T. 9/5318; brown and gold overall *striped* mohair; e.s.; f.j.; felt face with painted features; brown glass eyes; mint. The body, arms and legs are slender, ca. 1926-34. Advanced collectors look for color variations of a standard animal.

Roly Poly squirrel: 4"/10 cm.; green wooden base is 3"/7.5 cm. diam.; bushy mohair ears and tail; hard stuffed cotton; black glass bead eyes; black stitched nose/mouth; holding velveteen nut. Other rare Roly Poly animals shown in the 1937 Steiff catalogue are: rabbit, cat, dog, and fox. Unusual to find an older velveteen piece in mint condition. Courtesy Debbi Anton.

Deer family, (L-R): 6"/15 cm. long; STEIFF button, block capitals not underlined (found just after WWII, sometimes in conjunction with US-Zone tag; *woolly plush* (the baby spots are done by a resist method); black glass eyes; pearl cotton nose/mouth; ca. 1940s. Lying fawn: 16"/40 cm. long; RSB; S.T. 2335; mohair; Dralon chest and ear lining; successful design, ca. 1960. Male deer: 11"/28 cm. long; no I.D.; *flat wool plush*; stitched felt antlers; ca. early 1950s. Deer: 7¾"/20 cm. long; short mohair with seamed velveteen legs (at one time a perfect match, now mohair is faded); *squeaker*. If I.D. were present it would be FF button/yellow S.T. (1934-50). Roe: 12"/30 cm. long; C.T. "Original Steiff"; mohair; black *plastic* eyes; ca. 1960s. Fawn: 5½"/14 cm. long; RSB; spotted mohair; ca. 1950s. All six deer are excelsior stuffed and have a horizontal "shine" stitch on nose. Courtesy Vivienne Roche.

The rarest of Steiff fishes, the slender bodied Trout with a Mona Lisa smile accompanies *Cosy Sigi* the seahorse shown with a sequinned shell purse. Trout: 15"/38 cm.; non-durable rayon cotton plush in shades of turquoise, blue and purple; turquoise felt fins and tail; glass Teddy Bear eyes; made in 1948 only. *Cosy Sigi*: 11"/28 cm.; S.T. 4628; appropriately enough is a washable Dralon fish in (faded) aquatic colors splashed with day-glow pink; green glass cat eyes; porcine snout. Also available in 8" size, 1959 only. Retail, $8.00 and $5.50. Additionally, Steiff made a very rare BLACK seahorse with multi-colored markings.
Courtesy Mary Benavente.

Steiff's *Starly*: 13"/33 cm. high, 22"/60 cm. diameter; mohair gloriously airbrushed with a myriad of colors; e.s.; steel framed stool; leather pads. This elusive starfish was hunted for three years and was finally landed in So. Calif. Rare due to limited production, wear to a utilitarian object and fugitive dyes. Starfish are fragile creatures. TV stools are found more often as frogs, turtles and ladybugs; ca. 1960s.
Courtesy Jean Ann Smith.

TOYS

Fighters, spouters and zoo in a garden

The medium size *Paddy*, 5½"/14 cm. long is viewing himself in the Nov. 23, 1959 *Life*. The animal jungle was photographed in the conservatory of New York's Botanical Garden. Steiff toys in the foreground include *Dinos* ($6.00), *Brosus* ($5.50) and *Tysus* ($5.50). Paddy arrived in 1959 with the "Original Steiff" C.T. Later it was changed to *Paddy*.

Striking Christmas Fox: 12"/30.5 cm. high, 8"/ 20.5 cm. long; RSB; unknown stock number; red and white mohair, black mohair backs the ears, black airbrushing accents face and legs; e.s.; swivel head; orange glass eyes; twisted hard, black cotton floss nose/mouth; no claws or pads; squeaker; rarely seen animal from the late 1950s.
Courtesy Debbi Anton.

Tulla goose in *rare* large size: 11"/28 cm.; RSB; white mohair spotted black on wings and tail; e.s.; yellow felt backing accents the bright blue glass eyes; orange felt open bill and webbed feet, ca. 1950s. *Extremely desirable.*
Courtesy Barbara Baldwin.

Musical chimp: 13½"/35 cm. (one size only); RSB; S.T. 97/9/9335,3; typical open mouth mohair *Jocko*. "Music" is stenciled in gold on the felt circle. This felt is less compacted and the gold rubbed off easily. Press THREE times to engage the bellows music box. Rare in working condition; short production life, ca. 1957-58.
Courtesy Idele Gilbert.

Lion Family. (L-R), 4"/10 cm., running lion cub; 5½"/14 cm., running lioness; 6½"/ 17 cm. high, sitting lion cub, US-Zone tag; 6½"/17 cm. long, lying lion cub; 4"/10 cm., fully jointed lion cub; 4"/10 cm., sitting lion cub. Of special interest is the large sitting cub: spotted *wool plush*; e.s.; swivelhead; orange glass eyes/round pupil; light brown wool nose; dark stitched mouth; 3 floss claws; note the "sideburns." An easier to find 4" woolly plush cub was also made. During the late 1950s this model is found in the more common mohair (far right). Courtesy Debbi Anton.

Kangoo, male kangaroo: 11"/28 cm.; RSB; C.T.; shades of tan mohair, black accents; e.s.; jointed head and arms; glass eyes; grey felt lined ears; twisted hard, black cotton floss nose/mouth; three floss claws; no pouch or baby, but lacks none of that distinctive kangaroo appearance. In 1958 FAO Schwarz advertised him as "Brother Kangaroo" at a cost of $5.25. Courtesy Barbara Baldwin.

Pavian *Coco*: 13½"/35 cm.; RSB; S.T. 5335; C.T. *Coco*; silver-grey mohair, felt face and ears; e.s.; f.j.; brown glass inset eyes; airbrushed facial features; *open* peach felt mouth; grey felt hands and feet; squeaker; unusual horsehair mantle; long tail, ca. 1950-60 The only size of *Coco* made fully jointed. Strange but likeable.
Courtesy Debbi Anton.

White-handed Gibbon of the Malayan Peninsula: 9"/23 cm. high, 21"/53.5 cm. arm span; RSB; C.T. if present "Gibbon"; soft stuffed body, excelsior stuffed arms and legs; unjointed; airbrushed tan mohair; Dralon face with painted features; B&W googly glass eyes; brown felt pads on *white* Dralon hands; no tail. The larger of two sizes, ca. 1950-60. Striking and uncommon.
Courtesy Idele Gilbert.

Elephant and Steiff toys. *Jumbo*: 8½"/21.5 cm.; RSB; S.T. 4322,1; C.T. pet name; mohair; soft stuffed; jointed head and arms; B&W eyes; open peach felt mouth; painted toes; tan felt pads; squeaker; brass bell attached to trunk; red felt bib, ca. 1968-1975. Gym balls: 6"/15 cm., 8"/20 cm., 10"/25 cm.; long production, ca. 1950s-70s. Play Ring, 6"/16 cm.; S.T. 6413/16; Drumstick, 12"/30 cm.; S.T. 6414/30; ca. late 1960s-1970s. All of brightly colored mohair in mosaic pattern. Steiff cube: 4"/10 cm.; S.T. 6445/10, ca. 1980s. Musical Ladybird: 7"/18 cm.; IB; S.T. 6381/18; Dralon. Pull string to play "Sleep, Baby, Sleep"; pouch underneath to hang on crib, ca. 1977.
Courtesy Debbi Anton.

Merrythought's circus elephant *Nellie*: a large 18"/46 cm. high, 18"/46 cm. long; catalogue No. 2120/1; short mohair; e.s.; unjointed; amber glass eyes; felt tusks; brass bell sewn into nose. The felt cap matches blanket trimmed with small bells. Label sewn on tummy, "Merrythought, Ironbridge Shops, Made in England," ca. 1959. Note the comically long trunk. Astride is *Silly Basil*: 15"/38 cm.; made-to-body clown suit of synthetic plush; taffeta ruff with matching cap. Made by Bearly There Co. in 1985; retail $26.75.
Courtesy Kay Bransky.

Rare miniature tiger from the 1950s Circus Series: right, 2¾"/7 cm. high, 3"/7.5 cm. long; RSB; S.T. 5308; this smallest size was sold without a C.T.; tigered mohair; e.s.; f.j.; green glass eyes; twisted hard, *red* cotton floss nose/mouth; ROPE TAIL. Left, 4"/10 cm. high; RSB; S.T. 5310; fully jointed mohair tiger; three painted claws. Great demand for fully jointed Steiff miniatures.
Courtesy Idele Gilbert.

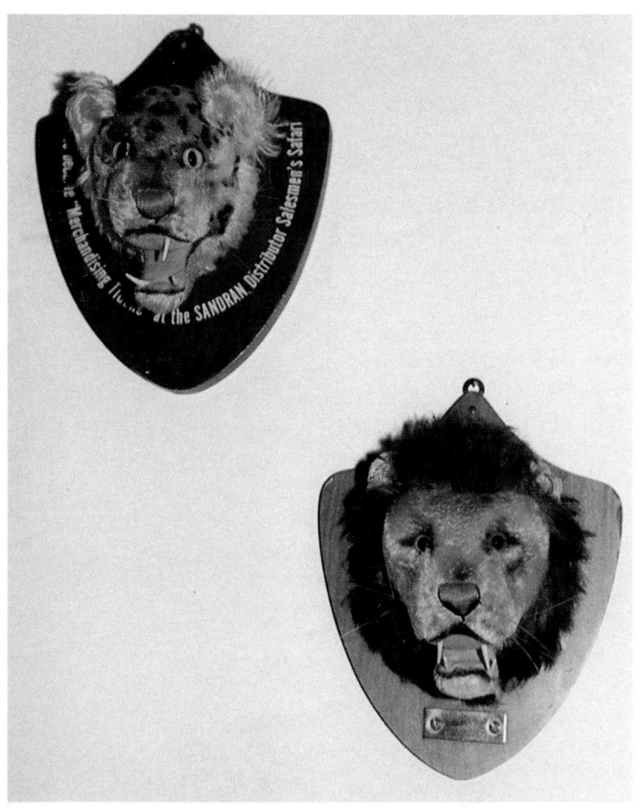

Trophy head leopard and lion: both are 6"/15 cm. (head to chin); RSB; S.T. 28; have golden mohair with airbrushed markings; excelsior stuffing; pink pearl cotton nose/painted nostrils; open felt mouth with four teeth; whiskers. The leopard has green glass cat eyes; lion has amber glass Teddy Bear eyes; Note the lion's full mohair ruff. These elusive pieces were also available in a 12" size and were made *primarily* for organizations, ca. 1950s.
Courtesy Barbara Baldwin.

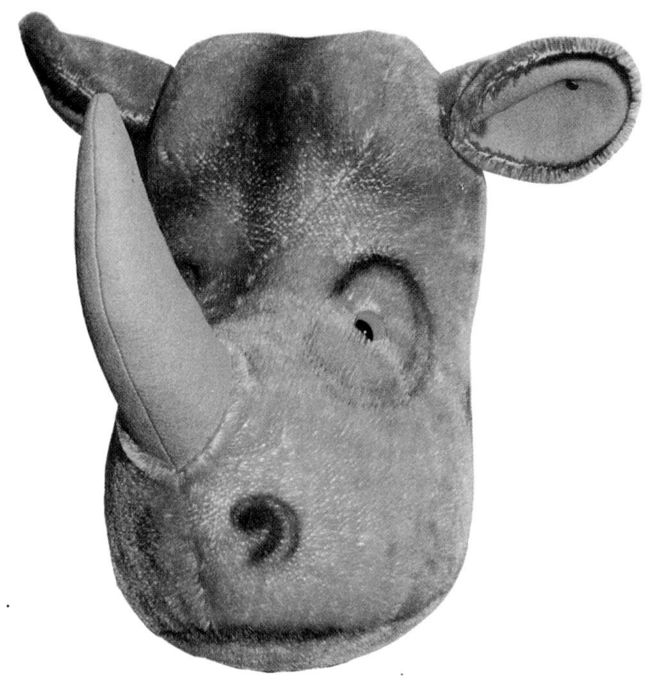

Rhino Trophy Head: 12"/30.5 cm. high; RSB; short tan pile tan mohair over excelsior; felt horn and lined ears; *unusual* amber glass eyes with black offset pupil. The airbrushed markings add personality to this *rare* piece, ca. 1950s.
Courtesy Barbara Baldwin.

STUDIO size *Nelly*, center: 6½"/16.5 cm. high (inc. soft vinyl antennae), 8½"/21.5 cm. long; rigid vinyl shell; velveteen body with white vinyl underside; e.s.; black glass beady eyes. The head has a GUSSET for shaping and a *stitched* nose/mouth. Extremely rare. Shown with 4½" size (see *TB & SA*, *Second Series*, pg. 178). Note *Nelly's* smiling face. The small snail is harder to find in blue.
Courtesy Idele Gilbert.

Lizzy searches for small bugs along a sandstone ledge: 1½"/4 cm. high, 8"/ 20.5 cm. long; RSB; velveteen with dappled green, brown and white markings; firmly cotton stuffed; unjointed; stickpin glass eyes and downward turned smile. Also made in 12" long size. One of the rare exotics, ca. 1959-60. Courtesy Mary Benavente.

Leopards and ocelots are often confused. The lepard has green glass (or plastic) cat eyes and side burns. The ocelot has bright orange plastic cat eyes and no sieburns. Leopards were made in several sizes both lying and running during the 1950s and 1960s. Ocelots were made lying only in 1964-65. Front: small ocelot, 6½"/17 cm., RSB; large ocelot, 11"/28 cm., RSB. Back: large leopard, 24"/60 cm. long, RSB; medium leopard, 11"/28 cm. long, RSB. All are mohair with airbrushed markings; excelsior stuffed and have three stitched claws; the largest leopard has a squeaker. The smallest (6½" long) lying leopard is the most common. Others are harder to find.
Courtesy Debbi Anton.

Man has always been in awe of the Begal tiger: 7ft./2.13 m. long plus tail (40"/100 cm. long); *large* RSB; tigered mohair; excelsior stuffed over steel armature; unjointed; *large* green glass cat eyes; rose color pearl cotton nose, open felt mouth airbrushed pink and red; four wooden teeth; three black stitched claws. The working pull-type growler resenbles the actual growl of a *large* animal. In the 1950s he was purchased from his display cage in a Cincinnati toy store. A real find in any condition and this one is mint. Baby: 17"/43 cm. high; RSB; description same as above. Made in greater numbers in the 8" size, ca. 1959. Exceptional animals. Note: "Bengal" C.T. is difficult to find; most Bengals have "Original Steiff" C.T.
Courtesy Barbara Baldwin.

STUDIO Crouching Lion, a regal mohair animal with natural coloring and flowing mane: 24"/ 61 cm. high, 40"/102 cm. long; RSB; excelsior over steel frame; unjointed; glass eyes; open felt mouth with four wooden teeth; ca. 1960s. An outstanding example of Steiff art. Courtesy Cynthia's Country Store.

Feelings come alive when viewing the STUDIO babies; zebra, 39"/99 cm. high, 39"/99 cm. long; RSB; S.T. 6399,90; bulbous glass eyes (1¼" diam.), blond horsehair eyelashes (1" long); strong face with solid black painted nose; wired ears (Dralon lined); salt and pepper horsehair mane; mohair ruff on tail; suede-like leather hoofs. Also made in 60"/ 152 cm. size. Okapi, 42"/107 cm. high, 45"/ 114 cm. long; mohair; excelsior stuffed, steel armature; the same convex glass eyes/horsehair eyelashes; open felt mouth outlined in black; brown leather life-like nose; cardboard cylinders inserted in ears for positioning; red/brown mohair ruff on tail; detailed leather hoofs. Note the *curvature* of the long neck giving an improbable look. The adult is 80"/203 cm.; shown in the 1955 special STUDIO catalogue. Rare STUDIO mohair animals made 1955-68 are: 24" goose, 30" turkey, panther with teeth, 115" snake, 32" seal, 48" gazelle, 60" antelope, 124" Jumbo elephant, adorable 20" Coco and others. The zebra is more common than the Okapi (fairly rare even in zoos), but harder to find than the giraffe. The Okapi is *special* because of his personable face and wonderful "look." He is priced accordingly.

Steiff STUDIO alligator: 100"/254 cm. long; beige mohair airbrushed in greens and yellows; excelsior stuffing over a steel frame; painted WOODEN eyes (many STUDIO types have wooden eyes, for example, the Basset Hound); open red felt mouth with numerous white felt teeth; green felt spine. An exciting stuffed toy, shown in 1967 Steiff STUDIO catalogue; extremely rare. Center, 28"/70 cm.; IB: S.T. 0970/70; C.T. *Gaty,* and 12"/30 cm.; RSB; S.T. 0970/30 same as above, but black rimmed green plastic cat eyes and four grey-brown felt claws on each foot. These reptiles fit nicely into a dinosaur collection. Courtesy Idele Gilbert.

Wotan Rams: 5"/12.5 cm. and 8½"/21.5 cm. high; RSB; S.T. 1512 and 1522; C.T. pet name; white short wool plush legs and face, thick brown woolly body; e.s.; unjointed; green plastic eyes; pink painted nose, brown floss mouth; airbrushed claws; white felt ruled horns; made only 1967-68. The woolly plush is unusual for this time period. Hard to find due to short production rather than demand.
Courtesy Debbi Anton.

FAO Schwarz Steiff squirrel: 8"/20.5 cm. high; begging posture; mohair airbrushed with greys and gold; e.s.; black plastic eyes; twisted hard, brown cotton floss outlines nose and mouth; felt paws and bushy tail. No I.D., but shown in 1967 Schwarz catalogue. Exclusives command higher prices. Realistic animal.
Courtesy Idele Gilbert.

White Gorilla: 10"/25 cm.; RSB; S.T. 6625,94; C.T. "Original Steiff"; Dralon; soft stuffed; unjointed; felt ears; bright blue plastic eyes; airbrushed facial features; pink chin and tummy with navel; seen in Steiff's 1961 German catalogue; distributed only by FAO Schwarz in 1967. Rare primate baby.

Wittie owl family: 13½"/35 cm.; 9"/22 cm.; 5½"/14 cm.; 4"/10 cm.; all have IB; new C.T. *Wittie*; all are mohair with spotted felt wings and tails; white felt feet; horsehair topknots and vinyl beaks. The two largest have swivel heads and bulbous green glass cat eyes (the same eyes used for large tigers). The two smallest have rigid heads and black-rimmed green plastic (glow-in-the-dark) eyes. Wool pompon owls: 3½"/9 cm. and 2½"/6 cm.; IB; S,T, 7480/09 and 06; swivel heads; orange plastic eyes; white felt beaks and plastic feet. All ca. 1971.
Courtesy Idele Gilbert.

Forest friends: raccoon and Steiff mohair owl puppet dressed up in *Klein Archie's* clothes commemorating the Enchanted Doll House's 25th anniversary. Soft raccoon designed for children: 12"/30.5 cm.; IB; S.T. 6205/30; fur of brown Dralon tipped in white, rust color mask; foam rubber stuffed; unjointed but head is made to wobble; plastic eyes have a black pupil rimmed in white; twisted hard, black cotton floss nose/mouth; brown flat feet with tan Trevira velvet pads; the bushy tail is not ringed, ca. 1977.
Courtesy Mary Benavente.

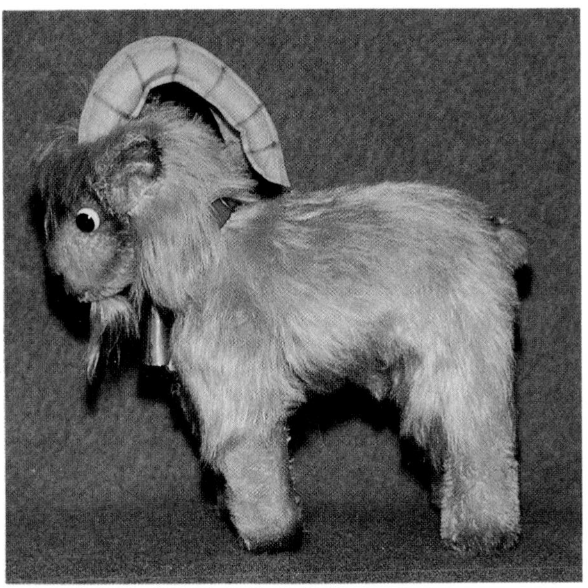

Clemen's (W. Germany) Billy Goat: 9"/23 cm. long; triangular metal and paper tag on blue rayon cord attached to chest; natural mohair (not spun into yarn); e.s.; unjointed; stuffed felt horns (no wire); black floss nose; airbrushed facial details and hoofs; plastic collar; cow bell; well designed and executed, ca. 1960-70. But the demand is for Steiff.
Courtesy Valerie Vann.

Cosy Koala: 8½"/22 cm. sitting; IB; S.T. 4770/22; Dralon; foam rubber stuffed; swivel head; painted features; felt nose, ca. 1971-77. A baby was made in 5" size. The ever popular Koala commands a higher price than other Cosys. This and the 16" *Molly Koala* (1973) are pleasant additions to a Steiff collection. Courtesy Rosemary Moran.

Cosy Camel: 11"/28 cm. high; RSB; S.T. 4890/28, excelsior stuffed legs for support; foam rubber stuffed body and head; unjointed; pinkish beige short and long pile Dralon; plastic eyes; brown floss nose/mouth with painted outline; felt ears; bifurcated hoofs. Introduced as a "Novelty" in 1968, discontinued after 1974. An artistic animal that should command a high price, but the Dralon covering is unpopular.
Courtesy Diane Hoffman.

New uses for Steiff frogs. No computer should be without one as a mascot. Frogs eat bugs! Only the *best* frogs will do. Left: 3"/8 cm. high, 3½"/9 cm. long; brass button; S.T. 2370/08; new C.T. *Froggy*; Trevira velvet (knitted velveteen, 100% polyester), ca. 1980s. Right: 5"/13 cm. high, 8"/20 cm. long; IB; riveted; S.T. 2380/20; C.T. *Froggy*; multicolored mohair; feet have stitched separate toes, ca. late 1960s. Reverse of C.T. reads, "Mottenecht Durch//Eulan//Bayer//Leverkusen," indicating moth proofing of the mohair. The popular frog is seldom found in this tissue mint condition.
Courtesy Valerie Vann.

Ponx: 6½"/16.5 cm.; IB; S.T. 5818/17; C.T. "Original Steiff"; Dralon; soft stuffed; unjointed; green plastic eyes; pink pearl cotton nose, brown stitched mouth; no claws or pads. Originally made in 1971 as a gift series in cardboard cage (box). Other members of the Dralon series: *Toccolino*, Chimpanzee; *Jacobombo*, elephant; *Simba*, lion; *Pinni*, penguin; *Aram*, cat; *Theophil*, dog. Little demand but hard to find.
Courtesy Debbi Anton.

Berg (Austria) lion finger puppet: 3"/7.5 cm.; paper tag in arm seam, metal heart (trademark) on chest; short gold mohair, synthetic plush tipped mane, felt cutout ears; excelsior stuffed head only; unjointed; plastic googly eyes; pink pearl cotton nose, black mouth; nylon whiskers; painted toes. Puppet operated by putting two fingers in glove-like legs, ca. 1970s. Right: 8½"/21.5 cm. tiger; possible Berg based on resemblance to companion finger puppet and high quality of materials. Note the many airbrushed details and complex seamed pattern. Mohair and plush; e.s.; swivel head; flat poseable metal strip in tail. Charming "cartoon" style expression, ca. 1970s.
Courtesy Valerie Vann.

Wizzi (Fitschew): 14"/36 cm.; IB; S.T. 2270/35; soft stuffed synthetic plush with animal markings; black belly; brown feet; small brown plastic eyes; leatherette nose; nylon whiskers; longish neck. Also made in 10"/25 cm. size. A Fitschew is the polecat of Europe. It preys on poultry. The Ferret is the domesticated variety. A rare Steiff toy produced 1977 only, but limited demand.
Courtesy Diane Hoffman.

Gaty: 12"/30 cm.; IB; S.T. 0980/30; C.T. *Gaty* on chest; Trevira velvet; foam rubber stuffed. Trevira is a registered trademark of Hoechst AG and is a particularly effective covering for this alligator. He has black rimmed green plastic eyes; painted teeth on closed mouth; four felt toes, ca. 1975-78. Also made in a 6" size. Used a short time, yet part of Steiff's history, Trevira velvet can also be found on the elephant, giraffe, lion, zebra, rhino, hippo and cow.
Courtesy Mary Benavente.

Wool mini woodsy rodents: skunk, 2¼"/6 cm.; RSB in *mohair* tail; S.T. 2506/40; green glass cat eyes; big bead nose, ca. 1950s-60s; desirable. Orange squirrel: 2"/5 cm. high; wool tail; black stick pin eyes and nose, ca. late 1970s. Bat was once part of a three set bat mobile: 2"/5 cm. long; S.T. 7088/05; brown wool body with green tummy; airbrushed undersides of wings; eyes are left to the imagination, ca. 1975; uncommon. Chipmunk holding a red berry (perhaps the only instance of a Steiff fruit): 2"/5 cm. long; *mohair* tail; stickpin eyes, ca. early 1950s-late 1970s. Rarest wool minis are the kittys, skunk, bat and pigeon.
Courtesy Mary Benavente.

Don't let him sneak up on you! "Elegante" by Dakin is an exceptional line of classic creations and storybook legends identified by their handsome leather tags. "A Wolf in Sheep's Clothing:" 20"/50.8 cm. tall, thick taupe-colored plush. The white satin-lined removable cloak is shaped like the sheepskin of the famous fable; plastic eyes; brown velvet nose; pink velvet tongue. Also made in a 13"/33 cm. size. Retail price 1985, $60.00; good investment potential. Steiff 8½"/21.6 cm. woolly plush lamb seen in "Domestic Animals."

PRICE GUIDE FOR TEDDY BEARS, STEIFF ANIMALS & ANNALEES

Page 4
13" Blond **$1,500.00**
16" Cinnamon **$2,800.00**
18" Blond **$3,800.00**
30" Gold **$2,900.00**
10" Honey **$1,000.00**
24" White **$2,100.00**
20" White **$1,300.00**
13" Champagne **$1,400.00**
24" Champagne **$1,800.00**
12" Honey **$1,400.00**
13" Cinnamon Red **$1,900.00**
Page 7
18" Bear/Pail **$200.00**
Page 12
Pincushion **$1000.00**
Rabbit **$350.00**
4¼" Cat **$450.00**
Pug Dog **$400.00**
Brwn./Wht. Dog **$400.00**
6" Kangaroo **$375.00**
Page 13
4½" Velvet Dog **$400.00**
Hambrick **$425.00**
Tin Bath **$75.00**
5½" Star Gazer **$550.00**
Pin Cushion **$250.00**
Page 14
Snow (Babies) Bears
ea. **$65.00**
3" Bisque Girl/
Teddy **$125.00**
5" Panda **$35.00**
2¼" Panda/Wheels **$45.00**
Page 15
6" 1960s **$200.00**
5" pre-1930s **$650.00**
5½" late 1940s **$275.00**
5½" 1950s Steiff **$200.00**
4" Teddy Baby **$900.00-**
$1,200.00
Page 16
3½" Chocolate **$300.00**
3½" White **$350.00**
3½" Caramel/Gold ... **$225.00**
3¼" Brown Mohair **$45.00**
5½" Panda 1950s **$95.00**
Page 17
5", 6", 4½" Family **$135.00**
6½" f.j. Mutzli **$95.00**
Berlin Bear **$25.00**
Page 19
20" Rod Bear **$8,000.00**
18" Ideal **$2,000.00**
Page 20
14½" Ideal **$1,200.00**
20½" Attikus **$14,000.00**
Page 21
Cinnamon **$5,000.00**
10" White **$1,300.00**
14" Honey **$2,100.00**
Harvard Bear **$2,500.00**
Wagon **$175.00**
Book **$125.00**
Page 22
24" Steiff c.s. ... **ea. $8,000.00**
28" 1905 Steiff **$9,000.00**
20" Steiff Teddys
ea. **$5,500.00**
Page 23
29" Teddy **$7,500.00**
25" Teddy **$6,000.00**
Dally **$750.00**
29" Steiff **$8,000.00**
24" Steiff **$6,000.00**
Polar Dog **$800.00**
Page 24
13" White **$2,000.00**
24" Cinnamon, c.s. **$8,500.00**
"Teddy" Photo **$40.00**
Page 25
16½" Oskar **$3,500.00**
13" Loved **$295.00**
Page 26
American 8" **$400.00**
16" **$600.00**
18" Ideal **$950.00**
12" Pale Gold **$300.00**
Book **$60.00**
Buttons ...... **ea. $30.00-60.00**
12" White Steiff **$2,000.00**
12" Ideal **$650.00**
Print **$65.00**
Page 27
Charly Jolly **$550.00**
14" Felt Nose **$1,400.00**
14" Ideal **$900.00**
Page28
18" Bruin **$3,000.00**
20" Steiff **$3,900.00**
Sled **$250.00**
Bushy **$1,200.00**
Bingley **$1,500.00**
Rugby **$500.00**
Puzzle Box **$125.00**
Page 29
13½" Bear **$900.00**
Humpty Dumpty **$350.00**
12" Peddler **$900.00**
15" Theodore **$1,600.00**
7" Wooly Teddy **$700.00**
Page 30
American 13" **$500.00**
American 18" **$650.00**
Blocks **$65.00**
Laughing Bear **$1,000.00**
Page 31
29½" Opera **$13,000.00**
Page 32
11½" White **$550.00**
12" Steiff **$1,500.00**
Mr. Perky **$475.00**
Page 33
30" Steiff 1917 .... **$6,000.00**
Tricycle **$300.00**
20" Aetna **$1,500.00**
Page 34
20" American **$1,200.00**
Old Glory **$250.00**
Page 35
Lifeguard **$1,000.00**
Barney **$325.00**
Reddy Kilowatt **$350.00**
Page 36
20" Electric Eye **$600.00**
14" Speaker **$225.00**
Page 37
26" f.j. Electric Eye .. **$675.00**
Page 38
15" Teddy **$550.00**
12" Mighty Bear **$400.00**
Page 39
18" Bing **$4,500.00**
24" Bing **$3,000.00**
Page 40
25" Gold Steiff . **ea.$4,000.00**
8" White Bear **$1,000.00**
Page 41
Teddy Red Socks **$325.00**
Artisan's Bear **$295.00**
White 1920s **$195.00**
Page 42
18" Petsy (worn) .. **$4,000.00**
1920s Tabby **$225.00**
Terrier **$65.00**
Blocks **$75.00**
18" Clown Bear **$3,500.00**
Page 43
Photograph **$40.00**
20" Amer. Gold **$375.00**
Page 44
Horse **$600.00**
20" Bear **$400.00**
11" Fisherman **$150.00**
Page 45
16" Frosted Teddy ... **$800.00**
5" Sitting Rabbit **$75.00**
10" Light Gold Mohair **$85.00**
Page 46
Inflatable Bear **$6,000.00**
Page 47
Miss Mildred **$600.00**
James **$135.00**
Page 48
Petz Teddy Bear **$500.00**
Petz Polar Bear **$75.00**
Bessie Kate **$125.00**
11" Brown **$175.00**
Page 49
15" Old Yellow **$300.00**
8½" Teddy Baby ... **$1,600.00**
5" Early Steiff,
(worn) **$275.00**
14" Brown **$175.00**
14" White **$175.00**
15" Character **$200.00**
13" Gold **$175.00**
Page 50
Pooh-Like Look .... **N.P.A.**
14" American **$350.00**
13½" "Tough Eddy" . **$300.00**
Page 51
Dirty Harry **$750.00**
22" Merrythought **$900.00**
18" English **$350.00**
Book **$15.00**
Page 52
Cut-Out Bear **$150.00**
25" Steiff Teddy **$3,500.00**
Dog **$475.00**
Austrian **$250.00**
German EM **$125.00**
Page 53
Jolly Boy **$350.00**
12" Two-sided **$65.00**
Page 54
17" Gold **$300.00**
16½" Hermann
Plush Co. **$300.00**
17" Mohair .... **ea. $225.00**
Page 55
Raggedies .... **pr. $600.00**
11" Bear (worn) **$175.00**
29" Raggedy Ann **$175.00**
15" Bear **$85.00**
Page 56
Ma Jong **$250.00**
O'Donnell **$75.00**
10½" Panda **$950.00**
Page 58
Buffy **$250.00**
Brother's Bear **$80.00**
17" Steiff **$1,600.00**
Page 59
17" 1930s (wear) **$900.00**
17" Brown 1940s .. **$1,700.00**
17" 1950s **$550.00**
16" Hugmee **$225.00**
Page 60
Bat Eared Bear **$150.00**
14" Cotton Plush **$100.00**
21" Dressed Teddy .. **$165.00**
Doll (mint) **$300.00**
Page 61
Minnie **$135.00**
Farnell Terrier **$65.00**

Farnell Bear **$250.00**
Farnell Cat **$125.00**
Book **$15.00**

Page 62
12" Anker-Munich ... **$175.00**
13" Cotton Plush **$25.00**
Carnival ...... **ea.$10.00-75.00**
Page 63
Walking Bear **$165.00**
28" Chad Valley **$700.00**
Page 64
6½" Zotty **$200.00-250.00**
10" White Zotty **$625.00**
10" Redwood **$225.00**
9" Zotty **$175.00**
10" Standard **$175.00**
17" Zotty 1965 .... **$375.00**
15" Standard **$225.00**
8" Zotty 1970s **$150.00**
8½" 1950s Orsi **$550.00**
Page 65
10½" Hermann Zotty . **$85.00**
9" Grisly **$45.00**
10" Steiff Zotty **$175.00**
20" Steiff Zotty **$425.00**
10½" Terrier **$75.00**
Page 66
Pip **$175.00**
10½" Chubby Mohair **$80.00**
8½" Coco **$75.00**
10" Cat **$25.00**
13" Character Bear .. **$125.00**
13" Pedigree Bear **$35.00**
Page 67
Schenker Cat **$30.00**
Large Bear (mint) **$125.00**
Smaller **$50.00-75.00**
Polar Bear **$25.00**
15" Pink .... **ea. $140.00**
Page 68
15" Schwika **$120.00**
11" Schwika **$110.00**
15" Pink **$100.00**
26" Chiltern **$150.00**
Page 69
Cheeky Bear **$95.00**
Open Mouth Fechters-
10" Goldie **$75.00**
15" Frosted Tan .. **$225.00**
8" Dk. Brown **$75.00**
8" Beige **$75.00**
16" Dk. Brown **$250.00**
16" Frosted **$250.00**
10" Frosted Tan .. **$125.00**
Cat **$60.00**
Page 70
7" & 5¾" Grey ..... **ea. $40.00**
9½" Gold **$70.00**
8" Taupe **$75.00**
12" Snowball **$150.00**
14" Cinnamon **$165.00**
13½" Blue **$200.00**
SAF **$75.00**
Page 71
UFB **$100.00**
Sebastian **$250.00**
Peky, sitting **$250.00**
60 cm. Mg. Strong
Cream **$750.00**
Page 72
Molly **$450.00**
50 cm. Mg. Strong ... **$900.00**
Dally **$400.00**
Rabbit **$90.00**
Manschli **$150.00**
Mouse **$65.00**
Teddy Rose **$230.00**
Grey Geingen **$135.00**
Page 73
Gae Sharp Bears **$75.00**
Teddy Baby/Wolf **$375.00**
Issue Price, 1988
269 DM **$155.00**
Page 74
27" Kodi **$600.00**
21" Oliver Fox **$400.00**
Page 75
Bears On Hat .... **ea.$75.00-$150.00**
2" Teddy **$85.00**
5" Golli **$125.00**
Page 76
Laurie Sasaki Bears **ea. $75.00-$150.00**
1" Bear **$60.00**
2" Rabbit **$65.00**
2½" Jester Bears ... **ea. $65.00**
2½" Rabbit/jacket **$75.00**
Page 77
22" Heinrich **$265.00**
30" Abernathy **$400.00**
30" Sgt. Major **$1,000.00**
13" McMurtry **$150.00**
13" Bear Brummels .... **pr. $300.00**
22" Bronwyll **$300.00**
Page 78
Phantom of the
Opera **$3,000.00**
Jennifer **$595.00**
Page 79
Kinser Frog **$250.00**
Tumbler Bears ...... **ea.$85.00**
Page 80
Teddy Rossebear **$295.00**
Bernie Bruin **$50.00**
Joshua **$180.00**
Chocolate Parfait **$110.00**
Page 81
Wee Wanderer **$160.00**
Na-Nooq **$175.00**
Blue Bear **$120.00**
Amanda **$100.00**
Page 82
Regis **$175.00**
Page 84
5¾" Wheeled Dog ... **$475.00**
32" Wheeled Bear **$3,500.00**
Decorative Goat ... **$1,000.00**
Page 85
10½" Bear on
Wheels **$1,000.00**
Record Teddy **$8,000.00**
6" Pull Toy **$600.00**
Page 86
9½" Brennessel **$1,000.00**
8½" St. Bernard **$1,200.00**
"Captain" Photo **$35.00**
Page 87
Rion **$2,500.00**
7½" Elephant **$750.00**
Page 88
Bing Elephant **$850.00**
Donkey Pull Toy .. **$1,200.00**
Cat & Dog (felt) **ea. $600.00**
Page 89
Bully/Wheels **$500.00**
Ball Mopsy **$125.00**
Raven Mobile **$65.00**
Molly **$500.00**
9" Fox/Wheels **$375.00**
Page 90
Record Peter **$1,000.00**
Coco On Wheels **$350.00**
Horse/Cart **$1,500.00**
Jocko **$475.00**
Page 91
Duck **$600.00**
Waddling Goose **$325.00**
16" Hermann **$165.00**
Duck (mint) **$200.00**
Page 92
20" Boxer **$375.00**
Push Dog **$95.00**
Doll (mint) **$250.00**
Page 93
Waldi **$225.00**
Hobby Horse **$225.00**
13½" Turtle **$350.00**
Page 94
Donkey/Farmer **$4,000.00**
Donkey/Cat **$1,000.00**
Page 95
Automated Pussy
Cat **$450.00**
Squeaker Dog **$95.00**
Hen, working **$25.00**
13" Standing Bear . **$4,500.00**
Page 96
Acrobatic Bear **$135.00**
6" Keywind Panda **$45.00**
Page 97
Dancing Bear **$100.00**
Pink Poodle **$45.00**
Mech. Tiger **$4,000.00**
Page 98
Village/Cars **$25,000.00**
Page 101
14½" Messenger ... **$3,000.00**
11" Messenger **$2,000.00**
14½" Bellhop **$3,000.00**
18" Pink Teddy **$3,300.00**
Violinist **$125.00**
Clown Bear **$100.00**
Bonzo **$75.00**
Yes/No Orange **$750.00**
Dime Store Bears,
ea. **$75.00-100.00**
Page 102
Yes/No Parrot **$600.00**
13" Yes/No Fox **$1,100.00**
7" Bulldog **$800.00**
Page 103
4½" Key-wind
Monkey **$165.00**
Yo-Yo **$500.00**
Blecky MIB **$250.00**
Perfume Monkey
MIB **$400.00**
2¼" Monkey **$175.00**
Page 104
Red Perfume Bear ... **$900.00**
Black Mini **$250.00**
Pink **$300.00**
Perfume Monkey **$375.00**
Bellhop Bear **$600.00**
Scotty **$135.00**
Mouse, Elf, Monkey
ea. **$165.00**
Boy/Stein **$135.00**
Page 105
Birds ...... **ea. $125.00-150.00**
10" Schuco Dwarf **$900.00**
Steiff Gnome **$1,200.00**
6½" Rabbit/wheels .. **$300.00**
3½" Steiff Bunnies
ea **$65.00**
Page 106
Louise **$225.00**
Schucie **$1,500.00**
Book **$20.00**
8" Tricky **$650.00**
8" Rolly Bear **$1,200.00**
Page 107
3½" Yes/No Panda .. **$700.00**

20" Schuco **$175.00**
8" White Chimp **$175.00**
Page 108
Noah's Ark Series
Animals .. **ea.$75.00-200.00**
Page 109
12" Rooster **$225.00**
Lg. Lady **$200.00**
Sm. Lady **$175.00**
Tramp **$175.00**
Page 110
Trip-Trap .... **ea. $350.00**
13" Schuco Bear **$125.00**
15" Dressed Bear **$175.00**
10" Character **$50.00**
Page 112
15" Tea Cosey **$3,500.00**
Book **$45.00**
Page 113
Rooster/Hen ...... **pr. $300.00**
Velvet Chick **$150.00**
Bear/ Swing **$150.00**
Glass Bear **$100.00**
Pitcher **$600.00**
Page 114
6" German Plate **$95.00**
Glass Plates .... **ea. $85.00**
Huld's Postmarked .. **$165.00**
Wood **$85.00**
Postcards
(mint) **$18.00-25.00**
Page 115
Steiff Pillow Dog **$300.00**
Molly Purse **$500.00**
Hankie **$10.00**
6" Corduroy **$85.00**
Page 116 & 117
Stamps .... **ea. $25.00**
Page 118
Gingerbread
House **$1,200.00**
7½" Santa **$250.00**
5½" Tom Cat **$75.00**
Witch Puppet **$35.00**
Record Cover **$25.00**
Paddy **$300.00**
Page 119
Turtle **$275.00**
Leopard Rug **$650.00**
Page 120
5" Felt Mickey **$900.00**
10" Schuco Mickey .. **$500.00**
Paper Dolls **$50.00**
Christopher **$750.00**
Page 121
Pooh Figures .... **ea. $20.00**
Donald Duck **$600.00**
20" "T.J." **$350.00**
17" Donald/Skis **$550.00**
Page 122
Dino **$175.00**
Thumper **$550.00**
Bonzo **$145.00**
Page 123
Rudolph **$30.00**
Scamp **$175.00**
19" Giraffe **$300.00**
Page 124
Reinhold **$375.00**
Mockie **$50.00**
6" Gogo **$125.00**
Page 125
Blue Camel **$25.00**
13½" Rupert **$35.00**
Page 126
Fireman Set .... **Pr. $3,000.00**
The Germ .... **N.P.A.**
Sleepy Bear ... compl. **$50.00**
Page 127
11" T.R. Bear **$65.00**
Tin Tray **$125.00**
Manatee **$20.00**
Mascot (small) **$30.00**
Mascot (large) **$50.00**
Page 128
Terrier **$35.00**
Spaniel **$75.00**
Bear **$50.00**
White Jocko **$150.00**
Tiger Cub **$75.00**
Gora **$75.00**
Mimic Puppets .. **ea. $225.00**
King Charles
Spaniel **$250.00**
1930s Jocko **$125.00**
Page 129
Terrier **$150.00**
Dally **$250.00**
Spaniel **$250.00**
Beppo **$100.00**
Poodle **$75.00**
Rabbit, Tiger, Cat. **ea. $55.00**
Teddy Baby **$85.00**
Tiger Cub **$75.00**
Page 130
Snaky **$500.00**
Marionette MIB **$95.00**
Page 132
Squeaker Book **$40.00**
22" Golly (1910) **$300.00**
Biscuit Tin **$2,500.00**
Child's Cup **$95.00**
Perfume **$250.00**
Pearse Book **$50.00**
20" Golly **$150.00**
Page 133
15" Celluloid **$110.00**
17" Bear 1905 .... **$1,600.00**
15" Ireland **$90.00**
11" Golly **$65.00**
Sugar Bowl **$35.00**
Truck **$15.00**
15" Golly (1940s) **$100.00**
12" Steiff Teddy **$1,500.00**
18" Golly (1930) **$165.00**
15" Blue Eyes **$125.00**
Block **$35.00**
Page 134
13" Chiltern **$75.00**
24" Chad Valley **$140.00**
13" Printed **$70.00**
10" Teddy **$200.00**
16" Chad Valley **$75.00**
17" Chad Valley **$100.00**
Page 135
18" Knitted **$55.00**
14" Knitted (1940s) **$70.00**
21" Knitted **$60.00**
18" Knitted **$55.00**
Doll **$100.00**
15" Dean's **$45.00**
13" Dean's **$35.00**
Cut-out **$25.00**
17" Dean's **$45.00**
Page 136
16" Flat Teddy **$70.00**
13" Chad Valley **$65.00**
19" Golly **$130.00**
Page 137
14" Pooh **$250.00**
8½" Golly **$45.00**
Bank **$200.00**
Toffee Tin **$35.00**
Trapeze Toy **$325.00**
15" Sign **$60.00**
30" Display **$1,500.00**
Page 138
Valentine **$35.00**
Match Box **$35.00**
Paperdoll **$30.00**
Furniture/box **$50.00**
Squeak Toy **$65.00**
Clickers .... **ea. $75.00**
Paper Bag **$35.00**
6" Golly **$55.00**
Notebook **$35.00**
Page 139
Pins (1930-55) ...... **ea. $55.00**
Pins (1956-on) .... **ea. $35.00**
Modern Pins .... **ea. $10.00**
22" Mr. Gollywog **$750.00**
Upton Book **$150.00-200.00**
Page 141
10" Country
Girl **$2,600.00-3,500.00**
10" Beauty .... **N.P.A.**
10" Water Skiier ... **$1,500.00**
Page 142
7" Baby Angel **$300.00**
7" Wee-Ski **$350.00**
12" Gnome **$300.00**
7" Gnome **$150.00**
Page 143
7" Boy/Girl .... **ea. $300.00**
10" Dancers
ea. **$100.00-150.00**
8" Monk **$75.00-100.00**
7" Cupid **$125.00**
7" Indian Boy **$150.00**
Page 144
7" Ghost Kid .... **C.S.P.**
10" Scarecrow **$325.00**
7" Mr./Mrs. Santa With
Skis .... **ea.$175.00**
18" Mrs. Santa
ea. **$150.00-200.00**
7" Mr./Mrs.Santa . **ea.$100.00**
Page 145
7" Santa Mouse **$125.00**
12" Nightshirt
Mouse **$150.00-225.00**
22" Jack Frost **$150.00-250.00**
10" Jack Frost **$150.00**
Christmas Elf .... **C.S.P.**
10" Workshop Elves **ea. $75.00**
7" Santa **$50.00**
Page 146
18" Candy Dolls . **ea.$150.00**
10" Gingerbread
Boy **$100.00-150.00**
5" Ornament **$30.00**
18" Saddle Bag .. **ea. $100.00**
36" Doe **$450.00**
18" Fawn **$225.00**
Page 147
7" Bear/Bee **$150.00**
18" Ballerina Bear ... **$275.00**
18" Valentine Bear .. **$175.00**
Page 148
10" Valentine
Panda **$200.00-350.00**
10" Christmas Panda **$100.00**
10" Fishing Bear **$200.00**
10" Bear/Bee **$200.00**
10" Girl Bear **$200.00**
Page 149
10" Bear/Sled .... **$30.00 UP**
10" Eskimo .... **C.S.P.**
7" Hunter Mouse **$250.00**
Jogger Mouse **$75.00**
Skateboard Mouse ... **$300.00**
7" Tennis Boy **$75.00**
Page 150
7" Bicycle
Mouse **$125.00-175.00**

7" Boating Mouse **$55.00**
7" Bowling Mouse **$75.00**
7" Iceskater Mouse .. **$150.00**
7" Cheerleader.
Mouse **$125.00-200.00**
Page 151
7" Cowboy Pair .. **ea.$150.00**
7" Retired (1974) **$125.00**
7" Retired (1984) **$100.00**
7" Yum Yum
Bunny .... **ea.$525.00**
Page 152
7" White Bunny **$125.00**
7" Country .... **pr. $100.00**
7"Rabbits(1978) . **pr. $200.00**
29" E.P. Boy **$150.00**
4 ft. Boy **$500.00**
29" Country Girl **$150.00**
Page 153
18" Victorian Bunnies
pr. **$250.00**
10" Boy Frog........... **$125.00**
18" Boy Frog........... **$150.00**
10" Willie Wog **$200.00**
10" Polly Frog **$200.00**
Page 154
18" Fox **$300.00-400.00**
12" Monkey **$225.00**
14" Dragon.. **$600.00-900.00**
Page 155
8" Ballerina Pigs
ea. **$200.00-250.00**
7" Ballerina
Bunny **$100.00-175.00**
12" Skunks .... **ea.$225.00**
5" Pilot Duck ... **$50.00-75.00**
5" Easter Parade
Ducks .... **ea.$50.00**
5" Duck (1984) **$40.00**
5" Sailor Duck .... **C.S.P.**
Duck/Santa Hat **$75.00**
Duck in Santa Hat **$75.00**
Page 156
12" Kitten **$35.00-50.00**
18" Clown (1978) **$250.00**
10" Clown (1980) **$100.00**
18" Clown (1985) **$200.00**
10" Clown (1977) **$125.00**
10" Clown (1981)....... **$95.00**
10" Clown (1984)....... **$75.00**
10" Clown (1987)....... **$75.00**
Page 158
13½" Steiff
Dolls .... **pr.$5,000.00**
Character Child **$1,600.00**
Pomeranian **$500.00**
16" Doll **$600.00**
10" Horse **$200.00**
4" Molly **$95.00**

Page 159
Alida & Hubertus
ea. **$3,000.00**
French Soldier **$2,500.00**
Goat on Wheels ... **$2,500.00**
21" Doll **$2,400.00**
Page 160
Missis/Captain **pr. $5,000.00**
12" Comic Farmer **$2,800.00**
Cow **$1,100.00**
Farmers .... **ea.$1,800.00-2,200.00**
Page 161
13½" Soldier **$3,200.00**
14" Schneid **$1,800.00**
14" Schus **$2,200.00**
5½" Bear **$200.00**
Bully **$2,500.00**
Ringmaster **$2,400.00**
Hooligan **$2,400.00**
Coloro Clown **$1,800.00**
Rooster **$700.00**
Page 162
12" Snik **$1,600.00**
17" Clown **$2,500.00**
Page 163
Mecki **$75.00**
Floppy Ele **$45.00**
5" Neander **$135.00**
7½" Neander **$165.00**
Page 165
25" Benham **$800.00**
Bird **$65.00**
Dog **$65.00**
Honey Crate **$65.00**
Goose **$475.00**
Page 166
Teddy/Bib **$450.00**
9" Dressed Dogs
(pair) **$900.00**
Navy Goat **$250.00**
Yale Bulldog **$800.00**
Princeton Tiger **$250.00**
Page 167
Mascot Donkey **$150.00**
Standard Donkey **$65.00**
6½" Army Mule **$325.00**
Alpine Donkey **$85.00**
Page 168
11" Monkey **$65.00**
Polar Bear **$125.00**
City Mouse House ... **$350.00**
Page 169
Pippy **$325.00**
Armadillo **$10.00**
Lix/Lixie .... **ea. $185.00**
Lix/Lixie (mint) ....
each **$325.00**
13½" Beige Teddy ... **$165.00**

Page 171
5" & 4½" Bunnies ea. **$450.00**
7½" Rattle **$450.00**
Hollander Rabbits
ea. **$1,500.00**
Page 172
10" Peter Rabbit . **$600.00 UP**
12" Jack Rabbit **$3,500.00**
9" Steiff **$600.00**
Artists Rabbits ea. **$45.00-75.00**
Page 173
9" Yes/No Rabbit **$700.00**
16" Rabbit **$1,500.00**
Colored Rabbits . **ea. $500.00**
Page 174
Felt Hopping **$1,500.00**
Mohair Hopping **$950.00**
5" Acrobat **$450.00**
23" Manni **$3,500.00**
Page 175
15" Rabbit **$65.00**
Kiwi Bird **$20.00**
13½" Bunny Belle **$500.00**
Dottie Dumbunnie .. **$800.00**
Posey Pet Bear **$375.00**
Page 176
5" Rabbit **$175.00**
20" Rabbit **$350.00**
Girl Rabbit **$125.00**
Hunter Rabbit **$150.00**
Girl in Dress **$100.00**
Painter Rabbit **$125.00**
Page 177
27½" Hansili ... **pr. $2,500.00**
10" Rabbit **$125.00**
Schuco Minis ..... **ea. $400.00**
Page 178
3¼" Thumper **$275.00**
Bib, Bibbie
(mint) .... **ea. $325.00**
Page 179
17" Lulac **$175.00**
26" Lulac **$550.00**
6½" Running Rabbit **$250.00**
Town Crier **$700.00**
Elephant **$250.00**
Quaggy & Kiki ... **ea $325.00**
Mother Rabbit **$450.00**
Baby Rabbit **$175.00**
Fox **$600.00**
Mini Schuco **$175.00**
Schuco Panda **$250.00**
Page 180
Nikili Rabbits .. **pr. $1,200.00**
25½" Rabbit **$850.00**
Replicas . **$145.00 & $195.00**
5½" & 6½" Nikki **$275.00**
11" Niki **$375.00**

13½" Niki **$475.00**
8½" Niki **$325.00**
Page 181
10" Nikili .... **pr. $850.00**
Yello/Yella .... **pr. $600.00**
10" Easter Rabbit **$300.00**
Page 182
18" Schuco **$75.00**
18" Steiff **$35.00**
Stroller **$100.00**
Steiff Bunnies .. **$15.00-30.00**
Asian Bunnies **$10.00**
Page 184
4" Siamy **$175.00**
Cat/Wheels **$475.00**
Cat w/o Wheels **$175.00**
Page 185
Kalac **$500.00**
Kitty Cat **$275.00**
Fechter **$30.00**
Fluffy **$250.00**
Black Cat **$50.00**
Siamese **$65.00**
Musical Steiff **$750.00**
Skiier Cat only **$50.00**
Cat/Skiis **$200.00**
English **$75.00**
Kersa **$75.00**
7½" Steiff Tabby **$700.00**
Page 186
Merrythought **$70.00**
FAO Schwarz Cats **$1,000.00**
10½" Schenker Cat **$90.00**
16" Schenker Bear ... **$150.00**
8" Schenker Puppy **$45.00**
Page 187
12" Dachshund **$800.00**
7" Felt Pup **$275.00**
Old Pug **$850.00**
Little Doggy **$175.00**
Page 188
8½" Spaniel **$475.00**
Left Treff **$375.00**
Center Treff **$900.00**
Right Treff **$275.00**
4½" Character Dog .. **$225.00**
Rattler **$425.00**
Foxy **$175.00**
Page 189
8" Scotty **$500.00**
3" Scotty **$250.00**
10" Terrier **$350.00**
Page 190
Peky **$100.00**
Rags **$275.00**
Airedale/wheels **$600.00**
Tessie **$250.00**
Biggie **$125.00**
8" Posey Pet **$85.00**

STUDIO Arco **$1,200.00**
36" Snobby Lac **$1,600.00**
Page 191
8½" Fellow **$375.00**
13½" Terry **$295.00**
11" Terry **$175.00**
13½" Foxy **$165.00**
Standing Chow **$125.00**
Sitting Chow **$175.00**
Hermann Chow **$55.00**
Page 192
11" Cockie **$225.00**
6" Butch **$275.00**
12" Maidy **$350.00**
Page 193
4" Boxer Sitting........ **$100.00**
5½" Boxer Sitting..... **$160.00**
4" Arco **$150.00**
4" Standing St. Bernard.................. **$125.00**
5" Sitting St. Bernard **$175.00**
4" Sitting Foxy **$150.00**
5½" Sitting Foxy **$275.00**
6½" Standing Foxy **$75.00**
Page 194
4" Collie Sitting **$95.00**
4" Biggie **$85.00**
6½" Biggie **$150.00**
8½" Basset **$250.00**
6" Basset **$150.00**
5" Basset **$125.00**
4" Rolly **$350.00**
Page 195
23" Doby **$75.00**
Dismal Desmond **$45.00**
Page 196
10" Pig **$550.00**
Holstein Cow **$1,600.00**
11" Oxy **$600.00**
Page 197
3½" Lying Lamby **$250.00**
15" Cow **$125.00**
Lg. Lying Zicky **$350.00**
Sm. Lying Zicky **$250.00**
Lamby **$75.00**
Cosy Lamby **$45.00**
Locky **$40.00**
Page 198
STUDIO Boar **$650.00**
5½" Boar **$55.00**

Mohair Donkey **$175.00**
8½" Mohair Horse ... **$250.00**
Panda **$150.00**
5½" Velvet Colt **$95.00**
Page 199
Blue or Orange Flossy,
small **$55.00**
medium **$75.00**
large .... **$275.00 UP**
Yellow/Brown Flossy -
small .... **$ 95.00**
medium **$150.00**
large .... **$350.00 UP**
10" Cosy Flossy **$40.00**
Coral Fish .... **ea. $30.00**
Angel Fish .... **ea. $15.00**
Flora Cow **$125.00**
Page 200
Parrot **$275.00**
9½" Rose Duck **$35.00**
10½" Chicken **$25.00**
Wind-up Chick **$50.00**
5½" Duckling **$65.00**
Schuco Lady Bug **$50.00-75.00**
7" Revue Susie **$225.00**
20" Peggy **$200.00**
10" Bessy **$200.00**
Page 201
Finch .... ea. **$250.00**
Birds .... **ea. $75.00-125.00**
Ballbody Chicks **$65.00-85.00**
Birdhouse **$85.00**
5½" Woolly Duck **$95.00**
Page 202
STUDIO Macaw **$500.00**
30" Turkey **$1,500.00**
Lora **$60.00**
Mini Parrots .... **ea. $25.00**
Cheerup Birds ..... **ea. $45.00**
Ladybug **$15.00**
Page 203
St. Pat's Bird **$50.00**
Pigeon **$45.00**
Metal Footed Birds **$30.00**
Plastic Footed Birds ... **$20.00**
Page 204
Swans .... **ea. $35.00**
18" Cockatoo **$135.00**

Page 205
12" Elephant **$1,100.00**
7" Fox **$650.00**
7½" Squirrel **$800.00**
10' Snake **$4,000.00**
Page 206
11" Striped Monkey **$675.00**
Roly Poly Squirrel ... **$350.00**
6" Deer **$150.00**
Lying Fawn **$135.00**
11" Male Deer **$175.00**
7¾" Deer **$150.00**
12" Roe **$175.00**
5½" Fawn **$75.00**
Page 207
Steiff Trout **$750.00**
11" Sigi (faded) **$375.00**
8" Sigi (mint) **$500.00**
Starly **$600.00**
5½" Paddy **$105.00**
Page 208
Red Fox **$650.00**
11" Goose **$550.00**
Musical Chimp **$1,000.00**
Page 209
4" Running Cub **$85.00**
5½" Running **$110.00**
6½" Sitting Cub **$225.00**
6½" Lying Cub **$85.00**
4" Fully Jointed **$95.00**
4" Sitting Cub **$75.00**
Kangoo **$135.00**
13½" Coco **$350.00**
Gibbon **$200.00**
Page 210
Jumbo **$125.00**
6",8",10" Balls.. **$60.00,95.00, & 125.00**
6" Play Ring **$55.00**
12" Drumstick **$75.00**
Cube **$35.00**
Musical Ladybug **$100.00**
Nellie **$375.00**
Silly Basil **$45.00**
2¾" Jointed Tiger **$275.00**
4" Jointed Tiger **$145.00**
Page 211
6" Trophy Heads **ea. $450.00**
12" Rhino Head **$850.00**
Studio Snail .... **N.P.A.**

4½" Nelly **$300.00**
Page 212
8" Lizzy **$300.00**
12" Lizzy **$350.00**
7 ft. Bengal **$2,500.00**
17" Bengal **$750.00**
6½" Ocelot **$200.00**
11" Ocelot **$375.00**
11" Leopard **$225.00**
24" Leopard **$550.00**
Page 213
Crouching Lion **$1,400.00**
39" Zebra **$1,500.00**
42" Okapi **$2,200.00**
STUDIO Gaty **$2,500.00**
28" Gaty **$200.00**
12" Gaty **$75.00**
Page 214
5" Wotan Ram **$150.00**
8½" Wotan Ram **$275.00**
8" Squirrel **$150.00**
10" Gorilla **$200.00**
Page 215
13½" Wittie **$250.00**
9" Wittie **$100.00**
5½" Wittie **$55.00**
4" Wittie **$35.00-45.00**
3½" Wool Mini Owl .. **$30.00**
2½" Wool Mini Owl .. **$20.00**
Owl Puppet **$45.00**
Raccoon **$45.00**
9" Goat **$125.00**
Page 216
8½" Cosy Koala **$65.00**
11" Cosy Camel **$125.00**
3" Velvet Frog **$40.00**
5" Mohair Frog **$145.00**
Page 217
Ponx Tiger **$85.00**
Ponx with Cage **$150.00**
3" Berg Puppet **$35.00**
8½" Mohair Tiger **$75.00**
14" Wizzi **$95.00**
Page 218
12" Trevira Gaty **$55.00**
Skunk **$50.00**
Orange Squirrel **$25.00**
Bat **$45.00**
Chipmunk **$30.00**
Wolf **$95.00**

Back Cover, "Amador," left: 12½"/32 cm.; mohair; FF button; e.s.; f.j.; shoe button eyes; pearl cotton nose/mouth; felt pads; *side squeaker*, ca. 1913. The original brown leather collar and muzzle make him SPECIAL. *Record Peter*: 8½"/22 cm. high, 8"/20cm. long; "STEIFF, Made in Germany, Imported D'Allemagne" impressed into each stained wheel; peacock blue mohair body/limbs (also made in orange or green); brown mohair *Jocko* head; e.s.; f.j.; shoe button eyes; purple yarn ruff; squeaker in seat. Both are extremely desirable. "Bear with Honey Pot and Bee" see page 7. 12½" Muzzle Bear $3,800.00; Record Peter $550.00.
Front Cover: See page 74.

Schroeder's Antiques Price Guide

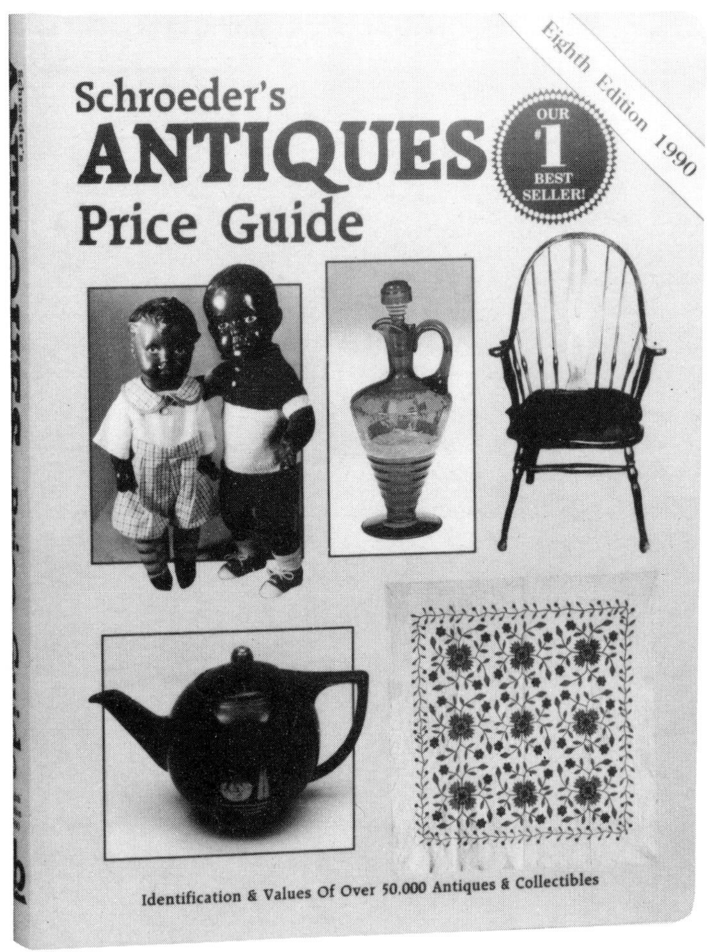

Schroeder's Antiques Price Guide has climbed its way to the top in a field already supplied with several well-established publications! The word is out, *Schroeder's Price Guide* is the best buy at any price. Over 500 categories are covered, with more than 50,000 listings. But it's not volume alone that makes Schroeder's the unique guide it is recognized to be. From ABC Plates to Zsolnay, if it merits the interest of today's collector, you'll find it in Schroeder's. Each subject is represented with histories and background information. In addition, hundreds of sharp original photos are used each year to illustrate not only the rare and the unusual, but the everyday "fun-type" collectibles as well -- not postage stamp pictures, but large close-up shots that show important details clearly.

Each edition is completely re-typeset from all new sources. We have not and will not simply change prices in each new edition. All new copy and all new illustrations make Schroeder's THE price guide on antiques and collectibles.

The writing and researching team behind this giant is proportionately large. It is backed by a staff of more than seventy of Collector Books' finest authors, as well as a board of advisors made up of well-known antique authorities and the country's top dealers, all specialists in their fields. Accuracy is their primary aim. Prices are gathered over the entire year previous to publication, from ads and personal contacts. Then each category is thoroughly checked to spot inconsistencies, listings that may not be entirely reflective of actual market dealings, and lines too vague to be of merit. Only the best of the lot remains for publication. You'll find *Schroeder's Antiques Price Guide* the one to buy for factual information and quality.

No dealer, collector or investor can afford not to own this book. It is available from your favorite bookseller or antiques dealer at the low price of $12.95. If you are unable to find this price guide in your area, it's available from Collector Books, P. O. Box 3009, Paducah, KY 42001 at $12.95 plus $2.00 for postage and handling.

8½ x 11, 608 Pages $12.95

COLLECTOR BOOKS

A Division of Schroeder Publishing Co., Inc.